Thanks for all
your support

Jim

Globalization and
National Financial Systems

Globalization and National Financial Systems

Edited by
James A. Hanson
Patrick Honohan
Giovanni Majnoni

**A copublication of the World Bank
and Oxford University Press**

© 2003 The International Bank for Reconstruction and Development/The World Bank
1818 H Street, NW
Washington, DC 20433
Telephone 202-473-1000
Internet www.worldbank.org
E-mail feedback@worldbank.org

1   2   3   4   06   05   04   03

A copublication of the World Bank and Oxford University Press.

Oxford University Press
198 Madison Avenue
New York, NY 10016

ISBN 0-8213-5208-3

Library of Congress Cataloging-in-Publication Data

Globalization and national financial systems / edited by James A. Hanson,
    Patrick Honohan, Giovanni Majnoni.
        p. cm.
    Includes bibliographical references.
    ISBN 0-8213-5208-3
    1. Finance. 2. Banks and banking. 3. International finance. 4. Monetary
    policy. 5. Globalization—Economic aspects. I. Hanson, James A.
    II. Honohan, Patrick III. Majnoni, Giovanni.

HG173.G638 2003
332'.042—dc21   2002191091

Contents

Foreword

Globalization of finance is a hugely important subject. Trade, technology, and international travel are making finance international despite attempts to isolate national financial systems. Too often, however, the potential gains from globalization are overlooked in the focus on how it complicates nationally oriented financial sector policy.

It is striking how few developing countries have financial systems that would match in size an average bank in the major financial centers. The Bank-Fund Staff Federal Credit Union, by way of example, is larger than the financial systems of several African countries. The small size of these national financial systems means higher financial intermediation costs, limited scope for risk diversification, limited liquidity in capital markets, and limited access to sophisticated financial services and risk-management products. Globalization of finance can reduce these shortcomings, although it also brings new risks that need to be managed.

This book thus looks at financial globalization in a somewhat different way, focusing on these problems and specific ways to mitigate them by taking advantage of the globalization of finance. The different chapters, prepared mainly by experts associated with the World Bank's financial sector staff, address such issues as banking offshore as a way to avoid high intermediation costs and risks, the use of on-shore foreign currency deposits, the performance of foreign banks in low-income economies, and the benefits of international diversification of equity portfolios. It also discusses the use of international linkages and information technology to improve the efficiency of banks and equity markets and to lower the cost of services needed by equity markets, pension providers, and other contractual savings institutions. A final chapter looks at the role of an emerging international "soft law" in strengthening and harmonizing regulation and supervision as promoted de facto by the joint World Bank–IMF Financial Sector Assessment Program (FSAP).

Financial globalization thus opens up hitherto unavailable opportunities, especially for small countries. With the right national policies, the risks can be controlled and the costs kept to the minimum. The key to ensuring the correct policy response is to keep our eye on the main objective of financial sector development, namely to ensure that the public benefits from the access to financial services and products needed to support steady development.

Cesare Calari
Vice President, Financial Sector
The World Bank

Contributors

Biagio Bossone is an associate director of the Bank of Italy and is currently advisor to the International Monetary Fund's Executive Director for Italy. He has been a member of several Organisation for Economic Co-operation and Development, Group of 10, and European Union task forces on financial and central bank issues. He has also been an adjunct professor at the Università degli Studi di Palermo and worked at the Asian Development Bank and the World Bank. His research focuses on money and banking, payments systems, international finance, and financial sector development and policy.

Stijn Claessens is a professor of international finance at the University of Amsterdam and a fellow of the Centre for Economic Policy Research. Prior to this he taught at New York University Business School and worked at the World Bank. His research on enterprise and financial sector restructuring, sovereign asset liability and risk management, corporate governance and capital market development, and the internationalization of financial services issues has been widely published.

Joost Driessen is an assistant professor of finance at the University of Amsterdam. His current research interests are asset pricing and financial econometrics, in particular, modeling the term structure of interest rates, derivative pricing, and credit risk. He holds a Ph.D. in econometrics from Tilburg University, the Netherlands, and also studied at the University of Chicago.

Thomas C. Glaessner is a lead economist in the World Bank currently heading the integrator group in the Financial Sector Vice Presidency and with prior experience in the Bank's Treasury and its East Asia and Latin America regions. He has been a senior strategist within Soros Fund Management LLC and previously spent five years with the International Finance Division of the Federal Reserve Board. Mr. Glaessner holds a Ph.D. in Economics and Finance from the University of Virginia.

James A. Hanson is a senior financial policy advisor at the World Bank. He has been the World Bank's resident lead economist in India and Indonesia, and also led economic work on international debt and Latin America. He has written extensively on macroeconomic and financial issues, as well as on India, Indonesia, and Latin American economies. Prior to joining the World Bank he taught at Brown University in the United States and in various Latin American universities.

Patrick Honohan is a senior advisor in the World Bank's Financial Sector Operations and Policy Department and Development Research Group. Previously he was economic advisor to the prime minister of Ireland and spent several years as a professor at the Economic and Social Research Institute in Dublin and at the Central Bank of Ireland. Based in Dublin he is a member of the Royal Irish Academy and a research fellow of the Centre for Economic Policy Research in London.

Gregorio Impavido has been a senior financial economist in the World Bank's Financial Sector Operations and Policy Department since 1998, specializing in insurance and pension regulation and supervision and in financial market development. Previously he taught at Warwick University in the United Kingdom, from which he holds a Ph.D. in economics. His recent research has focused on the interactions between contractual savings and financial market development.

Cally Jordan is a senior counsel at the World Bank. Formerly, she was an associate professor at the Faculty of Law, McGill University, and continues to teach international capital markets and corporate and comparative law subjects at Georgetown Law Center, Osgoode Hall Law School, and the University of Melbourne. She practiced international finance in New York City for a number of years and has been an advisor to the Financial Services Bureau of the Hong Kong government.

Luc Laeven is a financial economist at the World Bank, where his current research focuses on international banking, deposit insurance, and corporate finance issues. He studied at the London School of Economics and holds a Ph.D. in finance from the University of Amsterdam.

Jong-Kun Lee is a team leader at the Institute of Monetary and Economic Research of the Bank of Korea. Previously he was on secondment as a senior economist at the Financial Sector Policy Division of the World Bank. His main fields of research are financial and price stability. He holds a Ph.D. in economics from the University of Illinois at Urbana-Champaign.

Giovanni Majnoni is an advisor at the World Bank. Previously he was a deputy director in the Bank of Italy's Department of Bank Supervision. His recent research has focused on bank capital regulation, early warning indicators of bank fragility, determinants of financial volatility, and financial contagion. He has published extensively on issues related to financial regulation and risk management. He holds degrees in economics from the University of Rome and from Columbia University in New York.

Alberto R. Musalem has worked at the World Bank since 1985 and is currently lead economist in the Middle East and North Africa Region. Previously he was an advisor in the Financial Sector Development Department. His recent research has focused on contractual savings and financial markets. He holds a Ph.D. in economics from the University of Chicago.

Ajay Shah is a consultant for the Ministry of Finance in New Delhi and is on the faculty of the Indira Gandhi Institute for Development Research in Bombay. Previously he worked at the Centre for Monitoring Indian Economy in Bombay. His research and policy work has been in the areas of financial sector policy, including problems in securities markets, derivatives, and banking.

Anqing Shi is a research analyst in the Development Economics Research Group of the World Bank. Prior to this he was a visiting scholar at the Institute of Asian Studies at Columbia University, New York. He has participated in various World Bank research projects and published in the area of demographic dynamics and sustainable development.

Susan Thomas is a faculty member at the Indira Gandhi Institute for Development Research in Bombay. She has engaged in academic research and public policy work in the areas of time series econometrics, volatility models and risk management, market microstructure, credit risk, and commodity futures markets.

Salvador Valdés-Prieto is a professor of economics at the Catholic University of Chile in Santiago. He specializes in financial regulation and industrial organization and has published widely on these topics in professional journals and books. He has been an advisor to the governments of Bolivia, Chile, China, the Dominican Republic, El Salvador, and Mexico and has been a consultant to the World Bank in Brazil, Kazakhstan, Mexico, and the Philippines. He holds a Ph.D. in economics from the Massachusetts Institute of Technology.

Dimitri Vittas is a senior advisor at the World Bank. He specializes in financial sector issues, especially the promotion and regulation of pension funds, insurance companies, and mutual funds, and has published widely on these topics and related issues. He is currently focusing on second generation issues in pension reform, including the organization of individual accounts and the development of annuity markets.

1

Globalization and National Financial Systems: Issues of Integration and Size

James A. Hanson, Patrick Honohan, and Giovanni Majnoni

Globalization poses new challenges and constraints to the ways in which financial sectors have operated; however, it also offers new opportunities for those countries that take advantage of them by giving them and their citizens a better menu of risk and return on assets and liabilities and better financial services at lower costs. This volume explores these challenges, constraints, and opportunities.

The volume is divided into five traditional areas of finance: the macroeconomy, banking, securities markets, pension issues, and regulation. Four cross-cutting messages emerge. First, the erosion of national frontiers by trade, tourism, migration, and capital account liberalization means that residents of all countries have substantial financial assets—and often liabilities—denominated in foreign currencies at home or abroad. Any analysis of national financial systems must take this into account. More important, this

The authors are grateful to the contributors to the volume for their helpful comments and to Ying Lin for excellent research assistance.

factor constrains governments' use of macroeconomic and financial policy and may contribute to economic fluctuations.

Second, individuals and firms benefit substantially from the improved risk and return menu associated with global diversification. Diversification is of particular importance in developing countries where the lack of size and diversity of the national economy results in instability in the value of production.

Third, the small size of most developing countries limits the efficiency and quality of financial services: banking, equity markets, and pensions. Thus cross-border provision of financial services, one facet of globalization, has potential benefits for small economies. This volume provides some evidence of the rapid growth of cross-border services and suggests additional ways to use them, for example, by unbundling services and using foreign providers. The concern that cross-border providers may skew access to financial services away from small users appears to be unwarranted.

Fourth, taking full advantage of the opportunities presented by globalization and minimizing its costs depend on effective regulation and supervision to ensure good quality information, transparency, market integrity, and prudent investing by banks and pension funds. The entry of foreign participants and the offshore listing of firms both require this infrastructure and often help to improve it.

Introduction

Globalization has brought with it increased specialization and volatility, as well as some loss of policymaking independence. However, as discussed in this volume, globalization can ease some of the problems related to the smallness of financial systems.

National Financial Systems

Policymakers in developing countries often remain focused on domestic financial sector issues, seemingly believing that finance should be national, as far as possible. In this focus they echo Keynes' view expressed in 1933 (cited in Skidelsky 1992) and the approach of many academic economists in industrial countries. This focus harks back to the preglobalized, Bretton Woods era and an economic model inappropriate for small developing economies in today's globalizing world.

On becoming independent after World War II, many developing countries adopted a national currency to replace their use of a metropolitan currency or a currency board (see Hanke and Schuler

1994; Williamson 1995).[1] They set up a central bank and an adjustable peg exchange rate regime and joined the International Monetary Fund.[2] They usually also imposed foreign exchange controls. Exchange controls made supporting a currency peg easier,[3] allowed the government to allocate foreign exchange, and eased concerns about the scarcity of foreign exchange and the potential outflow of investible resources that were prevalent at the time. This institutional setup was similar to that in many industrial countries at the time and to that in the Latin American countries, which had long been independent and had their own currencies.[4]

This national approach to finance probably reflected not only a desire to establish a national identity, but also the need to finance the government and the prevailing development strategy, which relied on public sector-led import substitution. Governments used monetary creation and restrictions on the financial sector, including ceilings on interest rates, large cash reserves, and directed credit requirements on banks, to finance themselves, public enterprises, and other favored borrowers. Insurance companies and pension programs were also often forced to finance government deficits by requirements that they hold mostly government debt. To ensure that these financial sector policies were implemented, governments often set up public sector institutions to provide banking services, term loans, insurance, and pensions, which created vested interests in the national financial system. In addition, at the macroeconomic level governments used capital controls in an attempt to limit avoidance of these measures and increase the effectiveness of the inflation tax and financial repression (see, for example, Aizenman and Guidotti 1994; Alesina and Tabellini 1989; Leblang 1997). Nearly half a century later, the still strong attraction of the seigniorage from this nationalistic approach to currencies and finance is manifest in the adoption of national currencies by most of the new nations created out of the former Soviet Union and the former Yugoslavia and by the issuance of currencies by 14 Argentine provinces in 2002. Of course, when governments have relied on monetary creation excessively, the result has been high inflation and expanding directed credit programs, followed by capital flight, exchange rate pressures, and stabilization programs.[5]

The Globalization of Finance

Globalization has disrupted the national approach to the financial system. The globalization of finance increased in the 1960s as increased trade, travel, migration, and current account convertibility made capital account controls less effective for those willing to evade them.[6] First governments of developing countries, then large corporations, took advantage of expanded offshore borrowing opportunities and capital markets to reduce their financing costs. As time passed, political pressures developed to allow citizens to protect themselves against inflation and restrictions on interest rates in the financial system by holding foreign currency–denominated assets, first offshore and then—even more conveniently—onshore.[7] These domestic pressures, often resulting from the ease with which the well connected and the wealthy circumvented exchange controls, combined with international pressures to reduce the barriers to capital flows and trade in financial services, especially in the 1990s.

Casual observation suggests that finance has become increasingly globalized; however, measuring this change is not easy, and investigators have used many indicators (Eichengreen 2001). One indicator is the increased volume of offshore deposits by individuals and nonbank institutions of developing countries. Between 1995 and 1999 the ratio of offshore deposits in Organisation for Economic Co-operation and Development (OECD) countries' banks to onshore deposits increased in many of the countries listed in table 1.1, as shown by the points lying above the 45-degree diagonal line in figure 1.1.[8] For the countries as a group, the weighted average increase in the offshore deposit to onshore deposit ratio (weighted by domestic deposits) was more than 5 percentage points between 1995 and 1999.

Portfolio flows to developing countries have also grown since the 1980s, although they did experience some ups and downs during the 1990s (Hanson, chapter 4 in this volume; World Bank 2002). Country access also seems to be widening. For example, from September 2001 through January 2002 Costa Rica, the Dominican Republic, El Salvador, and Guatemala all floated international bond issues, even though they all lacked investment grade ratings from Standard & Poor's and Argentina was in the process of defaulting.

Another indicator of financial globalization was the widespread use and growth of foreign currency deposits during the 1990s, as shown in Honohan and Shi (chapter 2 in this volume). In addition, the use of industrial countries' currency is also extensive in many developing countries (Hanson 2002).

Smallness of Developing Countries' Financial Systems

Developing countries' financial systems are small. The only developing countries among the world's 25 largest banking systems are

Figure 1.1 Ratio of Foreign Deposits to Domestic Deposits, Selected Developing Countries, 1995 and 1999 (percent, log scale)

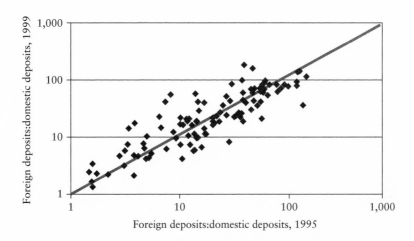

Sources: Bank for International Settlement, *International Banking Statistics;* International Monetary Fund, *International Financial Statistics;* International Federation of Stock Exchanges data.

China (2.5 percent of the world's bank deposits in 2000), India (1.1 percent), Brazil (0.8 percent), Thailand (0.6 percent), and Mexico (0.5 percent). A recent study found that M2 was less than US$1 billion in 59 countries and less than US$10 billion in 118 countries (Bossone, Honohan, and Long 2002). Of the 108 developing countries shown in table 1.1, 80 had total bank deposits of less than US$10 billion, of which 42 had less than US$1 billion in 2000.[9] In terms of equity markets, about 45 had no organized stock exchange, and of those that had, only 15 reported market capitalizations in excess of US$20 billion.

The small size of developing countries' financial systems largely reflects their modest gross domestic product (GDP). It is also often related to the impact of inflation and related forms of taxation of financial services under the nationalistic approach to finance (Bossone, Honohan, and Long 2002; Hanson, chapter 4 in this volume; Honohan and Shi, chapter 2 in this volume). In addition, the small size of developing countries' financial systems reflects

Table 1.1 Indicators of Financial Sector Size, Selected
Developing Countries and Years

Country	Deposits (US$ millions, 2000)	Number of banks (2000)	Average bank size (US$ millions, 2000)	Stock market capitalization (US$ millions, 1999)
China	464,745	105	4,426	330,703
India	206,055	103	2,001	184,605
Brazil	145,900	203	719	227,962
Thailand	106,773	13	8,213	58,365
Mexico	99,510	52	1,914	154,044
Malaysia	82,380	34	2,423	145,445
Argentina	77,983	107	729	83,887
Indonesia	69,093	165	419	64,087
Poland	62,837	80	785	29,577
South Africa	62,743	60	1,046	262,478
Egypt, Arab Republic	59,666	28	2,131	32,838
Turkey	42,157	62	680	112,716
Russian Federation	39,903	1,309	30	72,205
Philippines	36,307	51	712	48,105
Czech Republic	33,652	47	716	11,796
Lebanon	31,564	70	451	1,921
Syrian Arab Republic	30,873	—	—	—
Chile	30,691	30	1,023	68,228
Morocco	21,925	21	1,044	13,695
Pakistan	18,240	52	351	6,965
Hungary	17,814	42	424	16,317
Venezúela, RB	17,247	26	663	7,471
Colombia	16,861	33	511	11,590
Algeria	14,310	—	—	—
Peru	13,566	19	714	13,392
Bangladesh	13,073	50	261	865
Libya	12,066	—	—	—
Slovak Republic	11,265	—	—	723
Uruguay	8,958	22	407	168
Tunisia	8,772	14	627	2,706
Slovenia	8,277	24	345	2,180
Croatia	8,085	54	150	2,584
Jordan	7,653	16	478	5,827
Nigeria	6,785	51	133	2,940
El Salvador	5,605	14	400	2,141

Table 1.1 Continued

Country	Deposits (US$ millions, 2000)	Number of banks (2000)	Average bank size (US$ millions, 2000)	Stock market capitalization (US$ millions, 1999)
Dominican Republic	5,432	15	362	141
Costa Rica	5,170	20	259	2,303
Sri Lanka	5,095	26	196	1,584
Kenya	3,707	53	70	1,409
Ecuador	3,667	—	—	415
Guatemala	3,593	33	109	215
Trinidad and Tobago	3,433	6	572	4,367
Ukraine	3,387	—	—	1,121
Bolivia	3,220	14	230	116
Romania	3,180	36	88	873
Jamaica	2,874	6	479	2,530
Bulgaria	2,785	34	82	706
Vietnam	2,672	48	56	—
Honduras	2,246	22	102	—
Ethiopia	2,023	8	253	—
Nepal	1,990	13	153	417
Kazakhstan	1,981	—	—	2,265
Lithuania	1,946	9	216	1,138
Paraguay	1,913	21	91	423
Estonia	1,590	6	265	1,789
Yemen, Rep.	1,480	13	114	—
Latvia	1,447	24	60	391
Côte d'Ivoire	1,441	14	103	1,514
Nicaragua	1,317	—	—	—
Zimbabwe	1,256	13	97	2,514
Botswana	1,253	4	313	1,052
Tanzania	1,252	4	313	181
Namibia	1,201	5	240	691
Belarus	1,156	27	43	—
Cameroon	1,045	9	116	—
Haiti	1,037	—	—	—
Papua New Guinea	918	—	—	—
Mozambique	893	9	99	—
Senegal	870	10	87	—
Angola	760	—	—	—
Sudan	742	—	—	—
Uganda	649	18	36	—
Gabon	582	8	73	—

Table 1.1 Continued

Country	Deposits (US$ millions, 2000)	Number of banks (2000)	Average bank size (US$ millions, 2000)	Stock market capitalization (US$ millions, 1999)
Madagascar	560	6	93	—
Azerbaijan	546	—	—	—
Macedonia FYR	531	23	23	—
Zambia	511	17	30	280
Ghana	507	16	32	916
Guyana	394	7	56	—
Benin	371	5	74	—
Mali	368	9	41	—
Grenada	363	—	—	—
Burkina Faso	345	7	49	—
Cape Verde	289	—	—	—
Congo, Rep.	279	4	70	—
Lao PDR	266	—	—	—
Swaziland	246	4	62	97
Djibouti	244	—	—	—
Togo	210	6	35	—
Rwanda	205	5	41	—
Lesotho	203	3	68	—
Maldives	198	4	49	—
Albania	174	—	—	—
Moldova	170	20	8	38
Armenia	167	—	—	25
Malawi	159	5	32	179
Georgia	156	—	—	—
Guinea	154	6	26	—
Mauritania	105	6	18	—
Niger	100	8	12	—
Gambia, The	97	6	16	—
Burundi	85	7	12	—
Samoa	78	—	—	—
Kyrgyz Republic	68	—	—	—
Tonga	57	3	19	—
Chad	56	6	9	—
Guinea-Bissau	30	—	—	—
São Tomé Principe	10	—	—	—

— Not available.

Sources: Bank for International Settlement, *International Banking Statistics;* International Monetary Fund, *International Financial Statistics;* International Federation of Stock Exchanges data.

feedback from the tendency, discussed later, toward high margins and capital market transactions that reduce the demand for national financial services. The result is that small developing countries have smaller domestic financial systems relative to their GDP than larger developing countries (see, for example, Hanson, chapter 4 in this volume).

Issues in the Globalization of Finance

The globalization of finance affects the whole economy, raising particular issues with regard to banking, securities markets, and contractual savings. Legal and regulatory structures are also affected.

The Macroeconomy

Reducing barriers to international capital movements is theoretically thought to improve welfare, analogously to reducing barriers to trade in goods. The standard argument is that opening the capital account would tend to equalize rates of return, leading to more investment and higher growth in developing countries. However, investigators have found little empirical association between capital account liberalization and growth or investment rates (see, for example, Kraay 1998; Rodrik 1998).[10] One possible explanation for this result is the difficulty of measuring liberalization of the capital account, as Eichengreen (2001) points out. Another possible explanation is that capital account liberalization may not only be associated with increased capital inflows, but also with increased capital outflows, particularly when the domestic policy environment is inappropriate.[11] A third, more fundamental, issue is that risk-adjusted rates of return in many developing countries may be unattractive, meaning that whatever inflows are encouraged by capital account liberalization may largely be offset by outflows.

Globalization can, in theory, also help smooth variations in consumption, a potentially important benefit for small economies. Small countries are likely to be more susceptible to weather shocks, natural disasters, and agricultural and livestock diseases than large countries because of their smaller area and specialized production. On the international demand side, the more specialized a country's output, the more likely that export demand is variable. The higher volatility of small countries' commodity terms of trade and their private consumption (Bossone, Honohan, and Long 2002), as well as of their GDP (Easterly 2000), provides some empirical support for these hypotheses.

The ability to offset such shocks within a developing country is necessarily limited: the more risk-averse citizens can buy insurance from the less risk averse, but the economy as a whole cannot offset the shock. However, a number of mechanisms related to the globalization of finance offer some possibilities for increasing diversification and reducing its cost. Foreigners holding equity and risk-sharing assets will absorb part of national volatility (Reynolds 1965). More important, residents' holdings of foreign assets provide diversification against their own country experiencing a supply decline or a fall in export prices. Risk can also be reduced through forward contracts in commodities and foreign exchange, but these domestic markets may not be effective in developing countries, particularly the many small ones.[12] International insurance or reinsurance contracts against natural disasters or weather can hedge internationally against national risks. The questions remain, of course, to what extent capital account opening is necessary to obtain this ability to offset risk and how effectively the government can and will handle the hedging of risk and consumption smoothing, for example, by contra-cyclical international borrowing.

Moreover, many economists believe that capital account liberalization increases the volatility of GDP. Inflows of capital can suddenly turn into outflows that are augmented by runs on the currency by residents. All too familiar are the exchange rate and financial crises such as the Latin American debt crisis of the 1980s and the Mexican, East Asian, and Russian crises of the latter half of the 1990s. Despite these well-known crises, the statistical evidence linking capital account liberalization and crises is tenuous (see, for example, Easterly, Islam, and Stiglitz 2001; Kraay 1998; Rossi 1999).

Nonetheless, the riskiness of capital account liberalization without fiscal adjustment to at least offset the loss of seigniorage resulting from capital account liberalization, and without reasonably strong financial regulation and supervision and a sound domestic financial system, is well recognized (see for example, Demirgüç-Kunt and Detragiache 2001; Honohan and Shi, chapter 2 in this volume; World Bank 2001). The weakness of financial regulation and supervision is generally considered to have been a major factor in the East Asian crisis (see, for example, World Bank 2000).

As many authors and finance ministers have noted, opening the capital account also reduces a country's policymaking independence. Capital flows tend to offset changes in monetary policy, particularly in small countries, although they may make fiscal policy more effective, as Mundell (1968) points out. Countries could try to restore their monetary policymaking independence by adopting floating exchange rates. However, adopting a floating exchange rate may simply encourage financial contracts to be denominated in foreign currency, onshore as well as offshore, which would also tend to limit a country's policymaking independence. Another approach has been to use capital controls to limit such contracts and support the inflation tax and financial repression, as noted earlier. Indeed, a statistical correlation exists between controls and chronic macroeconomic imbalances.[13] For those countries that historically have used monetary policy to generate high inflation, a reduction in policymaking independence may not be a major loss. Indeed, many countries have tried to signal a change in their monetary policy regime, reduce inflationary expectations quickly, and cut inflation without much loss of output by opening the capital account and linking their currency to a foreign currency with a fixed exchange rate, opting for a currency board, or even adopting a foreign currency (see, for example, Bartolini and Drazen 1997; Hanson 2002).

Despite these risks and potential disadvantages, developing countries have increasingly opened their capital accounts, reflecting to some degree the increasing difficulty of maintaining capital account restrictions. With increased trade, migration, and tourism and with the massive improvements in telecommunications conducting financial transactions across frontiers is becoming increasingly easier. Capital account restrictions may work temporarily, may sustain some deviation from world interest rates (adjusted for risk), and may be able to affect maturities as discussed in Dooley (1996), Edwards (1999), and Arioshi and others (2000). However, attempts to maintain large deviations from market rates with controls create distortions, encourage corruption, and tend to be ineffective (Edwards 1989; Kaminsky and Reinhart 1999). In addition, capital controls have adverse distributional consequences, acting as a tax on those who lack access to foreign currency assets and liabilities and who are unwilling to violate the rules (Hanson 1994).

Capital account liberalization brings benefits to firms and high-income individuals by improving the risk-return menu facing residents; the further step of allowing foreign currency deposits and loans within the country widens access to those benefits. Various aspects of the benefits associated with globalization are discussed in this volume in Honohan and Shi; Driessen and Laeven; Glaessner and Valdés-Prieto; and Impavido, Musalem, and Vittas (chapters 2, 7, 8, and 9, respectively). In particular, foreign currency assets and liabilities provide individuals and firms with some protection against inflation, instability, and repression of interest rates, as discussed earlier.[14]

Governments that have pursued inflationary policies and face shrunken financial systems have sometimes authorized foreign currency deposits to try to reduce the loss of deposits to offshore banks and increase the volume of credit. To some extent, this approach has limited the decline in onshore deposits (Hanson 2002). However, Honohan and Shi (chapter 2 in this volume) provide some new empirical evidence that the growth in credit from allowing foreign currency deposits may be limited, because the banks may invest much of the foreign currency deposits offshore to reduce their risk.

The attraction of foreign currency assets to savers, particularly in inflationary, unstable environments, is obvious. The attraction of foreign currency liabilities is more complex and involves some micro-level as well as macroeconomic risks. Foreign currency liabilities have lower nominal rates than local currency liabilities, because they do not include a depreciation premium. Thus a borrower in foreign currency pays nothing for devaluation risk until a devaluation actually occurs, and the savings can be large given the possibility of a prolonged "peso problem" in which local currency interest rates are high in expectation of a devaluation and can bankrupt local currency borrowers. Only after a devaluation occurs does the borrower in foreign currency suffer a large capital loss compared with having borrowed in local currency, and only feels this loss as amortization takes place over the outstanding maturity of the loan, although this effect may be small given the typically short maturities of loans in developing countries. Finally, the borrower may be able to take advantage of a government bailout scheme for borrowers, such as has often followed devaluations.

Thus borrowers, as well as depositors, may opt for foreign currency instruments. These preferences of depositors and borrowers make it easier for financial institutions to hedge foreign exchange risk by matching their foreign currency deposits with foreign currency loans.[15] However, matching foreign currency loans with deposits is likely to turn the potential currency risk for the banks into a credit risk for the banks,[16] because the borrowers may not have access to hedging facilities.[17] Honohan and Shi (chapter 2 in this volume) find that more dollarized countries tend to have a more rapid pass-through of devaluation into local prices. While this reduces the effectiveness of devaluation in a dollarized economy, it also tends to reduce the potential credit risk from lending in foreign currency.

These characteristics of foreign currency loans may lead both the public and the private sectors to seek them despite their exchange risk. For the government, this lower cost of a foreign currency loan immediately translates into lower deficits as a percentage of GDP until a devaluation occurs, after which the rise in the local currency value of the principal is spread out over the amortization term of the obligations, and if the government's borrowings are offshore, then it does not need to set up a local government bond market. Finally, for both the public and private sectors the spreads on borrowings in foreign currency loans, compared with foreign currency deposits, may be lower. All these attractions are certainly factors in the growth of demand for foreign currency loans by the public sector in developing countries and by the private sector where permitted. An important question is whether public and private sector borrowers systematically underestimate the foreign exchange risk. On the supply side questions have arisen about whether government policies, bailouts, and the international financial architecture have not overly reduced the risks to foreign lenders, particularly lenders to governments, and thus overly encouraged the supply of offshore lending.

Banking

The small size of banking systems in most developing countries is likely to hinder achievement of economies of scale and scope and tends to reduce competition. Only 28 of the 108 developing countries in table 1.1 have enough deposits to support even one bank with US$10 billion in assets. The volume of bank deposits in 55 of the developing countries in table 1.1 would be too small to support even five banks with US$300 million in deposits (roughly the average size of commercial banks in the United States in 2000 and substantially below the average bank size in the other industrial countries). Moreover, because governments typically license many banks, about two-fifths of countries have an average bank size of less than US$300 million in deposits.[18] Indeed, in half of the countries average bank size is less than US$150 million.

Such banks are far smaller than necessary to reach economies of scale. As discussed in Bossone and Lee (chapter 3 in this volume) and the works cited therein, recent studies of the U.S. banking industry find scale economies in the United States on the order of 20 percent of costs for bank sizes up to about US$10 billion to US$25 billion in assets. There is also some evidence of gains in larger banks from geographic diversification of risk (Hughes and others 1999). Although econometric studies in the 1980s suggested no economies of scale in U.S. banking, more recent studies were better able to identify economies of scale by adjusting for the riskiness of assets held by banks—the larger banks not only benefit from risk diversification, but may take on more risky assets because they are better able to diversify. The studies of European and Japanese banking cited in Bossone and Lee suggest that economies of scale existed in these areas of the world even before the 1990s. The recent econometric findings are consistent with the numerous mergers and takeovers in U.S. banking and the rise in the average size of banks in the United States that occurred in the 1990s once interstate banking was allowed.[19]

The lack of economies of scale and of competition in developing countries is likely to translate into larger bank margins between the average rates on loans and the average costs of deposits in developing countries than in industrial countries. Private banks' high spreads were probably one political justification for starting public sector banks.[20] Of course, the public sector banks have had problems associated with poor-quality lending and a limited contribution to growth that proved far more costly than high spreads (see, for example, Barth, Caprio and Levine 2001; LaPorta, Lopez-de-Silanes, and Shleifer 2000).

Bossone and Lee (chapter 3 in this volume) systematically investigate the earlier suggestion that bank margins are indeed related to country size (Bossone, Honohan, and Long 2002).[21] Using a large cross-country and time series banking data panel in a model where banks are value maximizers, they show that banks operating in larger financial systems have lower production costs and lower costs of risk absorption and reputation signaling than banks operating in small systems. They explore different channels through which these systemic economies of scale work their effects on the banks and present various estimates of such effects. The study also finds that information transparency, the risk environment, and market concentration affect banks' production efficiency.

Risk diversification is also likely to be a problem in developing countries, especially small ones, and that may partly explain some of the lower costs in larger financial systems. As noted, small economies tend to be less diversified and probably face more supply-side shocks. Moreover, the small size of banks in small countries makes it difficult for them to diversify domestically. Difficulties in diversification may also be worsened by the lumpiness of investment: to the extent that an investment involves economies of scale its demand for credit will be large relative to the financial system (Bossone, Honohan, and Long 2002). To some degree, the higher risk in small economies is likely to create upward pressure on bank margins in these countries to generate enough profits to compensate owners for the risks they face.

The globalization of financial services—the use of offshore deposits and loan facilities—is one way that residents of small countries can offset the costs and service limitations of small banking systems. Hanson (chapter 4 in this volume) provides some indication of the role of offshore deposits. Small developing economies (excluding offshore financial centers) tend to have fewer deposits than larger developing countries, relative to GDP and taking into account per capita income and inflation rates. This result perhaps provides an indirect test of residents' negative reaction to the higher margins, lack of competition, and limited scope of banks in small economies. However, the small developing countries also tend to have larger deposits offshore than the larger developing economies (again taking per capita income and inflation rates into account), suggesting a substitution of external deposits for domestic deposits. Note that the sum of offshore and onshore deposits in small countries averages about the same fraction of GDP as in large economies—offshore deposits roughly make up for smaller onshore deposits in the small countries. The exception to this finding is African countries, where the much lower level of onshore deposits is not offset by offshore deposits. One explanation for this might be the poorer telecommunications network in African countries than elsewhere, which makes accessing offshore banking services more difficult. Residents with limited access to international means of communications may find that avoiding the higher margins in small countries is more difficult.

An issue here is whether the loss of deposits to offshore banks reduces access to financial services and raises their cost to depositors and to local small and medium borrowers in developing countries. One approach to offsetting these problems would be to offer deposit access through nonbank intermediaries, such as post office banks, taking advantage of the stunning developments that have occurred in information technology. The development of nonbank intermediaries may also be useful for small and medium borrowers. Access to credit for small borrowers can also be improved by the use of the new information technology, for example, by developing credit registries that provide information on small borrowers and credit cards, as well as by improving the titling and legal aspects of collateral.

Another aspect of globalization is the growth of foreign participation in developing countries' banking systems. A common argument is that foreign banks follow foreign investors from their own countries; however, this observation may simply reflect profitable opportunities for both foreign investment and foreign banks once restrictions on foreign entry have been reduced. Home country factors are also important, for example, deregulation in Spain and the low profitability of banking in Japan may have contributed to the expansion of Spanish banks in Latin America and Japanese banks in East Asia.

Foreign banks often tend to be more efficient than their developing country competitors and put competitive pressure on them (Claessens and Lee, chapter 5 in this volume; Claessens, Demirgüç-Kunt, and Huizinga 2000). The loss of profits and franchise value may lead the domestic banks to engage in riskier lending, and may thereby increase the fragility of the banking system. At the same time the expansion of access by well-capitalized and well-managed banks can also be quite beneficial. Although the presence of foreign banks can have a positive effect on bank regulation and supervision, reaping the full benefits of a foreign presence in banking is likely to depend on improving institutions in at least a few key regulatory areas, as well as limiting entry to reputable foreign banks, which will have incentives for sound banking in order to protect their reputation.

The foreign banks' activities are often quite varied, including credit card business and participation in nascent government debt markets. In lending, some evidence indicates that in Latin America large foreign banks have, on average, about the same fraction of credit to small and medium enterprises as large domestic banks (including public sector banks), but small foreign banks have fewer credits to small and medium enterprises than their domestic counterparts (Clarke and others 2003). However, experience with foreign banks has not been as successful in Africa, in terms either of loans or of deposit taking. Nonetheless, there are some indications that foreign bank penetration not only improves services for large borrowers, but, in the right environment, can even increase access.

Claessens and Lee (chapter 5 in this volume) focus on the role of foreign banks in low-income, mainly small, countries. They show that foreign bank participation has increased in low-income countries, albeit from a small base. They confirm that increased foreign bank participation combined with a commitment to open markets has improved the efficiency and competitiveness of low-income countries' financial systems. Moreover, foreign banks have also introduced improved risk management practices and "imported" supervision from their home country regulators, thereby helping to strengthen banking systems and improve financial stability.

National Securities Markets

Capital markets are small in developing countries for the same reasons that banking systems are small. GDP is small; costs are high; and the macroeconomic, legal, and accounting frameworks are weak. Many developing countries do not even have a market for government bonds, an important precondition for a sound market for private bonds.[22] The lack of a local government bond market typically reflects instability and the government's reliance on monetary issue, forced lending from banks, and offshore borrowing to finance its deficits.[23] But without a government bond market, developing an efficient private bond or commercial paper market is hard.

Most other developing country equity markets have market capitalizations in the US$1 billion to US$15 billion range. Even the largest equity markets in developing countries—Brazil, China, India, Malaysia, Mexico, South Africa, and Turkey—have market capitalizations of only about US$100 billion to US$350 billion, similar in size to those in Belgium, Denmark, Finland, and Sweden and much smaller than in Australia, Canada, Italy, Spain, and Switzerland, which are in the US$450 billion to US800 billion range. Turnover is often less than 50 percent of market capitalization in many developing country markets, particularly in the small country markets. The number of listed firms is typically less than 200, except for the largest markets (see Standard & Poor's 2001).[24] Of course, this should not be surprising, because in most industrial countries listed companies typically number less than 1,000. The exceptions are the United States with about 8,000 listings (according to Standard & Poor's 2001), Canada with 3,000, Japan with 2,500, and the United Kingdom with 2,000, and among the developing countries India with 6,000. These market sizes suggest that even some medium companies have floated shares in these countries.

Trading costs are relatively high in small markets because of low trading volumes relative to the capital cost of market infrastructure. In this sense, equity markets in developing countries face the same pressures to merge that exist in industrial countries' markets; however, the real problem in small markets may be their lack of liquidity.

Shah and Thomas (chapter 6 in this volume) show that, empirically, transaction costs tend to be higher and liquidity much lower in smaller markets, particularly in markets of less than US$20 billion capitalization, which represent three-fourths of developing country markets. For the smaller firms that account for much of developing country markets, liquidity is especially low, even in the relatively large Indian market or the NASDAQ. Shah and Thomas thus divide the problem of small markets into three issues: the inherent low liquidity of the small firms that account for most listed firms in developing countries; the problems of market governance and information, which may particularly affect small firms; and the economies of scale in financial markets.[25]

Shah and Thomas note that computerization and the falling prices of computing power and programs have reduced the direct costs of trading, depositories, and payments, lowering the potential gap in direct costs that larger markets enjoy in this area.[26] Moreover, costs could be reduced by outsourcing intermediary services or sharing services across multiple developing countries. Costs could also be reduced by combining various parts of the capital market in countries where regulations separate them.

Many developing countries suffer from problems related to market governance and information. Not only are the markets too small to support a good information infrastructure, the raw information itself is weak and the legal system leaves much to be desired. Accounting standards are unclear, companies are closely held, and rating agencies are weak. In addition, minority shareholders' rights are typically weak in developing countries. Thus improving the legal and accounting frameworks and market integrity could enhance the attractiveness of these markets.

Nonetheless, small markets have some inherent problems. Even in the best of circumstances bid-asked spreads and transaction costs are inherently going to be higher in developing countries than in industrial countries. Moreover, the large spreads and imperfect markets make it difficult for mutual funds to develop, in part because of the difficulty of pricing their portfolios and thus comparing their performance. Lack of liquidity, both in terms of market size and trading in shares of individual companies, also limits the interest of international portfolio managers, who want to be able to buy and sell quickly without affecting prices much.

Globalization has three main effects on developing country markets. First, the capital markets in developing countries, particularly large capital markets, may be attractive to foreigners for diversifying risk—often the correlation between a developing country market and a foreign market is low. Thus an attraction exists despite the aforementioned problems and despite such policies as limits on the repatriation of earnings, required divestitures, and restrictions on the size of holdings that often exist. Of course, foreigners' interest is in large markets and large companies because of liquidity concerns, and less interest exists in small markets and small companies. Typically foreign buyers bid up the market, thereby reducing the cost of capital. Thus listed firms benefit from lower costs of capital and some new companies go public. However, once foreign investors make their stock adjustment, inflows tend to slow. Trading by foreign investors tends to dominate trading, because many local investors buy and hold. Small day-to-day flows to and from the developing country market are usually sufficient to keep the market reasonably correlated with the industrial country markets, reducing the diversification incentive for large, new inflows. One indicator of the extent to which this process has occurred is the decline in single country equity funds in industrial countries (*Financial Times* 2002).

A second effect is the shift offshore of equity issues and trading of the larger companies once they are permitted to raise capital offshore. During the 1990s larger companies took advantage of the lower costs and greater liquidity and increasingly raised capital in industrial country markets by issuing depository rights,[27] or even shifted their primary listing offshore.[28] On average, companies accounting for about 55 percent of market capitalization in 15 middle-income countries and 27 percent in 25 low-income countries were listed offshore in 2000 (Claessens, Klingebiel, and Schmukler 2002). Not only are the shares listed offshore, but trading is shifting offshore. This is particularly true in middle-income countries where, on average, about 40 percent of the trading in firms listed offshore took place offshore in 2000 (Claessens, Klingebiel, and Schmukler 2002), suggesting that in many cases liquidity in these firms' shares may be greater offshore than onshore.[29] Moreover, in some cases large companies that were mainstays of the small, local markets have been taken over by foreign companies, in effect moving their listing to equity markets in these companies' home countries. Thus the net result has been to reduce the trading volume of shares in some of the largest companies in developing country markets, further reducing liquidity and the effectiveness of stock markets in developing countries.

Thus companies that are large enough and strong enough to attract international interest have benefited from globalization in terms of lower costs of capital. The foreign presence in the local market will also benefit other listed companies and those that take advantage of the initial wave of foreign investment to go public. After the initial inflow going public on the local stock exchange may not be much easier than before the foreign investors entered, partly because the entry of foreign investors may lead to much stronger regulation and market integrity. However, this is not much of an issue because, generally speaking, equity markets have not been sources of finance for medium companies. The attractiveness of the domestic equity market to foreigners and the development of the domestic commercial paper and bond markets can be stimulated by improving the legal framework and developing a local government bond market.[30] The development of a local commercial paper market is desirable, as it creates competition for banks. Such competition was an important factor in reducing bank lending rates in the United States.

A third effect of globalization on equity markets is the potential gain from international diversification of equity portfolios by investors located in developing countries. Thus if local investors are permitted to invest offshore, they benefit from a much wider range of options and can diversify better. Of course, to the extent that local investors invest offshore, the outflow of funds offsets the inflow of funds from international investors. In terms of local market volume the net effect can be either positive or negative.

The inability to diversify could be particularly costly for capital market investors in small countries, because of the small economies' high volatility. However, most of the literature on the benefits of international portfolio diversification takes a U.S. perspective and focuses on large economies. Driessen and Laeven (chapter 7 in this volume) document the benefits of international equity portfolio diversification across a range of countries, in each case from the perspective of a local investor. They measure the benefits of globalization to investors from investing in equities outside the national market, and investigate whether these benefits differ substantially between industrial and developing countries. They find that the benefits of investing abroad are large in general, and are largest for investors in developing countries. Unfortunately, investors in developing economies are often restricted in their offshore investments, which highlights the importance of further liberalization of international financial markets for offshore investment.

Contractual Savings

Pension funds and other forms of contractual saving in small economies exhibit the same problems of high costs, lack of competition, and lack of diversification as banking and capital markets. Economies of scale in pensions and other forms of contractual saving are an important issue (Ghilarducci and Terry 1999). In their exhaustive review of the subject, Glaessner and Valdés-Prieto (chapter 8 in this volume) break down the supply of pension funds into elementary functions and services. They argue that economies of scale are important in what are potentially separable subsegments of the pension industry, such as collecting contributions and payments, processing data, and maintaining records, but not in client services.

The economies of scale in pension funds and the resulting process of consolidation in pension funds raise the issue of competition in pension services, a problem that is exacerbated in small economies. In many countries where mandatory, fully funded pensions have been set up along the lines of the Chilean scheme, observers note definite tendencies toward a reduction in the number of providers consistent with the observation that economies of scale prevail.[31] Obviously, one response might be to create a single national scheme or provident fund. This might only apply to the areas where economies of scale exist as, for example, the Swedish approach and the U.S. Thrift Savings Plan for U.S. government employees, where a single provider is responsible for collections and payments, but contributors have a choice of mutual funds in which to invest. This approach can be operated in such a way as to limit the marketing expenses that have sometimes been a problem in Chilean-style schemes. However, such an approach is likely to be government operated, and experience in many developing countries suggests that government-operated funds run the risk of poor handling of individual accounts as well as low rates of return.[32]

Another alternative, discussed in Glaessner and Valdés-Prieto, would be to unbundle the various services and use global providers. An example is the split between collecting contributions and investing discussed in the previous paragraph. Unbundling would allow the small country to benefit from economies of scale by using domestic services where economies of scale are not present and international competitive bidding for provision of the other services. Reputable global banks can also provide custodial services to segregate pension assets from nonpension assets, an important element in protecting pension funds from poor performance by an individual institutions (see Impavido, Musalem, and Vittas, chapter 9 in this volume). A side benefit of globalization in this context is that the country will also import elements of the regulatory framework of the country of the provider of the service.

Fully funded pensions in small economies also face problems of diversifying their investments, unless they are allowed to invest globally (Glaessner and Valdés-Prieto and Impavido, Musalem, and Vittas, chapters 8 and 9 in this volume). Capital markets in developing countries tend to be small and illiquid, as discussed earlier. The growth of fully funded pensions does tend to stimulate larger markets by creating a demand for longer-term paper, but cannot resolve the problem. However, the pension funds are likely to swamp the domestic market, bidding up prices and becoming too large to undertake trades without generating substantial price movements given the domestic market's low liquidity.[33] Moreover, as noted previously, small economies tend to be more volatile than large economies, and so local capital markets may have relatively large swings. These problems may be worsened by erratic macroeconomic policy. As a result, some participants in fully funded pensions in small economies may become victims of country risk if they retire during bad years, a problem that may be more pronounced in small economies, and as a result receive much smaller pensions than others who retire a few years earlier or later.

One solution for these problems is global diversification of pension fund investment, as discussed in Glaessner and Valdés-Prieto and Impavido, Musalem, and Vittas. In practice, countries that have fully funded pension schemes typically restrict the amount of external investment, even when the capital account is fairly open, for instance, Canada, Chile, and Peru. This yields the paradoxical situation that individual investors can diversity more than institutional investors. Such restrictions represent a holdover from the national approach to finance, with the government seeking a local market for its debt and hoping to increase investible resources in the country. However, such an approach is, in effect, a differential, dedicated tax on the pension contributors in favor of the government and those firms that are eligible for pension fund investment. The differential in taxation is particularly large in countries where other capital flows are relatively free. Allowing greater global diversification by pension funds would improve the access of pension fund contributors to a better range of risk and return options and reduce the risks associated with retiring in a "down" year. Glaessner and Valdés-Prieto even suggest that requiring such diversification might be desirable.

Regulation

The quality of financial regulation and supervision, as well as of information and the legal system, are important factors in making the most of the globalization of finance. Strong regulation and supervision may help to encourage domestic depositors and investors and attract foreign investors. Most observers agree that weak financial regulation contributed to the East Asia crisis.

The globalization of finance can itself contribute to strengthening. For example, countries that want to list on one of the industrial country markets or to sell depository rights are required to improve their financial accounts and disclosure. Such disclosure can not only inform and protect the domestic investors in that company, but can even place pressure on companies that are not listing abroad to enhance their disclosure. Likewise, the entry of foreign banks can import good practices established in their home countries and cause local banks to respond lest their customers migrate to the newcomers.

To a degree, self-regulatory structures may emerge where official regulation is lacking (as happened in the case of the unregulated Euromarkets of the 1960s). However, self-regulation is rarely enough for consumer and systemic protection in finance, particularly in developing countries. Yet without a global financial regulator the reality has been one of uneven, and in many cases inadequate, official regulatory and supervisory structures in small developing countries. To some extent this has been the consequence of a skills deficit, and to some extent the result of a lack of political will.

The promulgation of a series of codes and standards of good financial regulation and information has created the embryo of what Jordan and Majnoni (chapter 10 in this volume) describe as an international soft law on these matters. The first of these statements was the Basel Core Principles for Effective Banking Supervision, adopted in 1997, which has been followed by a large number of parallel statements developed by international associations of regulators for the various segments of the financial system, or by international financial institutions for areas as diverse as insurance, securities markets, accounting, auditing, corporate governance, systemically important payments systems, and transparency of financial policies.

These principles will, no doubt, be modified in time, but for the moment, the readiness with which they have been accepted internationally is striking. Disseminated in part through the Financial Sector Assessment Program of the International Monetary Fund and the World Bank, they are beginning to form the backbone of "hard" financial sector law and regulation in many countries. The speed of this legal globalization process rivals that of financial services. Jordan and Majnoni argue that an important factor in their acceptance has been their blend of elements of market and regulatory discipline, which has helped to gain the support of traditionally opposed constituencies. Yet, as Jordan and Majnoni observe, for small countries with limited administrative capacity, to transplant and implement these principles effectively in the local legal and institutional environment will remain a challenge.

Conclusions

Small financial markets characterize the vast majority of developing countries. This volume finds that this tends to mean that financial services are more expensive for residents of these countries because of the lack of economies of scope and scale and of competition and because opportunities for diversifying risk are limited.

As the chapters in this book discuss, the globalization of finance tends to offset these countries' deficiencies by providing individuals and firms with better opportunities in regard to risk and returns and more and better services at lower costs. Whether for a depositor, a borrower, a stock investor, a firm raising equity capital, or a worker investing a pension, access to international markets provides more diversification; possibilities for higher returns on investments; lower costs of funding; and less costly, more competitive, and more diverse financial services. The availability of foreign financial assets and the location of foreign intermediaries onshore increase access to these benefits, and domestic capital markets and firms tend to benefit from inflows. Better legal frameworks and regulation and supervision can increase the attractiveness of local markets to foreign inflows and globalization can contribute to improving these frameworks.

Of course, as with freer trade there are some losers, namely, those who benefited from the national financial system. Citizens employed in domestic financial intermediaries and markets may lose their jobs because of competition from foreign banks, and governments and those few borrowers who benefited from below market credits will find their costs of borrowing increasing. Some have raised concerns about the provision of loans to small borrowers and, in Africa, about small depository services by banks; however, most evidence suggests that small borrowers did not benefit much from the national financial system (see Caprio, Hanson, and Honohan 2001 and the works cited therein). Moreover, some evidence suggests that large foreign banks provide as much credit to small borrowers as large domestic banks, including large public banks, and their credit card services are another source of small credits. In any case, traditional banks may not be the best way to reach small depositors and borrowers, and other institutions may be needed.

The globalization of finance has potential macroeconomic costs, however, that can affect individuals and firms indirectly. First is the well-known concern that globalization may increase macroeconomic volatility, which is already larger in developing countries than in industrial countries. Individuals and firms may be able to protect their assets better against volatility with globalization, but the variability of aggregate demand may increase and financial instability may become more of an issue.

Second, the globalization of finance complicates monetary and fiscal policy. Open capital markets reduce the independence of monetary policy. Of course, that may not be a great loss for countries that have pursued unstable monetary policy, but it could be an issue for some countries.[34] Fiscal policy becomes more effective with financial globalization—it reduces crowding out—but globalization raises its own risks. Globalization reduces the ability to rely on seigniorage, and so may require some fiscal tightening. In addition, whether the international financial architecture and domestic political governance provide appropriate discipline against excessive borrowing is not clear.

The globalization of finance is thus not an unmixed blessing, but it appears to be inexorable. Increased trade, travel, and migration make it difficult to maintain capital controls and government allocations of foreign exchange without risking worsening corruption and income distribution. In recognition of these problems and the net benefits of more open capital accounts, countries have increasingly liberalized finance internationally, thereby providing a "test of the market" for financial globalization. However, the issues mentioned in this chapter mean this must be done carefully. Strengthening financial systems through stronger regulation and supervision and allowing the entry of reputable foreign banks are important, both areas in which globalization can actually help. Macroeconomic policy, particularly offshore government borrowing, must be done carefully. Adjustments may also be needed in the domestic financial sector and the policy toward inflows to ensure that the incentives to borrow offshore are not excessive.

Notes

1. The currency boards of the two CFA zones in Africa and the eastern Caribbean countries were the best known exceptions.

2. The countries did not adopt floating exchange rates to isolate their economies and financial systems for a variety of reasons, including the Bretton Woods arrangements, which were based on adjustable peg exchange rate regimes; the political economy of the time, which involved government rather than market allocation of resources like foreign exchange; and the concerns that floating rates would be unstable.

3. Studies such as Leblang (1997) show a correlation between capital controls and pegged exchange rates.

4. The South American countries have had their own currencies for many years and have suffered from a history of high inflation. Panama used the U.S. dollar as its currency, and most Central American countries had their own currencies, but maintained fixed rates against the U.S. dollar until they succumbed to inflationary tendencies in the 1980s (Edwards 1995). Mexico

also maintained a fixed exchange rate against the dollar for many years, but experienced higher rates of inflation and frequent devaluations after 1983.

5. The tendency to finance directed credit with cross-subsidies, that is, higher rates on other borrowers, leads to pressures to expand directed credit as discussed in Caprio, Hanson, and Honohan (2001).

6. For example, as trade grew overinvoicing imports and underinvoicing exports to transfer funds overseas became easier.

7. For example, the 1991 Peruvian Constitution, passed after the hyper-inflation of the late 1990s, guarantees citizens the right to hold foreign exchange assets.

8. Hanson (chapter 4 in this volume) also provides some data suggest-ing that offshore deposits have risen. These calculations are based on Bank for International Settlements data on deposits in OECD banks by nonresi-dents. They understate offshore deposits because they exclude deposits in non-OECD financial centers and because nonresidents may use addresses in OECD countries for their banking.

9. The table excludes 26 other developing countries all of which had deposits of less than US$10 billion and none of which had stock markets. These countries were excluded either because their data appear to reflect a role as an offshore financial center or because of large movements in off-shore deposits during the period.

10. Of course, this also implies no significant growth benefit from restricting capital flows.

11. See Dooley and others (1986) and World Bank (1985) for Latin America in the 1980s, World Bank (2000) for East Asia before the 1997 financial crisis, and World Bank (2002) for China.

12. Broadly speaking these markets are ineffective because they are often limited by governments; because banks are often limited in their ability to engage in or lend for hedging; and because, as Mundell (1968) notes, their smallness may generate market power. The markets for foreign exchange hedging are also limited because residents with access to foreign exchange may choose to sell it directly or use it to self-hedge their own activities (see Mussa and others 2000, p. 15). Hence hedging mostly depends on nonres-idents, and their participation is often discouraged by the difficulty of col-lecting on contracts in the context of the weak legal framework. Small, off-shore futures markets have existed in a few currencies in Hong Kong (China), Singapore, and the United States. Governments sometimes offer hedges, often at subsidized rates, but these have proved costly, particularly during crises, for example, in Thailand in 1997.

13. See, for example, Alesina, Grilli, and Milesi-Ferreti (1994) and Garrett (1995, 2000). Of course the direction of causation in this relation-ship is hard to establish, that is, capital controls may be imposed because a government intends to engage in macroeconomic imbalances, as Dornbusch and Edwards (1991) and Eichengreen (2001) note.

14. Of course, individuals and firms also use offshore holdings of deposits and other assets to avoid taxes.

15. They may also hedge by placing funds offshore as discussed in Honohan and Shi (chapter 2 in this volume).

16. Note that much of the credit risk depends on national economic instability rather than on the loan being denominated in foreign currency as such. If borrowers were forced to take domestic currency loans instead of foreign currency loans (and assuming matching of deposits), then the institution would still have a large credit risk because of the high, variable domestic currency interest rates that prevail in unstable countries in which devaluation may occur.

17. Moreover, hedging would reduce the gains from borrowing in foreign currency. If perfect hedging facilities were available and a devaluation were perfectly forecast, then the cost of foreign and domestic currency loans would be equal, although hedging might still involve higher cash flow payments initially.

18. This includes all the countries with less than US$300 million of deposits, as well as those countries for which data are available on the number of banks that have an average size of less than US$300 million. The actual number with an average bank size of less than US$300 million is probably larger, because many of the countries in which the number of banks is unavailable have total bank deposits of less than US$2 billion.

19. The number of commercial banks in the United States declined from 12,300 in 1990 to 8,300 in 2000 and their average size more than doubled, rising from US$150 million in deposits in 1990 to US$330 million in 2000.

20. Another justification is that following countries' independence, foreign banks only dealt with traditional business and did not serve governments' developmental goals.

21. Lower wages may provide some offset. Bossone, Honohan, and Long (2002) attempt to take the effect of low wages on costs into account by using per capita GDP as a proxy for wages.

22. Another important precondition for private bonds is a sound legal framework for bondholders' rights.

23. In some cases a market does exist for short-term, central bank bonds that have been created to carry out open market operations for monetary policy. This market's infrastructure could also be used to set up a government bond market, but institutional changes would also be necessary to deal with the interaction of government and central bank bonds and any switch to the use of government bonds for open market operations.

24. Among the largest markets China has about 1,100 listed firms, Malaysia has about 800, South Africa has about 600, Turkey has about 300, Brazil has less than 450, and Mexico has less than 200.

25. Another factor pertinent to low liquidity in developing country markets, even large ones, may be prohibitions on bank lending for equity

trading. Developing countries often restrict this in an attempt to divert credit from what they consider financial speculation to the real economy.

26. For example, India's National Stock Exchange has had an electronic system linked to brokers' offices throughout the country since the mid-1990s. The South African (JSE) Securities Exchange recently initiated an electronic trading system based on the London Stock Exchange's system. Shah and Thomas (1999) argue that direct transaction costs in Indian markets were halved between 1993 and 1997, although they were still double the costs in U.S. markets.

27. Depository receipts are foreign currency–denominated instruments issued by international banks, mostly in New York (American depository receipts) or London markets (global depository receipts), that are linked to securities traded in developing countries and held by a custodian. Depository receipts and stock values typically move together in their home markets, because depository rights can be converted back and forth into the underlying shares inexpensively. Depository receipts thus differ from the special classes of shares that can only be held by foreigners, such as have existed in China and the Republic of Korea. Karolyi (1998) provides a useful summary of the options for international listings.

28. For example, South African Breweries and Anglo-American recently moved their primary listings from the Johannesburg Exchange to the London Stock Exchange.

29. In low-income countries the average trading offshore is only 7 percent of onshore trading.

30. As noted earlier, international banks often play a large role in government debt markets in developing countries.

31. Of course, large numbers of employee-based pension schemes continue to exist in many countries, but these have limited portability and piggyback on the company payroll system. Nonetheless, they often incur high costs, have poor records, and may use employee pensions as a source of investment funds as discussed in Impavido, Musalem, and Vittas (chapter 9 in this volume). These problems are particularly true in relation to small companies' employee pension funds.

32. Impavido, Musalem, and Vittas (chapter 9 in this volume) provide some evidence suggesting that rates of return are associated with the quality of governance in a society.

33. The illiquidity of the market makes it difficult to mark pension fund assets to market.

34. Moving toward more flexible exchange rates may restore some monetary policy independence. However, it may also encourage individuals and firms to move toward more foreign currency–denominated assets and liabilities, which also reduces the effectiveness of monetary policy. Moreover, the importance of foreign currency–denominated assets and liabilities in the

domestic financial system often seems to lead to countries aiming their policies at stabilizing the "flexible" exchange rate (Calvo and Reinhart 2000).

References

The word *processed* describes informally produced works that may not be commonly available through libraries.

Aizenman, J., and P. Guidotti. 1994. "Capital Controls, Collection Costs, and Domestic Public Debt." *Journal of International Money and Finance* 13(1): 41–54.

Alesina, A., and G. Tabellini. 1989. "External Debt, Capital Flight, Political Risk." *Journal of International Economics* 27(3–4): 199–220.

Alesina, A., V. Grilli, and G. Milesi-Ferreti. 1994. "The Political Economy of Capital Controls." In L. Liederman and A. Razin, eds., *Capital Mobility: The Impact on Consumption, Investment, and Growth.* Cambridge, U.K.: Cambridge University Press.

Arioshi, A., K. Habermeier, B. Laurens, I. Otker-Robe, J. Canales-Krijenko, and A. Kirilenko. 2000. *Capital Controls: Country Experiences with Their Use and Liberalization.* Occasional Paper no. 190. Washington, D.C.: International Monetary Fund.

Barth, J., G. Caprio, and R. Levine. 2001. "Banking Systems around the Globe: Do Regulation and Ownership Affect Performance and Stability." In F. Mishkin, ed., *Prudential Regulation and Supervision; Why Is It Important and What Are the Issues?* Cambridge, Mass.: National Bureau of Economic Research.

Bartolini, L., and A. Drazen. 1997. "Capital Account Liberalization as a Signal." *American Economic Review* 87(1): 138–54.

Bossone, B., P. Honohan, and M. Long. 2002. "Policy for Small Financial Systems." In G. Caprio, P. Honohan, and D. Vittas, eds., *Financial Sector Policy for Developing Countries—A Reader.* Oxford, U.K.: Oxford University Press.

Calvo, G., and C. Reinhart. 2000. "Fear of Floating." Working Paper no. 7993. National Bureau of Economic Research, Cambridge, Mass.

Caprio, G., J. Hanson, and P. Honohan. 2001. "Introduction and Overview: The Case for Liberalization and Some Drawbacks." In G. Caprio, P. Honohan, and J. Stiglitz, eds., *Financial Liberalization: How Far, How Fast?* Cambridge, U.K.: Cambridge University Press.

Claessens, S., A. Demirgüç-Kunt, and H. Huizinga. 2000. "The Role of Foreign Banks in Domestic Banking Systems." In S. Classens and M. Jansen, eds., *The Internationalization of Financial Services: Issues and Lessons for Developing Countries.* Boston: Kluwer Academic Press.

Claessens, S., D. Klingebiel, and S. Schmukler. 2002. "Explaining the Migration of Stocks from Exchanges in Emerging Economies to International Centers." World Bank, Washington, D.C. Processed.

Clarke, G., R. Cull, M. Martinez Peria, and S. Sanchez. 2003. "Foreign Bank Entry: Experience, Implications for Developing Economies, and Agenda for Further Research." *World Bank Research Observer* 18(1): 25–60.

Demirgüç-Kunt, A., and E. Detragiache, 2001, "Financial Liberalization and Financial Fragility." In G. Caprio, P. Honohan, and J. Stiglitz, eds., *Financial Liberalization: How Far, How Fast?* Cambridge, U.K.: Cambridge University Press.

Dooley, M. 1996. "A Survey of Literature on Controls over International Capital Transactions." *International Monetary Fund Staff Papers* 43(4): 639–87.

Dooley, M., W. Helkie, R. Tyron, and J. Underwood. 1986. "An Analysis of the External Debt Positions of Eight Developing Countries through 1990." *Journal of Development Economics* 21(2): 283–318.

Dornbusch, R., and S. Edwards. 1991. *The Macroeconomics of Populism in Latin America.* Chicago: University of Chicago Press.

Easterly, W. 2000. "Small States, Small Problems? Income, Growth, and Volatility in Small States." *World Development* 28(11): 2013–27.

Easterly, W., R. Islam, and J. E. Stiglitz. 2001. "Shaken and Stirred: Explaining Growth and Volatility." In B. Pleskovic and J. Stiglitz, eds., *Annual Bank Conference on Development Economics, 2000.* Washington, D.C.: World Bank.

Edwards, S. 1989. *Real Exchange Rates, Devaluation, and Adjustment.* Cambridge, Mass.: Massachusetts Institute of Technology.

_____. 1995. "Exchange Rates, Inflation, and Disinflation." In S. Edwards, ed., *Capital Controls, Exchange Rates, and Monetary Policy in the World Economy.* Cambridge, U.K.: Cambridge, University Press.

_____. 1999. "How Effective Are Capital Controls?" *Journal of Economic Perspectives* 13(4): 65–84.

Eichengreen, B. 2001. "Capital Account Liberalization: What Do Cross Country Studies Tell Us?" *World Bank Economic Review* 15(3): 341–66.

Financial Times. 2002. "Single-Country Funds Set to Dwindle as Economies Fall Closer into Line." June 6.

Garrett, G. 1995. "Capital Mobility, Trade, and the Domestic Politics of Economic Policy." *International Organization* 49(4): 657–87.

_____. 2000. "Capital Mobility, Exchange Rates, and Fiscal Policy in the Global Economy." *Review of International Political Economy* 7(1): 153–70.

Ghilarducci T., and K. Terry. 1999. "Scale Economies in Union Pension Plan Administration." *Industrial Relations* 38(1): 11–17.

Hanke, S., and K. Schuler. 1994. *Currency Boards for Developing Countries: A Handbook*. San Francisco: International Center for Economic Growth.

Hanson, J. 1994. "An Open Capital Account: A Brief Survey of the Issues and the Results." In G. Caprio, I. Atiyas, and J. Hanson, eds., *Financial Reform: Theory and Experience*. Cambridge, U.K.: Cambridge University Press.

_____. 2002. "Dollarization, Private and Official: Issues, Benefits, and Costs." In G. Caprio, P. Honohan, and D. Vittas, eds., *Financial Sector Policy for Developing Countries—A Reader*. Oxford, U.K.: Oxford University Press.

Hughes, J., W. Lang, L. Mester, and C. Moon. 1999. "Efficient Banking under Interstate Branching." *Journal of Money, Credit and Banking* 28(4):1045–71.

Kaminsky, G., and C. Reinhart. 1999. "The Twin Crises: The Causes of Banking and Balance of Payments Problems." *American Economic Review* 89(3): 473–500.

Karolyi, G. 1998. "Why Do Companies List Shares Abroad? A Survey of the Evidence and Its Managerial Implications." *Financial Markets, Institutions, and Instruments* 7(1): 1–60.

Kraay, A. 1998. "In Search of the Macroeconomic Effects of Capital Account Liberalization." World Bank, Development Economics Research Group, Washington, D.C. Processed.

LaPorta, R., F. Lopez-de-Silanes, and A. Shleifer. 2000. "Government Ownership of Banks." Harvard University, Cambridge, Massachusetts. Available on: www.economics.harvard.edu/faculty/laporta/laporta.html.

Leblang, D. 1997. "Domestic and Systemic Determinants of Capital Controls in the Developed and Developing World." *International Studies Quarterly* 41(3): 435–54.

Mundell, R. 1968. *International Economics*. New York: Macmillan.

Mussa, M., P. Masson, A. Swoboda, E. Jadresic, P. Mauro, and A. Berg. 2000. *Exchange Rate Regimes in an Increasingly Integrated World Economy*. Occasional Paper no. 193. Washington, D.C.: International Monetary Fund.

Reynolds, C. 1965. "Development Problems of an Export Economy: The Case of Chile and Copper." In C. Reynolds and M. Mamalakis, eds., *Essays on the Chilean Economy*. Homewood, Ill.: Irwin.

Rodrik, D. 1998. "Who Needs Capital Account Convertibility?" In S. Fischer, R. N. Cooper, R. Dornbusch, P. M. Garber, C. Massad, J. J. Polak, D. Rodrik, and S. S. Tarapore, eds., *Should the IMF Pursue Capital Account Liberalization?* Princeton Essays in International Finance no. 207. Princeton, N.J.: Princeton University, International Finance Section.

Rossi, M. 1999. "Financial Fragility and Developing Economies: Do Capital Controls, Prudential Regulation, and Supervision Matter?" Working Paper no. WP/99/66. International Monetary Fund, Washington, D.C.

Shah, A., and S. Thomas. 1999. "Developing the Indian Capital Market." In J. A. Hanson and S. Kathuria, eds., *India: A Financial Sector for the Twenty-First Century*. New York: Oxford University Press.

Skidelsky, R. 1992. *John Maynard Keynes: The Economist as Saviour 1920–37*. London: Macmillan.

Standard & Poor's. 2001. *Emerging Stock Markets Factbook*. New York: McGraw-Hill.

Williamson, J. 1995. *What Role for Currency Boards?* Washington, D.C.: Institute of International Economics.

World Bank. 1985. *World Development Report: International Capital and Economic Development*. New York: Oxford University Press.

_____. 2000. *East Asia: Recovery and Beyond*. Washington, D.C.

_____. 2001. *Finance for Growth: Policy Choice in a Volatile World*. New York: Oxford University Press.

_____. 2002. *Global Development Finance 2002*. Washington, D.C.

Part I

Macroeconomics and Globalization

2

Deposit Dollarization and the Financial Sector

Patrick Honohan and Anqing Shi

In many countries, usually following episodes of high inflation and sudden depreciation, banks and their customers have spontaneously shifted part of their business to foreign currency–denominated deposits and loans, a trend known as dollarization, even though other foreign currencies such as the deutschmark or euro have been involved in some countries.[1]

Although not altogether irreversible—macroeconomic stabilization and legislation prohibiting it have reduced dollarization in some countries—dollarization is a phenomenon that will likely persist for the foreseeable future. This chapter reviews recent trends in partial dollarization of bank deposits in developing countries, assembling an expanded dataset on deposit dollarization.[2] It identifies empirical regularities in the data and considers some implications for financial sector stability and performance.

Although the quality and comparability of the data are not uniformly high, quantitative information on deposit dollarization is now available for 60 emerging economies, several more than covered in Baliño and others' (1999) survey. In addition, we have added

Helpful comments were received from Gerard Caprio, Augusto de la Torre, James Hanson, Giovanni Majnoni, Maria Soledad Martinez-Peria, and Fernando Montes-Negret.

up to five years to those countries that were in the earlier paper, whose data ended at 1995. A comparison of the most recent data with those for dollarization in 1995 indicates a continued trend toward increased dollarization.

Much of the policy discussion has rightly focused on monetary stabilization issues, which are not discussed in this chapter, which instead examines issues of risk and pricing. At the level of the individual depositor, the availability of foreign currency deposits offers risk reduction possibilities, the importance of which will depend in part on the degree of macroeconomic volatility and the extent to which foreign currency is a useful inflation hedge. At the level of the system as a whole, however, increased deposit dollarization can be associated with a change in the system's vulnerability to shocks. It can also affect the supply and cost of credit, depending on how it influences the supply of deposits to banks and their currency composition. For example, banks need to hedge the currency risk and may not safely be able to pass it on by lending foreign currency to local borrowers who do not have foreign currency receivables. The market power of banks may also be affected, resulting in higher spreads. Finally, if increased dollarization is associated with a higher risk premium on local currency assets, real interest rates on large deposits and money market assets denominated in local currency may also increase to clear the market.

Recent papers have clarified many of the policy issues involved, but wide differences of opinion remain, some of them attributable to a lack of agreement on the ultimate causes and mechanisms involved. This chapter throws empirical light on several of the most important building blocks for understanding how dollarization works. In particular, it explores

- Whether pass-through of exchange rate changes tends to be higher with higher dollarization
- Whether an irreversibility or "ratchet effect" is involved
- Whether there is a relationship between dollarization and the degree to which nonbank residents have deposits in offshore banks
- Whether a link exists between deposit dollarization and the volume and currency composition of bank lending
- Whether bank interest margins are systematically associated with the degree of dollarization
- Whether real deposit interest rates increase with dollarization.

The chapter begins with a brief review of theoretical predictions about the relationships between dollarization, the supply of credit, interest rates and spreads, and the speed of price pass-through. This is followed by a description of recent developments in deposit dollarization as revealed by the data, including evidence on the supposed ratchet effect. The next section presents regression results based on the new data, followed by a consideration of the consequences for risk in the banking system and some remarks on policy implications.

Theoretical Review of the Causes and Consequences of Dollarization

The degree of dollarization in an economy is something that is endogenously determined by agents optimizing within the constraints presented by policy and technology. Therefore when observing correlations between the degree of deposit dollarization and other macroeconomic or financial sector variables, jumping to causal conclusions would be unwise. Nevertheless, a sizable body of theory about the behavior of different classes of economic agents faced with the choice between domestic- and foreign-currency denominated instruments does help in interpreting why some such correlations may be observed. This body of theory builds in part on an older literature on the use of noninterest-bearing foreign currency notes and coin—so-called currency substitution (see box 2.1).

Role of Pass-Through

Holding dollar deposits helps protect against devaluation of the local currency, but this protection is usually bought at a price in the form of lower nominal interest rates, inasmuch as interest rate differentials will adjust to offset, at least partially, the expected rate of depreciation.[3] However, nominal devaluation of the local currency is not the only risk. Real exchange rate fluctuations mean that holding dollar deposits is not a risk-free strategy for depositors whose consumption patterns include local as well as imported goods. To minimize the variance of a portfolio's real value the mix of foreign and local currency assets must be chosen with reference both to the variance of inflation and to the variance of the real exchange rate, as well as to covariances. The higher the variance of domestic inflation, the higher the share of dollars in the minimum variance portfolio, but the higher the variance of the real exchange rate, the lower the share of dollars. Note that the minimum variance approach is relevant to borrowers as well as to lenders.

The optimal portfolio will differ from the minimum variance portfolio to the extent that investors are prepared to accept a higher

> *Box 2.1* Currency Substitution
> and Transaction Dollarization
>
> Even in the absence of foreign exchange deposits, dollars may circulate freely and be used in transactions. The early literature on this phenomenon of currency substitution focused on agents holding non-deposit cash in multiple currency denominations. It examined the impact of increased currency substitution on macroeconomic volatility, and specifically on the way in which a shrinking domestic currency money base (resulting from currency substitution) risked increasing the amplitude of the response of equilibrium exchange rates and inflation to nominal shocks, such as a change in the rate of monetary expansion (Girton and Roper 1981; Kareken and Wallace 1981). As Berg and Borensztein (2000) note, McKinnon (1996) justifies his recommendation for an international monetary standard and a world monetary authority largely on the basis of this volatility of exchange rates under currency substitution.
>
> The major technical differences between currency substitution and dollarization are (a) currency notes and coin are not interest-bearing, with the result that an increased expected rate of depreciation cannot simply be compensated for by increased interest payments; and (b) bank deposits, as liabilities of market institutions, affect bank profitability and the credit market.
>
> The dollarization of transactions has also been widely observed, though difficult to measure in a systematic way. It can include posting the prices of goods and services in foreign exchange even if payment is made in local currency, as well as the actual use of dollars in transactions. The dollarization of transactions is often associated with rapid price pass-through.

risk in return for a higher expected return. Nevertheless, inasmuch as both borrowers and lenders can benefit from reduced real variance, the minimum variance calculations point to likely important influences on the equilibrium share of dollarization in the economy. Indeed, empirical results reported by Ize and Levy-Yeyati (1998) confirm the predicted correlations between the degree of dollarization and these determinants of the minimum variance portfolio.[4] Alternative specifications, for example, those expressed in terms of the risk of rare but large devaluations, may perform equally well, and other considerations may also be important.[5]

A rapid pass-through of exchange rate changes into local prices will tend to stabilize real exchange rates, which in turn will boost dollarization, according to Ize and Levy-Yeyati's (1998) reasoning. Yet even though the determinants of pass-through and dollarization certainly overlap, models differ as to how closely they are related.[6] The degree of correlation between the two is thus an empirical question.

Hysteresis or the Ratchet Effect

While the initial impetus for dollarization often comes from disruption or extreme volatility in financial markets, observers note that the share of dollarization often remains high even when domestic financial conditions settle down. For one reason or another, once depositors become used to holding foreign currency–denominated deposits, they are slow to divest themselves of them even if the initial cause that triggered the holdings is reversed. This hysteresis or ratchet effect could be due to the depositors' setup costs of establishing dollar deposits and adjusting their business accordingly. Once depositors have paid the setup costs they might as well continue to benefit from the risk-reduction benefits of holding a mixed portfolio of currencies (Guidotti and Rodriguez 1992; Uribe 1997).[7] Alternatively, the persistence of a high rate of dollarization long after the crisis could result from the persistence of long-lived, residual anxieties of a recurrence that one episode of volatility can cause.

Deposit Dollarization Versus Offshore Holdings

Even where foreign exchange deposits are permitted, depositors may prefer to place their foreign exchange deposits abroad, sometimes in banks that are officially offshore but also have a significant onshore presence.[8] They will do so especially if there is a risk of expropriation or of enforced conversion of onshore foreign exchange deposits at an unfavorable exchange rate.[9] Furthermore, several countries have experienced a form of round-tripping where offshore borrowing is fully backed by offshore deposits made by the borrower. The goals of such back-to-back arrangements may include tax avoidance and protection against expropriation.

Impact of Deposit Dollarization on Bank Lending

A shift by depositors in favor of dollars is unlikely to be associated with a corresponding one-for-one shift in the currency composition of the banks' lending. Faced with the need to hedge an increase in dollar deposits banks can denominate more of their loans in dollars, reinvest some of the deposited dollars abroad, or both. There is a limit to which the first route can be done safely because after all, dollar-denominated loans to local firms are an imperfect hedge for dollar liabilities, especially if the borrower has no foreign currency receivables (or more precisely, unless the borrower stands otherwise to benefit from a nominal depreciation). Many banks have found to their cost that they have merely substituted credit risk for exchange rate risk.

The sizable risk of an open foreign exchange position and prudential limitations thus implies that, once the limit to safe and profitable foreign exchange lending at home has been reached, the remainder of the resources raised through dollar deposits at the bank will be placed into the international money market.

An obviously relevant consideration in this regard is how fast exchange rate changes pass through into local prices. If the pass-through is rapid, then local borrowers may be able to assume the exchange risk of a foreign currency–denominated loan even if they have no foreign currency receivables. Furthermore, banks typically have more market power in lending than in deposits. This also indicates that the impact of changes in deposit dollarization on the share of dollars in bank lending could be limited. By the same token, an increase in the foreign exchange share of a constant total of deposits could result in a lower volume of lending overall.

Banks' Market Power

If overall lending declines for the reasons outlined earlier, this may be associated with higher bank lending spreads. The availability of foreign currency resources can open profitable new lines of business and help enhance the profitability of loan markets by segmenting submarkets.[10]

Dollarization and Currency Risk Premiums

If the experience or risk of sharp devaluation has often been the trigger for deposit dollarization, then the degree of dollarization might in turn influence the risk of a policy-induced devaluation. Where deposit dollarization is high, will governments be more tempted to engineer a surprise devaluation? If so, local currency depositors will protect themselves from such risks by insisting on a higher interest rate differential, which will show up as a higher real interest rate over a period when devaluation does not occur.

Despite the lack of general agreement on the point,[11] a plausible argument is that high dollarization and speed of pass-through might increase the risk of the authorities engineering a sizable devaluation to relieve fiscal pressure.[12] Consider a heavily indebted government wishing to impose a one-off capital loss on holders of government debt denominated in local currency to reduce the real value of the government's debt. If pass-through is rapid, then any change in relative prices will be short-lived. Indeed, relative prices and the real exchange rate will essentially be fixed. If, in addition, dollarization is high, then the impact of a devaluation on a well-hedged banking system will also be slight. The temptation for a surprise devaluation to improve the fiscal position will be especially high in such conditions, in that the real value of local currency–denominated debt can be reduced with little impact on competitiveness conditions or the banking system.[13] These are therefore the conditions for a high currency risk premium.

This can be seen as an application of the fiscal theory of the price level, according to which a major influence on inflation and exchange rate developments comes through the government's incentive to run a deficit. To finance this deficit, the government may have recourse to the inflation tax. If prices and wages are somewhat sticky, this will lead to exchange rate overshooting and a costly period of misaligned relative prices. The degree of dollarization and the speed of pass-through both influence the incentive for reliance on the inflation tax, and hence the degree to which shocks affecting the fiscal accounts will pass through to the exchange rate. In particular, the base for the inflation tax may be lower if dollarization is higher, a factor that increases the size of the devaluation needed to generate a given amount of revenue. This might stay the hand of government, making it more reluctant to adopt inflationary policies (Calvo 2000a; Calvo and Vegh 1996). By contrast, the perceived cost of devaluing may be smaller where pass-through is high, as the relative prices of goods will be relatively unaffected by currency movements. Thus with the inflation tax often being a residual source of funds rather than being planned to achieve tax rate smoothing, a combination of dollarization (reducing the inflation tax base) and higher pass-through (lowering the real economy effects of nominal devaluation) would tend to increase nominal exchange rate volatility and thereby add a risk premium to real interest rates.

Where government macroeconomic policy lacks credibility, currency risk and country risk (as measured by the premium paid on the government's foreign exchange borrowing) will both be high.[14] They are indeed correlated across Latin America, suggesting a wide variation in policy credibility across this region, but not elsewhere, suggesting that other considerations can also be important. The foregoing discussion suggests that the degree of dollarization could influence currency risk more than country risk.

Recent Trends in Deposit Dollarization

Even though the availability of data is still quite patchy, it continues to improve, and as it does it confirms the growing importance of deposit dollarization in emerging economies. Our dataset, shown in the appendix tables, contains data for 60 emerging economies.

The share of dollar-denominated deposits in total onshore bank deposits for countries in the sample grew by about 1.7 percentage points per year during the 1990s. (This is a regression-based estimate, drawn from a panel regression covering the period 1990–2000 that includes country fixed effects and a first-order autoregressive coefficient.)

For the 25 emerging economies for which we have data for both 1995 and 1999, the unweighted mean share of foreign currency deposits in total bank deposits rose from 37.1 to 44.2 percent and the median share rose even more sharply from 31.6 to 43.2 percent.

The more traditional measure, foreign currency deposits as a share of money supply M2, is available for both years for 32 emerging economies. It rose from 25.8 to 30.9 percent, while the median rose from 21.2 to 25.9 percent, and the regression estimate of its annual rate of increase over the 1990s is 1.2 percentage points per year.

In 22 countries data for recent years show that half or more of deposits are denominated in foreign currencies (table 2.1).

The increase in average dollarization reflects increases in most of the individual countries also, as seen in figure 2.1; however, a sharp decline is apparent in a handful of East European countries. Without denying that a form of ratchet effect could apply with spontaneous dollarization, the recent declines in several countries do indicate that the process is not impossible to reverse. Poland probably provides the most striking example of an apparently sizable and sustained decline in dollarization. The figures for Estonia and Lithuania are also interesting in that they suggest a decline, followed by a gradual resumption of the use of foreign currency deposits as the 1990s progressed. Egypt provides a further example of a decline.

The data certainly suggest that substantial movements in the dollarization percentage are possible, but because there may be a number of hidden breaks in the series definition, these movements need to be viewed with especial caution. The year-to-year absolute value of the change in dollarization averages 4.5 percentage points (the median is

Table 2.1 Highest Rates of Dollarization Recorded (foreign exchange deposits as a percentage of M2, peak year)

Country	Rate	Country	Rate
Cambodia	94.0	Nicaragua	71.0
Bolivia	90.9	Peru	68.0
Angola	83.2	Belarus	63.5
Zaire	78.3	Lithuania	62.7
Georgia	78.1	Argentina	62.3
Lebanon	77.7	Guinea Bissau	60.9
Croatia	73.7	Bulgaria	55.9
Tajikistan	72.4	Egypt	55.6
Armenia	72.2	Mozambique	54.0
Azerbaijan	71.9	Paraguay	53.7
Laos PDR	71.5	Turkey	51.9

Source: See table A1.

Figure 2.1 Trends in Deposit Dollarization, Selected Countries, 1995 and 1999–2000 (foreign exchange deposits as a percentage of M2)

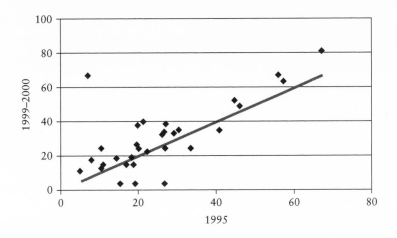

Source: See table A1.

2.5 percentage points), and there are several instances of annual changes of more than 25 percentage points.[15]

Evidence from Regression Results

This section reports on initial attempts to assess the empirical sign and size of the five remaining relationships (aside from ratchet effects, which have already been considered) highlighted in the introduction. Note that most of the variables in the regressions are endogenous, so these preliminary regression results need to be interpreted with caution. In particular, no causal interpretation has been established.

Is Faster Pass-Through Associated with Deposit Dollarization?

As mentioned earlier, some theoretical considerations suggest that higher pass-through and higher dollarization should be associated, which would increase local borrowers' capacity to assume exchange rate risk. Does an association exist in reality?

We examined this question using our new data. The main result is illustrated in figure 2.2, where an estimated pass-through coefficient (with its 95 percent confidence interval), estimated over the period 1980–2000, is plotted against the mean dollarization ratio. The upward-sloping trend is unmistakable, and a simple regression of the point estimates of the pass-through on dollarization reveals that a 10 percentage point increase in dollarization is associated with an 0.08 (8 percent) increase in pass-through (t-statistic of 4.5).

The pass-through coefficient shown in figure 2.2 is measured as follows from a simple panel of quarterly data from more than 50 countries for 1980–2000.[16] The dependent variable p is the log of the consumer price index; changes in it are modeled as impacted by changes in the log dollar exchange rate e with a lagged four-quarter change in p as well as the real exchange rate q (local consumer prices compared with dollar-adjusted U.S. wholesale prices) as an error correction or catch-up term. Thus the estimated equation is

$$\Delta p = \alpha_0 + \alpha_1 \Delta e + \alpha_2(p_{-1} - p_{-5}) + \alpha_3 q_{-4} \tag{2.1}$$

The coefficient α_1 is taken as the pass-through coefficient. (Little difference is made by employing some combination of α_1 and α_3 instead, such as the cumulative pass-through after one year, or the half-life.) Even using common coefficients for all countries, this model explains two-thirds of the sample variability, as can be seen from regression A in table 2.2. Making α_1 a function of the mean dollarization rate, as in regression B, improves the fit significantly,

Figure 2.2 Estimated Pass-Through Coefficient
and Dollarization, Selected Countries, 1980–2000

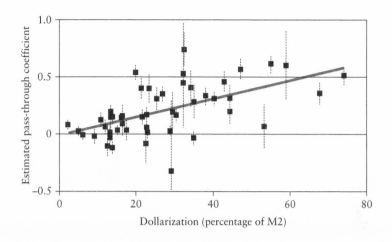

Source: Authors' calculations.

and the coefficient is positive and highly significant. An increase of 10 percentage points in dollarization increases estimated pass-through by 0.064 (more than 6 percent). Allowing country-specific values of α_1 improves the fit even more. The pass-through coefficients used in figure 2.2 are the point estimates from regression C of the country-specific coefficients α_{1i}.[17]

The conclusion must therefore be that a strong positive correlation exists between the degree of dollarization and the speed of pass-through.

Does Deposit Dollarization Shrink the Availability of Credit?

Placing dollar funds abroad insulates a bank more effectively against exchange rate risk, but reduces the availability of credit to local firms. Regressing the banking system's net foreign assets (as a percentage of M2) on the dollarization ratio suggests an approximate 50 percent pass-through of increases in dollarization to foreign asset holdings. This is the implication of the coefficient value of 0.538 in regression C of table 2.3. The higher figure in regression B should be discounted because of the residual autocorrelation, and the lower figure in regression D reflects the smaller numerator of the dollarization variable used in that regression.[18]

Table 2.2 Estimate of Dynamic Model of Pass-Through, Equation (2.1) (dependent variable: Δp)

Category	A Common model		B Role of dollarization		C Country-specific pass-through		D Country-specific pass-through	
	Estimate	t-statistic	Estimate	t-statistic	Estimate	t-statistic	Estimate	t-statistic
c	0.0109	(4.7)	0.0153	(8.3)	0.0207	(3.7)	0.0169	(12.9)
Time ($\times 10^3$)	−0.125	(3.4)	−0.134	(4.5)	−0.206	(2.5)	−0.177	(8.9)
$q(-4)$ ($\times 10^2$)	−0.396	(1.7)	−0.681	(3.2)	−0.194	(2.8)	−0.192	(8.9)
$p(-1) - p(-5)$	0.134	(47.1)	0.127	(44.4)	0.107	(34.8)	0.113	(37.2)
Δe	0.278	(36.7)	0.076	(7.6)	Country		Country	
dollar*Δe			0.00609	(17.2)				
Countries/ observations	49	2,493	49	2,493	49	2,493	49	2,493
Dates	1980Q1–1999Q4		1980Q1–2000Q4		1980Q1–2000Q4		1980Q1–2000Q4	
Method	SUR		SUR		Unweighted panel		SUR	
RSQ/DW	0.669	1.52	0.698	1.58	0.741	1.82	0.739	1.76

DW Durbin-Watson statistic.
Q Quarter.
RSQ Squared multiple correlation coefficient.
SUR Seemingly unrelated regressions system estimate of pool coefficients.
Note: "Country" means country-specific coefficients estimated (not individually reported).
The variable *dollar* is the share of foreign currency deposits in M2.
Source: Authors' calculations.

Some of this effect, especially where change in the dollarization rate is an explanatory variable as in regression A, could be seen as a mechanical valuation change effect, in that appreciation of the dollar would increase both dollarization and net foreign holdings as a share of the portfolio even if no other change occurred. Nevertheless, albeit mechanical, it is real. A simple if rough way of gauging the importance of the mechanical exchange rate effect is to include the rate of the exchange rate change in the previous year as an additional explanatory variable. Regression E shows that this still leaves a sizable and significant nonmechanical effect about twice the original estimate of regression A. Including the exchange rate change in the other regressions in which dollarization enters only in its level, and not in the rate of change, suggests that there is no significant mechanical valuation effect influencing those estimates (compare regressions F through H with B through D).

Dollarization thus does appear to shrink the availability of credit compared with a situation where the same amount of deposits is held onshore, but in local currency.

However, this conclusion raises the question whether increased dollarization is merely a substitute for offshore deposits. In other words, does low dollarization imply that depositors have simply placed their funds directly in banks located abroad, whether in violation of exchange controls or not? If so, more dollarization might reflect less holding of offshore deposits, in which case the finding that only half the dollar deposits were on-lent would be less worrying. Although this possibility seems plausible, we were unable to confirm it using regression analysis employing the Bank for International Settlements data on the country of origin of cross-border, nonbank deposits placed in reporting banks in the main industrial countries. Indeed, the regressions in table 2.4 suggest the existence of a strong positive association between changes in the degree of dollarization and offshore deposits. This may reflect the influence of offshore centers on the data on international deposits. Undoubtedly this relationship needs further examination. For one thing a mechanical valuation effect is again potentially at work. Correcting for this by including the rate of exchange rate change confirms that there still is a nonmechanical effect of about half the original estimate (compare regressions E through H with A through D).[19]

Does Dollarization Increase Interest Spreads?

If increased dollarization does squeeze credit availability, then an increase in interest spreads is likely. Indeed, this appears to be the

Table 2.3 Dollarization and the Net Foreign Assets of Banks
(dependent variable: *f* is log net foreign assets of banks)

Category	A Δf Estimate	t-statistic	B f Estimate	t-statistic	C f Estimate	t-statistic	D f Estimate	t-statistic
c	0.405	(0.4)	Country		Country		−3.551	(0.9)
Δdollar	0.527	(5.1)						
f(−2)	−0.198	(9.7)						
dollar			0.697	(5.8)	0.538	(5.5)	0.291	(4.2)
dollar(−2)	0.0177	(0.6)						
Δexch. rate %								
ar(1)					0.676	(24.3)	0.768	(34.1)
Countries/ observations	53	275	53	410	53	350	48	260
Years	1990–2000		1990–2000		1990–2000		1990–2000	
Method	Unweighted panel		Unweighted panel		Unweighted panel		Unweighted panel	
RSQ/DW	0.310	2.49	0.546	0.47	0.871	2.35	0.826	1.90

DW Durbin-Watson statistic.
RSQ Squared multiple correlation coefficient.
Note: "Country" means country-specific coefficients estimated (not individually reported).
Dollar is the share of foreign exchange in M2 (*A, B, C*); in deposits (*D*). *ar*(1) is the first-order autocorrelation coefficient.
Source: Authors' calculations.

Table 2.4 Dollarization and Offshore Deposits
(dependent variable: Δ*f:* change in nonbank holdings of deposits in reporting offshore banks as a percentage of M2)

Category	A Estimate	t-statistic	B Estimate	t-statistic	C Estimate	t-statistic	D Estimate	t-statistic
c	1.519	(1.5)	0.254	(0.3)	0.648	(0.6)	−0.310	(0.3)
Δdollar	0.546	(4.6)	0.602	(5.0)	0.441	(4.6)	0.492	(4.3)
lagged f	−0.096	(3.9)	−0.016	(0.6)	−0.098	(3.9)	−0.015	(0.6)
lagged dollar	−0.019	(0.7)	−0.012	(0.5)	0.010	(0.5)	0.011	(0.5)
Δexch. rate %	8.894	(5.1)	9.040	(6.1)	9..070	(5.2)	9.293	(6.0)
ar(1)	−0.239	(4.1)	−0.447	(4.8)	−0.256	(4.4)	−0.452	(4.5)
Countries/ observations	45	127	45	83	45	117	45	74
Years	1995–2000		1995–2000		1995–2000		1995–2000	
Method	Unweighted panel		Unweighted panel		Unweighted panel		Unweighted panel	
RSQ/DW	0.282	2.16	0.362	1.82	0.298	2.27	0.324	2.09

Note: Dollar is the share of foreign exchange in M2 (*A,B*); in deposits (*C,D*); lag length: 1 year (*A,C*); 2 years (*B,D*). *ar*(1) is the first-order autocorrelation coefficient.

E Δf		F f		G f		H f	
Estimate	t-statistic	Estimate	t-statistic	Estimate	t-statistic	Estimate	t-statistic
–0.869	(0.9)	Country		Country		–1.769	(0.4)
0.256	(2.3)						
–0.198	(10.2)						
		0.750	(5.8)	0.623	(5.2)	0.251	(3.4)
0.0178	(0.6)						
11.12	(5.5)	–3.50	(1.5)	0.498	(0.3)	3.039	(1.9)
				0.682	(23.9)	0.757	(31.9)
53	275	53	364	53	350	48	260
1990–2000		1990–2000		1990–2000		1990–2000	
Unweighted panel		Unweighted panel		Unweighted panel		Unweighted panel	
0.275	2.44	0.551	0.45	0.878	2.48	0.830	1.97

E		F		G		H	
Estimate	t-statistic	Estimate	t-statistic	Estimate	t-statistic	Estimate	t-statistic
1.129	(1.2)	0.161	(0.2)	0.207	(0.6)	–0.749	(0.9)
0.250	(2.1)	0.262	(2.4)	0.191	(1.9)	0.195	(2.0)
–0.115	(5.1)	–0.043	(2.2)	–0.117	(5.2)	–0.044	(2.1)
–0.032	(1.3)	–0.017	(0.9)	0.009	(0.0)	0.006	(0.3)
8.894	(5.1)	9.040	(6.1)	9.070	(5.2)	9.293	(6.0)
–0.274	(5.2)	–0.576	(7.0)	–0.279	(5.4)	–0.595	(6.5)
45	127	45	82	45	117	45	74
1995–2000		1995–2000		1995–2000		1995–2000	
Unweighted panel		Unweighted panel		Unweighted panel		Unweighted panel	
0.408	2.13	0.560	1.42	0.434	2.20	0.546	1.49

Table 2.5 Dollarization and Domestic Intermediation Spread (dependent variable: difference between quoted loan and deposit interest rates *spr*)

Category	A		B		C		D	
	Estimate	t-statistic	Estimate	t-statistic	Estimate	t-statistic	Estimate	t-statistic
c	8.209	(3.9)	Country		6.474	(3.8)	Country	
dollar	0.155	(2.7)	0.344	(2.5)	0.144	(3.9)	0.113	(1.0)
spread-fx	1.240	(3.8)	1.375	(4.1)				
ar(1)	0.470	(16.7)	0.343	(10.0)	0.423	(15.1)	0.330	(8.8)
Countries/ observations	50	182	50	182	48	168	48	168
Years	1994–2000		1994–2000		1994–2000		1994–2000	
Method	Unweighted panel		Unweighted panel		Unweighted panel		Unweighted panel	
RSQ/DW	0.621	1.44	0.798	2.38	0.614	1.67	0.731	2.37

Note: *Dollar* is the share in M2 (A,B); in deposits (C,D). *spread-fx* is the difference between quoted loan and deposit interest rates for FX-denominated business. *ar*(1) is the first-order autocorrelation coefficient.

case, using the differences between loan and deposit interest rates quoted in *International Financial Statistics*. A simple panel regression as shown in table 2.5 indicates a correlation with a sizable impact of increases in dollarization: the point estimates associate a 10 percentage point increase in deposit dollarization with an increase of about 150 basis points in quoted spreads (regressions A and C). Of course, these can be seen as extremely underspecified equations, especially insofar as the coverage of country characteristics is concerned. Nevertheless, the inclusion of country fixed effects to partially adjust for this does not reduce the size of the effect or eliminate the significance of dollarization, at least when expressed as a share of M2 (regression B).

However, the data do not seem to support Catão and Terrones's (2000) interesting hypothesis that an increase in dollarization widens interest spreads for local currency borrowers more than for foreign currency borrowers. Using the limited data available for foreign currency spreads (for just eight countries, see figure 2.3), table 2.6

Figure 2.3 Intermediation Spreads, Local Currency and Foreign Exchange Business, Selected Countries, Monthly Average 1997–99

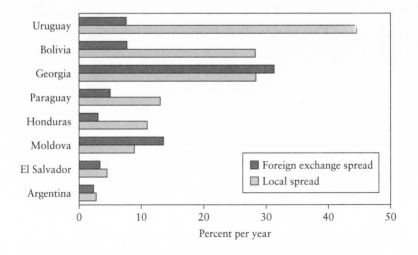

Source: International Monetary Fund, *International Financial Statistics*.

implies that the level of dollarization does not influence the relationship between dollar-based spreads and local currency-based spreads.

Does Dollarization Increase Currency Risk?

A possible correlation between the degree of dollarization and the currency risk premium was discussed earlier. Preliminary examination of this issue suggests that a positive statistical association

Table 2.6 Dollarization and Intermediation Spreads, Domestic and Foreign (dependent variable: difference between quoted loan and deposit interest rates *spr*)

	A		B	
Category	*Estimate*	*t-statistic*	*Estimate*	*t-statistic*
c	–4.357	(0.2)	9.935	(0.5)
dollar	–0.106	(0.5)	–0.218	(1.4)
spread-fx	1.240	(3.8)	1.375	(4.1)
ar(1)	0.947	(17.0)	0.934	(19.5)
Countries/ observations	7	19	7	19
Years	1994–2000		1994–2000	
Method	Unweighted panel		Unweighted panel	
RSQ/DW	0.931	2.18	0.938	2.55

Note: *Dollar* is the share in M2 (*A*); in deposits (*B*). *spread-fx* is the difference between quoted loan and deposit interest rates for FX-denominated business. *ar*(1) is first-order autocorrelation coefficient.

Table 2.7 Dollarization and Real Interest Rates (dependent variable is real deposit interest rate *r*)

	A		B		C		D	
Category	*Estimate*	*t-statistic*	*Estimate*	*t-statistic*	*Estimate*	*t-statistic*	*Estimate*	*t-statistic*
c	3.516	(0.8)	Country		–1.582	(0.3)	–2.859	(0.6)
dollar	0.247	(2.7)	0.194	(1.0)	0.255	(2.8)	0.206	(2.1)
deficit					1.322	(2.7)	1.084	(2.1)
bop ca							0.764	(2.5)
ar(1)	0.474	(9.1)	0.235	(3.2)	0.378	(6.1)	0.440	(6.8)
Countries/ observations	34	147	34	147	34	109	34	108
Years	1990–1999		1990–1999		1990–1999		1990–1999	
Method	Unweighted panel		Unweighted panel		Unweighted panel		Unweighted panel	
RSQ/DW	0.403	1.84	0.559	1.94	0.370	1.32	0.406	1.50

Note: "Country" means country-specific coefficients estimated (not individually reported); *dollar* is the share of foreign currency deposits in total deposits. *ar*(1) is the first-order autocorrelation coefficient.

between dollarization and real interest rates may indeed exist; however, whether the relationship is a robust one is not clear.

We used real deposit interest rates, as these are available for a much wider range of countries than wholesale rates. Included on its own in a panel regression (along with the first-order autocorrelation coefficient), dollarization does appear to increase the level of real deposit interest rates (regression A of table 2.7). The effect becomes insignificant when country fixed effects are included, though this should not be considered decisive given the small number of cross-sections (regression B). More important, the effect stays at a similar size and is still significant when data on the fiscal deficit (regression C) and the current account of the balance of payments (regression D)—variables that are used to explain the real interest rate—are also included. However, these results hold only when dollarization is expressed as a percentage of deposits. When M2 is the denominator, the variable becomes insignificant (regressions E through H). Nevertheless, this preliminary analysis suggests that dollarization may indeed increase the real rate of interest.

Dollarization and Banking System Risk

Drawing the strands together and simplifying illuminates the elements of a potential structural problem: factors leading to increased deposit dollarization could result in higher interest rates, lower credit supply, and greater vulnerability of the banking system. Even

E		F		G		H	
Estimate	*t-statistic*	*Estimate*	*t-statistic*	*Estimate*	*t-statistic*	*Estimate*	*t-statistic*
12.62	(3.0)	8.200	(1.8)	2.327	(0.4)	1.923	(0.3)
0.006	(0.1)	0.163	(1.4)	0.201	(1.5)	0.134	(1.0)
				1.544	(2.8)	1.181	(2.1)
						0.754	(2.2)
0.563	(4.5)	0.522	(11.3)	0.445	(7.5)	0.494	(8.2)
51	249	34	176	34	125	34	124
1990–1999		1990–1999		1990–1999		1990–1999	
Unweighted panel		Unweighted panel		Unweighted panel		Unweighted panel	
0.467	1.95	0.450	1.89	0.411	1.47	0.435	1.63

if bank margins widen, the net impact of increased dollarization on banks' sustained profitability is unclear. For example, to the extent that dollar lending does also grow, this may increase vulnerabilities to indirect currency risk when borrowers cannot absorb the foreign exchange risk.

There may also be an increase in banking risks associated with waves of currency speculation when depositors can choose the currency of denomination. This may not be obvious at first sight, after all, if deposit dollarization were not allowed, an increase in the perceived risk of a major devaluation would tend to result in deposit outflows, presenting each bank with a liquidity problem.[20] Thus, at first sight, the availability of dollar deposits appears to have the potential to insulate banks against deposit outflows triggered by a change in exchange rate expectations. Depositors need not withdraw their deposits if they can simply adjust the currency denomination of their deposit portfolio with a telephone call to the bank (though this will not be enough for depositors who fear that their dollar deposits might be frozen as part of the currency crisis).

However, currency switching by depositors, notably in response to shifting expectations about future exchange rate movements, is a source of volatility to banks, increasing their need for liquid assets and further reducing the supply of loanable funds. Thus, faced with an abrupt change in the currency composition of its deposits, a bank suddenly finds itself exposed to foreign exchange risk and will need to hedge this, effectively putting pressure on the value of the local currency. Clearly the bank will need to have sufficient liquidity to face the risk of this happening suddenly, perhaps more so because of the ease with which local depositors can make these switches (again putting downward pressure on the availability of loanable funds).

Even with adequate liquidity in local currency, the bank is vulnerable in these circumstances. After all, forced sale of these local currency liquid assets will, unless the central bank intervenes, depress the currency and result in capital losses for the bank. The bank can meet this risk by means of adequate procedures to ensure that the rates of exchange offered by the bank's retail deposit desks are up-to-date and embody a risk cushion. However, especially where a quasi-fixed exchange rate regime has been in effect for some time, such procedures may not be fully in effect. Overall, the bank may not maintain its hedge sufficiently current, and indeed may be implicitly assuming that the central bank will look after it.

The scenario depicted is one in which banks, fearful of exchange rate risk and of currency switching by depositors, hold high liquid reserves both in local currency and in foreign placements, driving up local real interest rates, yet still retaining a residual indirect exchange risk. This may in turn imply an unrecognized implicit risk for a government if it will face the costs of a bank bailout in the event of a devaluation.

Although the data are not rich enough to allow much quantification of these dimensions of banking risk, the scale of dollarization and the speed of some changes in dollarization rates noted in the dataset suggest that they are not negligible.

Concluding Remarks

Despite declines in a few countries, the general trend toward increased use of foreign currency–denominated deposits in emerging market banking systems has continued in the last few years. This trend has not been innocuous. In addition to its propensity to complicate monetary stabilization policy, deposit dollarization presents a number of structural challenges.

This chapter presents empirical evidence suggesting that even though dollarization may in part be a substitute for holding deposits abroad, a sizable fraction (about half on average) of funds switched to dollar deposit accounts are effectively exported through the banking system, thereby reducing the supply of credit. This may explain the finding that dollarization is associated with an increase in banking spreads. The conjecture that dollarization would tend to raise wholesale interest rates systematically through a peso premium receives some, though far from conclusive, support, but needs further empirical examination.

In dollarized economies where banks are imperfectly hedged against exchange risk, for example, where they have substantial foreign currency–denominated loans to local firms, the risk to bank solvency from devaluation is considerable. Especially where the dollarization is accompanied by a faster pass-through of exchange rate changes, as appears to be commonly the case, fiscal pressures may induce governments to adopt policies that can result in steep devaluations. However, if they neglect the consequences of such actions on the solvency of the banking system, they may find that the inflation tax fails to yield any net revenue after taking the implicit knock-on liabilities to the state from bank failure into account.

Although some transition economies have managed to reverse or slow dollarization by establishing credible currencies and a stable macroeconomic environment, dollarization is not going to wither away. Proscribing it is unlikely to be the most effective policy response, and could be counterproductive. Short of this, many other policy tools influence the degree of dollarization. These include the design of various taxes and tax-like measures, including reserve requirements. Lender of last resort and other safety net features, to the extent that they offer equal cover to dollar-denominated and local currency deposits, are often seen as providing an implicit subsidy to the expansion of dollarization (Broda and Levy-Yeyati 2002). Relevant policy will also include the level of inflation tax, whether one-off (surprise) or steady-state.

There are obviously implications for optimal monetary, exchange rate, and financial sector policy. Most authors assert that high dollarization implies the desirability of currency stability because of the risks of exchange rate volatility in the presence of dollarization (see Berg and Borensztein 2000),[21] although this begs the question whether a currency peg regime actually delivers the hoped-for stability, or whether it transforms a probability distribution with heavy weight on small monthly exchange rate changes to one with a low but nonnegligible weight on high monthly exchange rates.

Dollarization reinforces the need for offsetting structural policies. The key needs are first, to help ensure that the various participants internalize social risk, and second, to help strengthen the infrastructure supporting the importation of loanable funds from abroad. Internalizing social risk is an attempt to move the system closer to incentive compatibility. This could include stricter rules, taxes, or risk weights limiting indirect exposure to foreign exchange risk. Mechanisms for importing funds from abroad could include the use of structured finance or securitized loans sold to foreign lenders. The practicality of all such policies would need to be reviewed, but such a review is beyond the scope of this chapter.

Appendix: Data Tables

Table A1 Foreign Currency Deposits as a Percentage of M2, Selected Countries, 1990–2000

Country	1990	1991	1992	1993	1994	1995	1996	1997	1998	1999	2000
Albania	2.1	1.3	23.8	20.4	18.8	18.7	21.9	18.3	16.8	18.2	19.9
Angola	—	—	—	—	—	7.3	29.4	42.9	53.0	66.9	67.6
Argentina	33.7	34.9	35.4	40.7	43.8	45.1	45.7	47.3	49.0	52.5	—
Armenia	—	—	—	—	40.5	20.4	21.0	33.5	39.5	38.2	—
Azerbaijan	—	—	—	—	—	26.3	22.1	24.6	28.9	32.9	—
Belarus	—	—	—	40.6	54.3	30.7	—	27.3	—	—	—

Table A1 Continued

Country	1990	1991	1992	1993	1994	1995	1996	1997	1998	1999	2000
Bolivia	66.2	67.1	69.5	71.1	69.2	67.3	80.3	79.9	80.8	82.7	81.3
Bulgaria	12.0	34.0	25.8	20.5	32.5	27.2	50.5	43.6	39.2	39.1	—
Cambodia	—	—	26.3	36.3	51.4	56.3	63.1	62.5	54.2	60.9	68.0
Comoros	—	—	—	—	—	—	—	—	0.1	0.3	0.8
China	—	—	—	—	—	10.3	8.8	7.9	7.3	7.4	7.8
Congo, Dem. Rep.	—	—	—	—	35.8	29.0	—	—	—	—	—
Costa Rica	23.5	30.7	28.3	26.5	26.6	34.5	31.7	34.1	37.5	—	—
Croatia	—	—	—	53.8	50.3	57.5	59.6	61.7	66.3	64.0	—
Czech	—	—	—	8.1	7.0	5.3	6.0	11.4	11.3	11.7	11.6
Dominica	—	3.0	3.9	3.5	2.5	1.5	—	—	—	—	—
Ecuador	3.3	3.6	5.3	6.3	8.7	15.7	18.6	25.1	—	—	—
Egypt	46.1	47.9	32.2	27.7	27.5	27.2	23.4	20.6	19.6	20.8	24.7
El Salvador	3.4	2.9	4.2	3.7	4.5	5.0	6.4	7.5	7.8	—	—
Estonia	—	—	23.0	3.8	9.9	10.9	10.8	16.0	16.1	14.7	13.7
Georgia	—	—	—	—	80.1	30.8	14.8	20.8	29.1	35.4	—
Guinea	—	6.5	6.9	10.0	9.4	9.6	12.6	12.9	12.8	—	—
Guinea-Bissau	41.5	34.7	31.6	30.9	31.1	31.2	38.3	—	—	—	—
Honduras	1.4	3.0	5.3	6.9	12.8	17.0	25.3	23.4	23.9	—	—
Hungary	12.2	16.5	14.3	18.7	20.4	26.6	—	6.7	5.0	4.4	—
Jamaica	—	—	11.9	12.5	18.7	16.9	19.6	16.3	18.6	—	—
Lao, PDR	42.0	39.4	36.8	41.4	34.4	42.4	40.4	56.7	67.1	—	—
Latvia	—	—	—	27.2	27.5	31.1	—	—	—	—	—
Lebanon	—	—	—	—	—	65.1	59.9	71.3	75.3	—	—
Lithuania	—	—	—	44.2	26.9	26.8	24.8	21.3	24.2	30.4	34.0
Macedonia, FYR	—	—	—	—	—	14.8	13.2	19.2	21.5	19.2	—
Malawi	—	—	—	—	10.6	8.0	—	10.3	22.0	12.0	17.9
Mexico	11.1	11.8	9.7	11.1	16.5	17.5	18.0	12.7	11.9	—	—
Moldova	—	—	—	—	10.3	11.0	9.9	9.5	22.6	27.5	24.6
Mongolia	—	—	7.5	33.0	19.5	20.5	24.2	29.0	23.8	24.7	—
Mozambique	—	11.8	16.7	23.2	25.3	41.3	41.4	34.9	34.9	35.2	—
Netherlands Antilles	15.3	17.0	16.6	16.3	15.9	17.4	15.9	15.4	14.5	15.6	15.3
Nicaragua	27.3	26.2	33.6	46.1	48.2	57.1	59.2	62.9	64.7	—	—
Pakistan	2.6	8.9	11.9	13.9	13.6	18.0	22.8	23.8	9.6	—	—
Paraguay	—	—	—	35.0	32.5	27.6	32.7	37.6	44.0	—	—
Peru	38.6	55.5	57.8	58.9	58.9	57.1	61.5	53.9	54.1	—	—
Philippines	17.4	18.0	21.0	22.6	20.9	21.5	—	—	37.3	—	—
Poland	31.4	24.7	24.8	28.8	36.4	19.3	12.5	9.9	6.9	4.5	—
Romania	2.9	3.9	15.3	29.0	22.1	21.8	23.4	28.5	32.6	37.6	40.4
Russia	—	—	—	29.5	28.8	20.0	19.4	17.6	30.4	29.5	26.9
São Tomé and Príncipe	—	—	—	—	38.3	29.6	34.9	37.9	39.2	33.5	—
Saudi Arabia	22.9	21.5	19.2	21.3	20.2	19.2	17.0	16.5	17.9	16.5	15.6
Slovakia	—	—	—	11.2	12.9	11.3	10.2	10.5	14.7	14.5	15.6
Slovenia	3.4	2.9	4.2	3.7	4.5	5.0	6.4	7.5	7.8	—	—
Tajikistan	—	—	—	—	—	33.7	16.1	13.5	21.4	25.1	—
Trinidad and Tobago	—	—	—	6.9	16.1	16.5	18.9	17.9	—	—	—
Turkey	23.2	29.7	33.7	37.9	45.8	46.1	44.8	46.4	42.9	44.7	49.4
Uganda	—	—	—	10.1	11.2	11.7	12.8	13.2	13.0	—	—
Ukraine	—	—	—	19.4	31.7	22.6	16.6	13.0	20.8	24.5	22.7

Table A1 Continued

Country	1990	1991	1992	1993	1994	1995	1996	1997	1998	1999	2000
Uruguay	80.1	78.5	76.2	73.3	74.1	76.1	—	—	—	—	—
Uzbekistan	—	—	20.1	5.1	22.5	15.5	—	8.0	6.9	4.2	—
Venezúela, RB	—	—	—	—	0.1	3.4	2.2	2.3	2.2	—	—
Viet Nam	—	—	25.9	20.9	20.4	19.7	19.3	22.0	25.3	26.6	—
Yemen	—	10.8	12.1	19.7	20.7	20.9	—	—	—	—	—
Zambia	—	—	—	—	8.4	17.0	23.1	23.8	36.0	—	—

— Not available.

Note: Where conflicts existed between different sources we generally used the longest time series.

Sources: Baliño and others (1999); International Monetary Fund, *International Financial Statistics* (20 countries); individual International Monetary Fund country reports (30 countries); national central bank sources (including 10 collected and generously provided by Maria Soledad Martinez Peria); for China: unpublished estimate by Xiaofan Liu and Min Zhao based on official flow of funds statistics.

Table A2 Foreign Currency Deposits as a Percentage of Total Deposits, Selected Countries, 1990–2000

Country	1990	1991	1992	1993	1994	1995	1996	1997	1998	1999	2000
Albania	—	—	—	—	30.8	30.6	31.8	28.9	23.5	25.2	28.1
Angola	—	—	—	—	—	9.3	36.0	57.7	72.1	80.6	83.2
Argentina	47.2	48.1	47.1	52.2	55.5	57.4	56.4	57.2	58.2	62.3	—
Armenia	—	—	—	—	68.7	52.5	58.4	72.2	69.5	62.6	—
Azerbaijan	—	—	—	—	—	49.1	50.2	56.8	62.8	71.9	—
Belarus	—	—	—	—	—	—	—	34.6	63.5	35.6	—
Bolivia	79.8	77.3	78.6	79.1	77.8	76.8	89.8	89.1	89.5	90.9	89.5
Bulgaria	—	38.4	29.1	23.0	35.8	30.4	55.9	55.8	53.2	53.3	—
Cambodia	—	—	—	84.3	84.3	91.8	94.0	94.0	92.5	92.3	93.2
China	—	—	—	—	—	11.8	9.9	8.8	8.2	8.4	8.8
Comoros	—	—	—	—	—	—	—	—	0.2	0.5	1.2
Congo, Dem. Rep.	—	—	—	—	68.1	78.3	—	—	—	—	—
Costa Rica	26.8	34.8	32.4	30.4	31.1	40.9	35.7	38.5	41.9	—	—
Croatia	—	—	—	—	59.3	66.6	67.6	68.9	73.7	71.6	—
Czech	—	—	—	8.9	7.8	5.9	6.7	12.7	12.7	13.3	13.3
Dominica	0.2	2.7	3.5	3.1	2.2	1.3	0.9	1.7	2.2	—	—
Ecuador	3.8	4.2	6.1	7.2	9.8	17.4	20.5	27.6	—	—	—
Egypt	54.3	55.6	37.0	32.0	32.0	31.6	27.2	24.0	22.9	24.5	28.7
El Salvador	4.1	3.4	4.9	4.1	5.0	5.5	7.0	8.1	8.4	—	—
Estonia	—	—	—	—	—	17.2	15.5	21.0	20.6	18.9	16.9
Georgia	—	—	—	—	—	—	46.4	58.3	68.4	78.1	—
Guinea	—	—	—	—	—	19.0	22.6	23.9	24.4	—	—
Guinea-Bissau	—	—	—	—	—	—	60.9	—	—	—	—
Honduras	1.8	3.9	6.6	9.0	16.9	21.2	30.6	27.4	27.6	—	—
Hungary	—	—	—	—	—	—	—	7.9	5.8	5.3	—
Jamaica	—	—	11.9	12.5	21.0	18.9	22.1	18.4	21.0	—	—
Lao PDR	—	—	—	—	—	53.0	48.8	63.4	71.5	—	—
Latvia	—	—	—	—	—	—	1.7	2.0	—	—	—
Lebanon	—	—	—	—	—	68.2	62.5	73.8	77.7	—	—
Lithuania	—	—	—	62.7	38.8	40.6	38.2	32.7	36.4	43.7	45.6
Macedonia, FYR	—	—	—	—	—	20.9	19.3	26.4	28.5	24.6	—

Table A2 Continued

Country	1990	1991	1992	1993	1994	1995	1996	1997	1998	1999	2000
Malawi	—	—	—	—	—	—	—	13.5	27.9	16.1	23.4
Mexico	13.0	13.6	11.1	12.7	18.9	19.6	20.1	14.2	13.4	—	—
Moldova	—	—	—	—	—	—	20.3	19.3	43.8	49.6	41.8
Mongolia	—	—	—	—	—	—	36.4	41.0	35.9	40.9	—
Mozambique	—	—	—	—	—	53.6	54.0	44.0	43.1	43.2	—
Netherlands Antilles	16.8	18.6	18.2	17.7	17.3	18.8	17.3	16.6	15.5	16.7	16.4
Nicaragua	40.3	36.2	46.0	60.2	59.6	67.8	66.9	69.6	71.0	—	—
Pakistan	—	—	—	—	—	25.2	30.8	31.0	12.6	—	—
Paraguay	—	—	—	43.4	40.4	34.1	39.1	45.6	53.7	—	—
Peru	48.7	65.1	66.8	66.4	67.2	65.0	68.0	58.9	58.5	—	—
Philippines	—	—	—	—	—	—	—	—	40.9	—	—
Poland	—	—	—	—	43.2	23.7	15.1	11.7	8.0	5.3	—
Romania	3.6	4.7	20.4	37.9	27.9	27.6	28.4	33.4	37.3	43.2	47.0
Russia	—	—	—	39.9	39.2	28.3	27.4	24.6	43.3	40.4	36.8
São Tomé and Príncipe	—	—	—	—	—	38.7	42.7	46.4	50.5	45.0	—
Saudi Arabia	30.0	27.2	24.0	26.3	25.1	23.4	20.4	19.8	21.3	20.2	18.7
Slovakia	—	—	—	12.5	14.2	12.5	11.4	11.8	16.4	16.3	17.6
Slovenia	4.1	3.4	4.9	4.1	5.0	5.5	7.0	8.1	8.4	—	—
Tajikistan	—	—	—	—	—	—	41.5	43.6	62.8	72.4	—
Trinidad and Tobago	—	—	—	—	16.6	16.8	19.1	18.1	—	—	—
Turkey	26.4	33.0	37.4	42.2	49.9	49.8	47.6	49.1	45.2	46.9	51.9
Uganda	—	—	—	15.7	16.3	17.2	18.0	17.9	17.4	—	—
Ukraine	—	—	—	—	42.1	36.4	29.3	25.5	38.9	44.0	38.5
Uzbekistan	—	—	—	—	—	—	—	13.8	13.0	7.5	—
Venezúela, RB	—	—	—	—	0.1	3.8	2.5	2.6	2.5	—	—
Viet Nam	—	—	44.9	42.0	41.8	34.6	32.1	34.1	36.6	39.1	—
Zambia	—	—	—	—	10.2	20.1	27.3	28.2	42.6	—	—

— Not available.

Note: Where conflicts existed between different sources we generally used the longest time series.

Source: See table A1.

Notes

1. As the case of Bulgaria recently demonstrated, the dominance of the U.S. dollar can survive even when a currency board with a peg against the euro has been established.

2. Partial dollarization is to be distinguished from official or full dollarization, that is, formal adoption of the U.S. dollar as the sole legal tender and unit of account in a country as recently occurred in Ecuador. Related but distinct concepts are the use of foreign currency bills or notes, which is known as currency substitution, and the adoption of a fixed peg against the dollar backed by a currency board, as in Hong Kong, China. Indeed, currency board arrangements have sometimes been associated with prohibitions against denominating bank deposits or loans in a foreign currency.

3. As people often say in Latin America, they have to choose between eating (higher interest rate) and sleeping (protection against devaluation).

4. Ize and Levy-Yeyati's model has depositors choosing between three assets: onshore local currency and both onshore and offshore foreign exchange deposits. Simple diversification arguments suggest holding some of each. The minimum variance portfolio depends on the variance of the real return of each asset and their covariances. Deviations from the minimum variance portfolio will be reflected in inflows or outflows. Their calculations (the authors' equation 14) show that the dollarization ratio should increase with volatility of inflation, but decline with the volatility of real exchange rate depreciation. This implies, somewhat counterintuitively, that allowing the exchange rate to float while targeting inflation could have the effect of reducing dollarization, whereas a pegged exchange rate will reduce dollarization even if it also reduces inflation and inflation volatility.

5. Hausmann (2000) introduces an additional dimension of covariance, namely, of exchange rates and interest rates with income. He argues that devaluation expectations may be correlated with income (low-income periods having high devaluation expectations), and suggests that because of the perverse correlation between financial returns and income, people will prefer to save in foreign currency.

6. For example, Calvo (2000b) works with a model of imperfect competition between firms with staggered price setting; and his model generates little influence of bank loan dollarization (which he calls liability dollarization) on pricing decisions, and hence on pass-through.

7. Guidotti and Rodriguez review early experience with dollarization in four Latin American countries: Bolivia (1986–90), Mexico (1972–81), Peru (1978–84), and Uruguay (1972–89). Regarding the irreversible nature of dollarization they conclude as follows: "Two of the four dollarization episodes examined—those of Mexico and Peru . . . ended with a forced de-dollarization. In addition, Bolivia experienced a forced de-dollarization in November 1982 . . . In all of these cases, de-dollarization took the form of a *de facto* conversion of foreign currency deposits held by the private sector into domestic currency. In all cases, the de-dollarization implied devaluations. In addition, de-dollarization was accompanied, in all cases, by the imposition of capital and exchange controls, designed to impede any rapid reconstitution of private foreign assets holdings. Foreign currency deposits were allowed back in Bolivia in 1984 and in 1990 in Peru. The fact that dollarization has been reversed only through confiscation schemes suggests a stylized fact: in itself dollarization appears to be, to a large extent, an irreversible phenomenon" (Guidotti and Rodriguez 1992, p. 8). In Uribe's model, society accumulates a stock of "dollarization capital" depending on the proportion of transactions carried out in dollars during the last period, which lowers the cost of doing so in the future. But some goods are infi-

nitely costly to buy in dollars, so a demand for local currency always exists. He shows that such an economy has two steady states, one with no dollars, another with both currencies in use.

8. Banks in several countries are restricted in the extent to which they are allowed to offer foreign currency-denominated deposits and loans to domestic customers. For example, dollarization is outlawed in Brazil and Venezuela, but was not in Argentina during the currency board period.

9. Hanson (chapter 4 in this volume) shows that small countries with disproportionately small values for money supply M2 have higher than average offshore holdings of deposits as recorded in the statistics of the Bank for International Settlements.

10. Catão and Terrones (2000) provide a model in which oligopolistic banks segment the two classes of borrowers, international trading or not, making the strong assumption that dollar loans are offered only to the former. They explore the theoretical impact of changes in the international interest rate on the degree of dollarization and the intermediation spread.

11. For instance, Hausmann, Panizza, and Stein (2000) argue that countries that are unable to borrow in their own currencies will have a "fear of floating" regardless of the speed of exchange rate pass-through to prices. By contrast, countries able to borrow will float only if they have a low pass-through. If the banking system is dollarized, then the government may see this as an implicit liability and put it into the same category as if it were directly borrowing in foreign currency (see World Bank 2001, p. 188, for a discussion of these issues).

12. An alternative motivation for engineering a surprise devaluation is to respond to a loss of price and wage competitiveness. Rapid pass-through increases the scale of nominal depreciation needed to achieve a given improvement in competitiveness.

13. With the bulk of banking being carried out in foreign currency and prices essentially determined externally, the real value of local currency-denominated debt (including currency) has no fixed anchor, and the efficiency costs of surprise inflation are low. In such conditions government debt denominated in local currency (including banknotes) may take on some of the character of lottery tickets.

14. Powell and Sturzenegger (2000) suggests that such a correlation is a significant indicator of a lack of macroeconomic policy credibility or trustworthiness. An alternative and more traditional measure of this state of "original sin" (as it is known in the literature) is when a country's currency is not used to denominate long-term contracts or for borrowing abroad.

15. The median of the coefficient of variation (standard deviation divided by mean) of deposit dollarization is 25 percent.

16. Except where specified, all quarterly data used are from the International Monetary Fund's *International Financial Statistics* and all annual data are from the World Bank's *World Development Indicators.*

17. A wide variety of methods is available to model pass-through, and there is also the question of time-varying pass-through. Following Gonzalez (2000) we also estimated annual pass-through coefficients for each country using monthly data. Once again a regression of the estimated pass-through coefficients reveals a highly significant coefficient on dollarization. (This contrasts with Gonzalez's results with a smaller sample.)

18. The regression approach used in this chapter is designed to detect broad cross-country trends. The data are still not good enough to pretend to estimate structural models, and the relationships we report vary in their statistical robustness, as noted where appropriate. The regressions of annual relationships reported in table 2.3 represent a specification style that we have found useful through the remainder of the chapter. Thus we estimate a panel relationship with a single first-order autocorrelation correction to take account of detected serial correlation. The panel is usually between 7 and 11 years long, with many missing observations. Where the explanatory variable is country specific, we rely on estimates made with a common intercept, as the use of country fixed effects in these very short duration panels tends to wash out any differential impact of the variable being examined. Where the explanatory variable is common across all countries, we may rely on estimates with country fixed effects. The regressions do not use the data for China or Slovenia, which became available later.

19. Note that we were unable to examine directly the various forms of round-tripping that may occur, notably the practice of dollar borrowing from local banks with the proceeds placed abroad or in local dollar deposits for tax, exchange control, or other reasons.

20. The ability of the central bank as lender of last resort to compensate for such outflows may be limited, in practice if not in law, by its attempt to maintain the parity (Fischer 1999).

21. Another question Berg and Borensztein address is whether the link between money and prices is stronger if foreign currency deposits are included. They conclude that this is indeed the case.

References

The word *processed* describes informally produced works that may not be commonly available through libraries.

Baliño, Tomás J. T., Adam Bennett, Eduardo Borensztein, and others. 1999. *Monetary Policy in Dollarized Economies.* Occasional Paper no. 171. Washington, D.C.: International Monetary Fund.

Berg, Andrew, and Eduardo Borensztein. 2000. "The Choice of Exchange Rate Regime and Monetary Target in Highly Dollarized Economies." *Journal of Applied Economics* 3(2): 285–324.

Broda, Christian, and Eduardo Levy-Yeyati. 2002. "Dollarization and the Lender of Last Resort." In Eduardo Levy-Yeyati and Federico Sturzenegger, eds., *Dollarization.* Cambridge, Mass.: Massachusetts Institute of Technology Press.

Calvo, Guillermo A. 2000a. "Capital Markets and the Exchange Rate: With Special Reference to the Dollarization Debate in Latin America." University of Maryland, College Park. Processed.

_____. 2000b. "Notes on Price Stickiness: With Special Reference to Liability Dollarization and Credibility." University of Maryland, College Park. Processed.

Calvo, Guillermo A., and Carlos A. Vegh. 1996. "From Currency Substitution to Dollarization and Beyond: Analytical and Policy Issues." In Guillermo A. Calvo, ed., *Money, Exchange Rates, and Output.* Cambridge, Mass.: Massachusetts Institute of Technology Press.

Catão, Luis, and Marco Terrones. 2000. "Determinants of Dollarization: The Banking Side." Working Paper no. WP/00/146. International Monetary Fund, Washington, D.C.

Fischer, Stanley. 1999. "On the Need for an International Lender of Last Resort." *Journal of Economic Perspectives* 13(4): 85–104.

Girton, Lance, and Don Roper. 1981. "Theory and Implications of Currency Substitution." *Journal of Money, Credit, and Banking* 13(1): 12–30.

Gonzalez, José Antonio. 2000. "Exchange Rate Pass-Through and Partial Dollarization: Is There a Link?" Working Paper no. 81. Stanford University Center for Research on Economic Development and Policy Reform, Palo Alto, Calif.

Guidotti, Pablo E., and Carlos A. Rodriguez. 1992. "Dollarization in Latin America. Gresham's Law in Reverse?" *IMF Staff Papers* 39(3): 518–44.

Hausmann, Ricardo. 2000. "The Pros and Cons of Dollarization." Paper presented at the conference on Dollarization: A Common Currency for the Americas, March 6–7, Federal Reserve Bank of Dallas.

Hausmann, Ricardo, Ugo Panizza, and Ernesto Stein. 2000. "Why Do Countries Float the Way They Float?" Working Paper no. 418. Inter-American Development Bank, Washington, D.C.

Ize, Alain, and Eduardo Levy-Yeyati. 1998. "Dollarization of Financial Intermediation: Causes and Policy Implications." Working Paper no. WP/98/28. International Monetary Fund, Washington, D.C. Revised version forthcoming in the *Journal of International Economics.*

Kareken, John, and Neil Wallace. 1981. "The Indeterminacy of Equilibrium Interest Rates." *Quarterly Journal of Economics* 96(2): 207–22.

McKinnon, Ronald. 1996. *The Rules of the Game: International Money and Exchange Rates.* Cambridge, Mass.: Massachusetts Institute of Technology Press.

Powell, Andrew, and Federico Sturzenegger. 2000. "Dollarization: The Link between Devaluation and Default Risk." Paper presented at the conference on Dollarization: A Common Currency for the Americas, March 6–7, Federal Reserve Bank of Dallas.

Uribe, Martin. 1997. "Hysteresis in a Simple Model of Currency Substitution." *Journal of Monetary Economics* 40(1): 185–202.

World Bank. 2001. *Finance for Growth: Policy Choices in a Volatile World.* New York: Oxford University Press.

Part II

Banking

3

Bank Efficiency
and Financial System Size

Biagio Bossone and Jong-Kun Lee

As finance essentially involves increasing returns to scale of various
sorts, expecting economies to bear costs that vary inversely with the
size of their financial systems is not unreasonable. These costs may
range from a narrow growth potential for market intermediaries, to
limited opportunities for risk pooling and portfolio diversification,
to inadequate competition and market incompleteness, to larger
transaction and intermediation costs caused by a suboptimal scale
of financial infrastructure.

Bossone, Honohan, and Long (2001) provide a first shot at this
problem. Noting that in modern economies intermediaries increasingly rely on infrastructural systems, they argue that the efficiency
of financial intermediation should reflect not only the production
efficiency of the individual intermediation unit, but also the efficiency of the systems in which (or through which) they operate. In
other words, all else being equal, an intermediary of any given size
operating in a large domestic financial system should likely be able
to use resources more efficiently than if it were to operate in a
smaller system. Individual intermediaries might therefore realize

The authors wish to thank G. Dell'Ariccia, A. M. Gulde, J. Hanson, and
G. Majnoni for their helpful comments on this and earlier versions of the
study. They are particularly grateful to P. Honohan for detailed suggestions.

increasing returns by operating in larger-scale systems, which implies that intermediaries in small financial systems suffer from the small scale of their operating environment.

If this hypothesis were supported by empirical evidence, its main implication would be that intermediaries in small financial systems face greater challenges in achieving market viability than those in larger systems. This would have obvious welfare and policy implications, in that access to financial services by users in small financial systems would be systematically penalized, unless policies aimed at broadening that access were implemented.

This study investigates the hypothesis of systemic scale externalities. It discusses the channels through which systemic externalities affect bank production and formulates a testable proposition, and then tests the externalities' quantitative relevance on a cross-country and time series banking data panel in a model where banks are assumed to maximize value rather than profits.

Systemic Scale Externalities and Bank Efficiency

The new literature on scale economies in banking indicates the presence of significant scale efficiency effects. Economies of scale in bank production are detected when measurement techniques are used that allow for endogeneity in risk taking. Moreover, large efficiency gains from scale are found in risk management and reputation signaling functions (see Bossone, Honohan, and Long 2001 for a comprehensive review and references). Evidence shows that a larger production scale enhances the potential for risk diversification through a wider mix of financial products and services supplied, as well as through increased geographic spread of activities. More specifically, as the scale of production increases, banks economize on the use of financial capital both to cushion risks and to signal their strength to the market, and save on the costs of the labor and physical capital resources used to manage risks and to preserve financial capital. In addition, more geographically diversified banks have relatively lower deposit volatility, higher expected returns, and lower levels of risk.

We would like to further extend the analysis of scale economies in banking by showing that the efficiency of bank production is higher the larger the size of the financial systems in which the banks operate. In other words, we want to test the hypothesis that larger and more efficient financial systems enhance banks' efficiency in managing risks and in signaling their reputation to the markets.

This hypothesis should also capture the observed increasing returns embodied in financial infrastructure systems (such as payment systems, organized securities markets, and regulatory systems) resulting from scale economies and network externalities and from their interaction.[1] Because banks are increasingly integrated into these systems, expecting that their production efficiency somehow reflects the systems' efficiency is reasonable.

Our hypothesis can be expressed in the following testable proposition: all else being equal, banks operating in larger financial systems have relatively lower costs of production, risk absorption, and reputation signaling than banks operating in smaller systems.

This systemic type of scale externality can operate through various channels. First, if the scale efficiency effects incorporated in financial infrastructural services feed back into bank production, the average production cost should be expected to be higher (lower) for banks operating in small (large) systems, and would decrease with the increase in size of the financial system where the banks operate. As an example, a larger payment system, a larger bank credit bureau, or a larger infrastructure for the dissemination of financial information should offer more inexpensive (implicit or explicit) service charges to accessing banks, and should thereby afford banks a lower production cost structure than if they were to use smaller infrastructure.

Second, as banks need to raise their financial capital when expanding production, larger financial systems should allow them to economize on capital resources by enabling them to diversify their asset portfolios more efficiently across a broader borrower base, a wider spectrum of sectors of activity, and different geographic areas. As a result, an increase in the output of banks operating in larger systems should require proportionately less financial capital than that of banks in smaller systems.

Third, the cost structure of banks should be expected to change differently over time in response to changes in the technology embodied in financial infrastructure, depending on the size of the financial system in which they operate. Banks operating in larger financial systems should benefit more rapidly from the technological developments that improve the efficiency of infrastructure services used as production inputs.[2] This effect could be measured by observing a more (less) rapid pace of cost decline for banks operating in larger (smaller) systems. The more rapid decline would be caused by the interaction between network externalities and the scale economies that typically characterize infrastructural network services.

These three types of systemic scale externalities derive from the absolute size of the financial system, as opposed to its size relative to that of the economy. Therefore a level variable should be used in an empirical, cross-sectional comparative analysis. This level variable should also include information about the system's degree of openness to international transactions, as this would reflect the extent to which the domestic financial system is integrated into wider networks of international financial infrastructure.

Fourth, banks use financial capital as a buffer against risks and as a device to signal their reputation to investors. As the financial environment becomes more competitive, investors are increasingly reactive to changes in the quality of bank assets, and banks need to accumulate financial capital. However, the systemic externalities might be such that banks' demand for financial capital grows less than in proportion to the size of the financial markets where the banks operate for a number of reasons, namely:

• Deeper and more efficient financial markets help banks improve their screening of potential borrowers, monitor their investment more efficiently, and signal their risk attitude through information other than (and possibly complementary to) financial capital.[3] As a result, banks operating in large systems should attain the same degree of protection against financial distress, and the same reputation signaling effect, with a lower capital to asset ratio than those in smaller systems.

• Deeper and more efficient financial markets should enable banks to manage and protect their financial capital with relatively fewer nonfinancial resources. More specifically, as banks increase their output and adjust their financial capital position accordingly, they may need to mobilize additional nonfinancial resources to manage and protect their financial capital. The presence of systemic scale externalities should imply that banks operating in larger financial systems are able to perform these functions with relatively fewer nonfinancial resources than those operating in smaller systems. For example, the availability of better information provision and more efficient contract enforcement systems may allow banks to economize on additional human resources needed to manage an increase in risk positions.

• Better information provision, that is, more and higher-quality information, and a higher signal extraction capacity on the part of investors result in signaling becoming more efficient, and banks can thus economize on the financial capital needed to signal a given level of reputation or risk safety. The same holds if investors can rely on greater regulatory and rule enforcement capacity.

• Larger and more efficient financial markets allow banks to raise new financial capital at a less than proportional increase in their costs because, all else being equal, achieving a higher level of capital would signal a stronger position in relation to risks.

This fourth type of systemic externality should be captured more efficiently through a relative size indicator, because financial market depth and efficiency are better proxied by variables that measure the scale of the markets relative to the size of the overall economy.

The next section will seek to estimate the existence of systemic scale externalities in banking. Two features need to be considered before embarking on methodological and estimation issues: first, that risk taking in bank production is endogenous; and second, that banks should be seen as pursuing value rather than profit maximization.

As regards the first feature, the estimation of systemic scale efficiency effects must control for the impact of endogenous risk decisions on costs. If a larger system scale decreases the marginal cost of risk taking for individual banks, and hence increases the banks' marginal returns to risk taking, the banks have an incentive to take on additional risks, that is, to reduce asset quality for a higher expected return. However, as higher risks generate additional risk management costs (including higher financial capital, more labor inputs, and higher risk premiums on borrowed funds), the banks may actually use up the initial cost savings. As a result, estimates that did not duly account for risk endogeneity would not capture the cost effects of the system scale.

As for the second feature, the profit maximization (cost minimization) objective assumed in the standard models used to measure bank production efficiency may be inappropriate. As risks create the potential for costly episodes of financial distress, banks seek to maximize value and are prepared to trade higher profit for lower risk. By incorrectly assuming profit maximization, standard models may fail to detect the responsiveness of the bank risk/return tradeoff to scale effects: risk-averse bankers may find the level of financial capital implied by profit to be unacceptably low. Their demand for capital would have to be modeled by a broader objective than profit maximization (for a thorough discussion of these issues and their applications see Hughes 1999; Hughes, Mester, and Moon 2001; Hughes and others 2000). However, high banking market concentration or too large to fail expectations may reduce the perceived risk of individual banks (at least of the dominant ones) and weaken their incentive to accumulate financial capital in relation to given levels of risk. Failing to control for market concentration would therefore lead to a biased estimation of systemic scale externalities.

Both corrective features need to be incorporated in the methodology used in the next section.

Testing the Hypothesis

This section begins by setting out the model and methodology used, then describes the data used, before proceeding to a description of the results.

Model and Methodology

We assume that, in the short run, banks act to minimize their variable costs (the sum of the cost of physical inputs and deposits), subject to a transformation function in which the input of equity capital is treated as quasi-fixed $k = k^0$. In this we follow most banking studies in assuming the intermediation hypothesis, which regards deposits d as an input into production. The transformation function explicitly includes a bank-specific measure of asset quality q to incorporate the risk endogeneity effect discussed in the previous section. It also includes country-specific control variables ϕ that summarize aspects of the environment for banking, such as the quality of information available, and a time trend t as a proxy for technological progress.

Minimized variable (or cash flow) costs C_V are thus defined as follows:[4]

$$C_V(Q, w_l, w_c, w_d, k, q, \phi, t) = \min (w_l x_l + w_c x_c + w_d x_d) \text{ s.t.}$$
$$T(Q, x, k{:}q, \phi, t) \leq 0 \text{ and } k = k^0, \tag{3.1}$$

where

$\quad T(\cdot) =$ transformation function
$\quad Q =$ output (total loans and other earning assets)
$\quad w_l, w_c =$ price of physical inputs (labor l and physical capital c)
$\quad w_d =$ price of deposits d
$\quad x =$ quantity of variable factor input $= \{x_l, x_c, x_d\}$
$\quad k =$ financial (equity) capital
$\quad q =$ asset quality (micro)
$\quad \phi =$ banking environment (macro)
$\quad t =$ state of banking technology at time t.

The bank's value-maximizing problem is to minimize the economic cost resulting from the sum of the cash flow cost in the short run and the additional opportunity cost of equity capital at the given time of evaluation.[5] Thus the long-run (total) economic cost function (C_T) is specified as

$$C_T(Q, w_p, w_c, w_d, w^*_k, q, \phi, t) =$$
$$C_V(Q, w_p, w_c, w_d, k(Q, w_p, w_c, w_d, q, \phi, t), q, \phi, t) + w^*_k k, \quad (3.2)$$

where

w^*_k = shadow price of financial capital = $-\partial C_V / \partial k$.

For the purposes of estimation, we assume that the cost function can be approximated by the flexible translog functional form

$$\ln C_V = \alpha_0 + \sum_i \alpha_i \ln Z_i + \frac{1}{2} \sum_i \sum_j \beta_{ij} \ln Z_i \ln Z_j, \quad (3.3)$$

where the explanatory variables Z are the elements of the transformation function discussed earlier, $Z = \{Q, w_p, w_d, w_c, k, q, \phi, t\}$, and the parameters satisfy symmetry $\beta_{ij} = \beta_{ji}$.

The share S_j of each factor in variable cost can be derived from equation (3.3) by differentiating C_V with respect to the factor prices w_p, w_d, w_c, and the shadow price of the quasi-fixed factor capital w_k can be derived by differentiating C_V with respect to k. This provides the estimating equations. Substituting the observed market rate of return on equity w_k for the shadow price of financial capital w^*_k,

$$S_j = -\partial C_V / \partial w_j = \alpha_j + \sum_i \beta_{ij} \ln Z_i, \ j = l, d, c; \ \Sigma S_j = 1 \quad (3.4)$$

$$w_k = -\partial C_V / \partial k = (\alpha_k + \sum_i \beta_{ik} \ln Z_i) \frac{C_V}{k} \quad (3.5)$$

Following Hughes and Mester (1998) we specify the demand for capital as depending on risk-related asset quality as follows:

$$\ln k = \gamma_0 + \gamma_1 \ln Q + \gamma_2 \ln FS + \gamma_3 \ln FSD + \gamma_4 \ln CN + \gamma_5$$
$$\ln npla + \gamma_6 \ln R + \gamma_7 \ln \Pi, \quad (3.6)$$

where

FS = absolute financial system size (in billions of U.S. dollars)
FSD = relative financial system depth ($FS/GDP * MS$), where
GDP = gross domestic product and MS = financial
market size
CN = banking market concentration ($0 \le CN \le 1$)
$npla$ = adjusted nonperforming loan ratio
R = liquidity asset ratio
Π = profitability (spread between loan and deposit interest
rates).

Measurement of Scale Economies in Banking

Once a translog cost function is explicitly specified, we can derive parametric estimates of scale economies. We use four measures of scale economies ε as follows (defined more fully in the appendix). The first, ε_V, measures whether variable costs increase more or less than in proportion to an increase in output (without holding quality constant). The second, ε^q_V, is the same, but holds quality constant (thereby recognizing that the traditional measure may be contaminated by the fact that larger banks may incur higher costs in controlling for a potentially riskier portfolio) and is conditional on financial capital. The third and fourth measures, ε_T and ε^q_T, measure whether total costs increase as output increases, taking account of the induced change in the shadow price of capital. We may regard ε_V and ε_T as traditional measures inasmuch as they do not hold loan quality constant, whereas ε^q_V and ε^q_T are the more sophisticated measures. Note that in the following $\varepsilon > 1$ implies economies of scale, whereas $\varepsilon < 1$ implies diseconomies of scale.

Data and Sources

A sample of 875 commercial banks from 75 countries was drawn mainly from the International Bank Classification Agency's Bankscope database as of 2002, which contains banking information for more than 1,900 commercial banks with more than US$1 billion in total asset size. The sample was almost equally divided into three subgroups based on their reported total asset size:[6] 292 small banks (less than US$2.4 billion), 292 medium banks (US$2.4 billion to US$8 billion), and 292 large banks (more than US$8 billion). As a complete set of variables is required for the analysis of the bank cost structure, almost half of the banking observations for which information was partially missing or misreported had to be dropped. In cases where the necessary banking data were not available in the Bankscope database, we referred to banks' financial statements (available on official web sites) directly, or to official reports on countrywide banking prepared by national financial supervisory authorities, as an alternative or complementary source.

In addition to these micro banking data, we used macro-related variables to control for each country's specific financial structure and level of economic development. The information was obtained from the World Bank's *World Development Indicators* and *Global Development Finance;* the International Monetary Fund's *International Financial Statistics;* and from Beck, Demirgüç-Kunt, and Levine (1999); La Porta and others (1997, 1998); and Levine, Loayza, and Beck (2000).

In the case of missing information for some important variables in the Bankscope database, we used average values of peer group banks in each country instead. To collect comparable international data from different countries we simplified the data structure by aggregating variables that for some countries were not available on a disaggregated basis, and by removing some country-specific banks from the sample. The data were extracted from nonconsolidated income statements and balance sheets from 1995–97. All banking data except quantity variables are reported in U.S. dollars and are adjusted by consumer price index inflation in each respective country.[7] The resulting dataset is a pooled sample of cross-sectional time series of 2,625 observations over the three years considered, that is, 875 observations for each year. Summary information about the variables is shown in tables 3.1 and 3.2.

Following the intermediation approach to estimate economies of scale in banking, our main specification for the bank's cost function is characterized by one single output and four inputs. Output Q is defined as the sum of total loans and other earning assets, which are measured as the average dollar amount at the end of each year, and the corresponding output price P is calculated by dividing the total interest revenue by the inflation-adjusted value of total earning assets. The inputs are two nonfinancial factor inputs, labor x_l and physical capital x_c, and two financial inputs, deposits x_d and financial (or equity) capital k.

The price of labor, w_l, was obtained by dividing total salaries and benefits paid by the total number of employees. The price of physical capital, w_c, was derived by dividing other operating expenses, including occupancy expenses, by inflation-adjusted fixed assets x_c.[8] The input price of deposits, w_d, was obtained by dividing total interest expenses by the total inflation-adjusted amount of deposits x_d. The input quantity of financial capital, k, was directly obtained from the inflation-adjusted figures for equity capital reported in the balance sheets. However, as no information was available on the cost of financial capital, the return on average equity ($ROAE$) and an estimate of the market rental price of capital based on the bank production function were used as proxies for the price of financial capital, w_k, reflecting the opportunity cost of equity capital.

Finally, we used the accounting standard index from La Porta and others (1998) as a proxy for information transparency. To capture the different asset quality of banks across sample countries we used the ratio of nonperforming loans to total assets for

Table 3.1 Data Structure and Sources

Variable		Definition	Calculation	Sources
Q		Output	Total loans + other earning assets	
P		Price of output	Interest income/output (Q)	Banks' annual reports and financial statements (if necessary)
w_i	w_l	Price of labor	Personnel expenses/number of employees (x_l)	
	w_c	Price of physical capital	Other operating expense/fixed assets (x_c)	
	w_d	Price of deposits	Interest expense/volume of deposits (x_d)	
	w_k	Price of financial capital	Return on average equity or alternative estimate of opportunity cost	Bankscope
k		Financial capital	Equity capital	
C_v		Variable cost	Personnel expenses + interest expenses + other operating expenses	
ϕ	FS	Financial system size	Domestic credit + demand deposits + foreign assets + foreign liabilities	Beck, Demirgüç-Kunt, and Levine (1999); *International Financial Statistics*
	FSD	Financial system depth	Same as a share of GDP	
	MS	Financial market size	(Market capitalization/GDP) × (total value traded/GDP) × (turnover/GDP)	Beck, Demirgüç-Kunt, and Levine (1999); Levine, Loayza, and Beck (2000)
	AS	Information transparency	Accounting standards	La Porta and others (1997, 1998)
q	npl	Asset quality	Nonperforming loans/total assets	Bankscope
	R	Risk factor	Liquid asset ratio	
Others		Time trend variable (t), country dummy variables	t = 1, 2, 3 for 1995–1997 dummy country = 1, otherwise 0	*World Development Indicators; Global Development Finance; International Financial Statistics*

Source: Authors.

76

Table 3.2 Descriptive Statistics

Variable	Description	Average	Minimum	Maximum
Micro banking variables (875 banks)				
Q	Aggregate output (US$ billions)	19.4	0.4	629.4
x_l	Total number of employees	4,554	8	87,933
x_d	Total deposits (US$ billions)	15.0	0.1	454.4
x_c	Fixed assets (US$ billions)	0.3	0.0	7.2
x_k	Equity capital (US$ billions)	1.0	0.03	24.0
R	Liquidity asset ratio (%)	24.4	0.0	667.7
npl	Nonperforming loan ratio (%)	4.0	0.0	81.8
$npla$	Adjusted nonperforming loan ratio = npl/AS	6.6	0.0	149.0
P	Price of output (US$ thousands)	0.080	0.027	0.441
w_l	Price of labor (US$ thousands)	52.1	1.8	227.0
w_d	Price of deposits (US$ thousands)	0.07	0.01	5.75
w_c	Price of physical capital (US$ thousands)	1.01	0.01	11.15
w_k	Price of financial capital (real %)	10.8	−111.5	73.7
C_v	Variable cost (US$ billions)	12.3	0.0	38.0
Macro financial variables				
MS	Financial market size (US$ billions)	36.5	0.0 (Costa Rica)	1,326.8 (Taiwan, China)
FS	Financial system size (US$ billions)	967.5	2.4 (Bermuda)	20,467.2 (Japan)
$M2$	(US$ billions)	233.7	1.3 (Estonia)	5,261.4 (United States)
AS	Accounting standards (% of theoretical maximum)	58.3	24.0 (Bangladesh)	83.0 (Sweden)
CN	Banking market concentration ratio	0.62	0.19 (United States)	1.00 (5 countries)[a]

a. Algeria, Bermuda, Ethiopia, Liechtenstein, and Monaco.
Source: Authors.

each bank, q, adjusted for the accounting standards country index from La Porta and others (1998), so that poorer accounting standards translated into higher values of the adjusted ratio *npla* (*npl/ accounting standards index*).

In addition to this micro-based, bank-specific information, we collected country-specific variables from La Porta and others (1998) and Beck, Demirgüç-Kunt, and Levine (1999) to control for the effect of various financial sector structural characteristics and for the different level of financial sector development in each country. For the absolute size of the financial system of each country, *FS*, we constructed a comprehensive indicator for open economies by summing the banking system's domestic credits, domestic deposits, foreign assets, and foreign liabilities, expressed in billions of U.S. dollars.[9] Ignoring 3 very small countries because of data difficulties, we divided the remaining 72 into three subgroups: 24 small economies (*FS* less than US$35 billion), 25 medium economies (*FS* more than US$35 billion to US$300 billion), and 23 large economies (*FS* more than US$300 billion).[10]

To capture the relative size of the financial system we used the *FSD* ratio (*FS/GDP*) as a proxy for financial depth. We also constructed a composite size indicator of domestic capital markets (*MS*) by multiplying the three stock market ratios reported in Beck, Demirgüç-Kunt, and Levine (1999): stock market capitalization to GDP, stock market total value traded to GDP, and stock market turnover to GDP. Note that as the indicator reflects relative market size and includes the turnover ratio, it captures both the depth and the efficiency of the domestic capital markets.

On empirical estimation, the intercept terms α_0 in equation (3.3) and γ_1 in equation (3.6) were allowed to vary across countries to mitigate the heterogeneity of the underlying sample, thereby enabling us to take further account of country-specific differences. The model was estimated simultaneously by applying an iterative, seemingly unrelated regression estimation technique. The estimates obtained are asymptotically equivalent to maximum likelihood estimates. The estimation results for pooled cross-section time series are not shown here, but most of the parameter estimates are statistically significant at the 5 percent level.[11] The R^2s in the system equation regressions are high.[12]

Results

The results reveal the presence of significant scale economies associated with different indicators of financial system size (table 3.3). Note that systemic scale externalities are not detected by the con-

Table 3.3 Scale Economies and Financial Variables

Financial variable	Subsample	Conventional measure		Quality-adjusted measure	
		ε_V	ε_T	ε^q_V	ε^q_T
Financial system size (US$ billions) (*FS, M2*)	*FS* Small (126)	1.04	0.99	0.92	0.89
	Medium (252)	0.93	0.97	0.98	1.02
	Large (2,226)	0.87	0.98	1.04	1.18
	M2 Small[a] (105)	1.06	0.99	0.92	0.87
	Large (2,505)	0.88	0.98	1.03	1.06
Financial system depth (*FSD*MS*)	Low (675)	0.95	0.98	0.98	1.02
	High (1,950)	0.87	0.98	1.05	1.19
Financial market size (*MS*)	Small (1,329)	0.92	0.98	1.01	1.09
	Large (1,296)	0.85	0.97	1.05	1.21
Adjusted asset quality (*npla*)	High (1,746)	0.91	0.98	1.02	1.11
	Low (879)	0.84	0.97	1.05	1.22
Information transparency (*AS*)	Low (330)	0.98	0.98	0.95	0.96
	High (2,295)	0.87	0.98	1.04	1.17
Market concentration (*CN*)	High[b] (609)	0.95	1.03	0.98	1.03
	Low (2,016)	0.87	0.98	1.04	1.18

Note: The shaded area represents higher-scale economies for each classification of financial variables. The figures in parentheses represent the number of observations. All the parametric estimates reported above are statistically different at the 5 percent significance level. Differences refer to comparisons of conventional versus adjusted measures, small versus large classes, and low versus high classes.

a. $M2 < 10$.

b. More than 0.5.

Source: Authors' calculations.

ventional measures,[13] and turn out to be greater than 1 and increasing when the adjustment factors are incorporated in measurement, that is, as one moves from ε_V to ε^q_V to ε_T to ε^q_T.

This suggests that the systemic scale externalities in financial capitalization and risk management are relevant in bank production. In particular, small financial systems display fewer scale economies than large ones (figure 3.1 and table 3.3). Furthermore, scale economies change markedly in response to changes in the bank risk environment as proxied by the information transparency and asset quality indicators, that is, banks operating in highly transparent environments can expand production with a less than proportional increase in the costs of nonfinancial and financial resources needed to manage risks compared with banks operating in more opaque environments. Moreover, reputation signaling for banks with sound assets can be more efficient than for risky banks. For example, low-risk banks may be able to signal added levels of risk protection with fewer additional

Figure 3.1 Relationship between Scale Economies
and Financial System Size

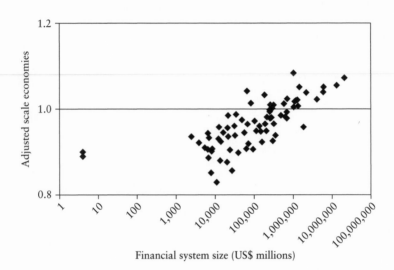

Financial system size (US$ millions)

Source: Authors' calculations.

resources than high-risk banks, and can possibly save on risk management costs, or even reduce their cost of funding, by signaling more
financial strength.

Consistent with the importance of the factors relating to risk and
information is what might otherwise appear to be a counterintuitive
finding, namely, that lower market concentration increases scale
efficiency.[14] Where competition is stronger, which is typically the
case in larger and more developed financial systems, investors' sen-
sitivity toward risk is higher, and signaling and signal extraction can
be done more efficiently. That is why scale economies associated
with financial capitalization and risk management are greater where
competition is strong.

This evidence in support of systemic scale externalities is confirmed by regressing the quality-adjusted measure of scale
economies (ε^q_T) on different size indicators of financial systems and
markets and on a number of variables reflecting bank market structure and risk environment characteristics (table 3.4).

Following Claessens and Lee (2002); Claessens, Demirgüç-Kunt,
and Huizinga (2001); and Demirgüç-Kunt and Huizinga (1999),[15]
weighted least squares regressions were run for banks grouped by
country and by the size of each country's financial system, *FS.*[16] The

Table 3.4 Determinants of Systemic Scale Externalities

Variables	Country observations[a]	Banking observations		
Dependent variable ε^q_T	(1) Total	(2) Total	(3) Small & medium systems	(4) Large systems
Independent variables				
Financial System Size	0.0244**	0.0275**	0.0144**	0.0289**
FS_{jt}	(5.9)	(11.4)	(3.4)	(9.9)
Financial System Depth	0.0230**	0.0140**	0.0384**	0.0125**
FSD_{jt}	(4.2)	(4.0)	(7.7)	(3.1)
Financial Market Size	0.0198**	0.0091**	0.0162**	0.0086**
MS_{jt}	(3.5)	(8.1)	(13.8)	(6.9)
Market Concentration	–0.0181	–0.0146**	0.0328**	–0.0139*
CN_{jt}	(–1.3)	(2.5)	(2.6)	(2.2)
Adjusted Asset Quality		–0.0105**	–0.0172**	–0.0105**
$npla_{ijt}$		(22.6)	(11.2)	(20.8)
Constant	–0.4113**	–0.4268**	–0.3631**	–0.4389**
	(12.0)	(15.8)	(13.2)	(12.5)
Adjusted R^2	0.903	0.429	0.790	0.397
Number of observations	75	2,625	399	2,226

* Indicates statistical significance at the 5 percent level.
** Indicates statistical significance at the 1 percent level.

Note: Regressions are estimated using weighted least squares, pooling bank-level data (i) across 75 countries (j) for 1995–97 (t). The inverse of the number of domestic banks in each country is used to weight the observations in the regressions to correct for varying numbers of bank observations in each country. The dependent variable is the adjusted scale measure of ε^q_T. All are log variables. The figures in parentheses beneath the parameter estimates are heteroskedasticity-corrected t-statistics.

a. Based on country observations averaged across their banking samples over 1995–97.

Source: Authors' calculations.

results are all statistically significant at the 1 percent level, indicating robustness across different subgroups of sample observations. They indicate that both the size of the financial system and the bank risk environment have considerable explanatory power. Financial system and market-related variables (*FS, FSD, MS*) show a positive relationship with scale economies.

By contrast, we find mixed evidence on the impact of market concentration, *CN,* on scale economies, depending on size of the financial system. The parameter estimate for *CN* is, on the whole, negative, which supports the conclusion that a more competitive market leads to higher scale efficiency. Running the same regression for separate subsamples of financial system size shows that the *CN* parameter takes a positive sign in the case of small and medium systems. This implies that lower market concentration in smaller systems up to a certain size may mean a suboptimal scale for individual banks. In other words, all else being equal, the minimum size for a bank to be viable varies inversely with the size of the financial system where it operates.[17] This result is quite powerful in that it suggests that stronger competition can fully translate into higher scale efficiency for individual banks only in systems above a certain threshold size.

Finally, looking at the effect of the composite index of asset quality, *npla* (the raw value of *npl* divided by the index of information transparency *AS*), the parameter estimates are negative as expected. Thus the lower the raw asset quality (*npl*) and the higher the information transparency (*AS*), the higher the scale efficiency.

The relevance of the risk environment variables is consistent with the findings in table 3.3. This leads to the presumption that systemic scale externalities are a product of the relationship between financial system size and the quality of the risk environment for banking intermediation: a larger, deeper, and more efficient system helps banks to save on the resources needed to manage the higher risks associated with larger production. The positive relationship between financial system size and scale efficiency in financial capitalization and risk management is illustrated quite clearly by tables 3.5 and 3.6, which report the values of coefficients ε_V and ε^q_V estimated for subgroups of

Table 3.5 Conventional Scale Economies (ε_V) by Size of Bank and Financial System

Bank size (US$ billions) (*ta* = total assets)	Financial system size (FS) (US$ billions)			
	Small	Medium	Large	Total[a]
Small (*ta* < 2.4)	1.05 (96)	0.94 (84)	0.86 (690)	0.90 (876)
Medium (2.4 < *ta* < 8.0)	1.05 (24)	0.92 (102)	0.87 (738)	0.89 (876)
Large (*ta* > 8.0)	0.97 (6)	0.94 (66)	0.87 (798)	0.88 (873)
Total	1.04 (126)	0.93 (252)	0.87 (2,226)	0.89 (2,625)

Note: The figures in parentheses are the numbers of sample bank observations. All are mean values calculated for 1995–97 for each subgroup.

a. Another fourth subgroup of three countries (21 total observations) was included in the calculation of the total average.

Source: Authors' calculations.

banks by bank scale and financial system size. Whereas conventional measures indicate the existence of modest scale economies only for small banks in small systems, adjusted measures show economies of scale increase with both bank scale and system size.

Two interesting observations from table 3.6 are that small banks in large systems are considerably more cost-efficient than small banks in small systems (1.06 and 0.93, respectively) and that, on the whole, bank scale does not make much of a difference within classes of financial system size.

Additional evidence in support of systemic scale externalities in production and risk management can be found by analyzing bank cost structures. From production theory, the elasticity of variable cost to output can be expressed as the ratio of marginal cost to average cost.[18] Using a hypothetical total cost function that incorporates the shadow cost of financial capital, $C_T = C_V + (-\partial C_V/\partial k)k$,[19] we estimated the average cost/marginal cost ratio for each subgroup of banks by bank scale and financial system size (table 3.7).[20] Note that ratio values larger (smaller) than 1 imply economies (diseconomies) of scale. Both average and marginal costs decrease as the size of the banks and the financial system increases. In addition, scale economies increase with the size of the financial system.

Table 3.6 Adjusted Scale Economies (ε^q_V)
by Size of Bank and Financial System

Bank size (US$ billions) (*ta* = total assets)	Financial system size (FS) (US$ billions)			
	Small	Medium	Large	Total[a]
Small	0.93 (96)	0.99 (84)	1.06 (690)	1.04 (876)
Medium	0.91 (24)	0.98 (102)	1.05 (738)	1.03 (876)
Large	0.95 (6)	0.96 (66)	1.02 (798)	1.01 (873)
Total	0.93 (126)	0.98 (252)	1.04 (2,226)	1.03 (2,625)

Note: The figures in parentheses are the numbers of sample bank observations. All are mean values calculated for 1995–97 for each subgroup.

a. Another fourth subgroup of three countries (21 total observations) was included in the calculation of the total average.

Source: Authors' calculations.

Table 3.7 Average and Marginal Total Cost
by Size of Bank and Financial System

Bank size (US$ billions) (*ta* = total assets)	*Financial system size (FS) (US$ billions)*			
	Small	Medium	Large	Total
Small	0.094 (0.093)	0.120 (0.110)	0.083 (0.075)	0.087 (0.080)
Medium	0.120 (0.120)	0.082 (0.078)	0.079 (0.073)	0.079 (0.074)
Large	0.071 (0.068)	0.073 (0.070)	0.068 (0.065)	0.068 (0.066)
Total	0.098 (0.095)	0.091 (0.086)	0.076 (0.071)	0.078 (0.073)

Note: Marginal costs are reported in parentheses. All are mean values calculated for 1995–97 for each subgroup. Fifteen outlier observations for *MC* (negative or close to 0) are excluded in the calculation of average in the case of small and medium financial systems.

Source: Authors' calculations.

Conclusion

Based on the general assumption that finance involves increasing returns to scale of various sorts, this study has formulated and tested empirically the hypothesis that banks' production efficiency increases with the size of the system where the banks operate. Using a large cross-country and time series banking data panel, the study has shown that banks operating in systems with large markets and infrastructures have lower production costs and lower costs of risk absorption and reputation signaling than banks operating in small systems. In particular, the results show that

• Systemic scale externalities can be detected when risk is endogenized in bank production decisions and market concentration is controlled for in a model where banks are modeled as value maximizers.

• Larger, deeper, and more efficient financial systems enable banks to save on the resources needed to manage the higher risks associated with larger production.

• The cost-efficiency effects of technological changes spread more rapidly across banks operating in larger systems.

• Small banks in large systems are more cost-efficient than small banks in small systems.

• The minimum size for a bank to be viable decreases with the size of the financial system where it operates. As a consequence, stronger competition (or lower market concentration) can fully translate into higher scale efficiency for individual banks only in systems larger than a certain threshold level.

Overall, the evidence has shown that banks operating in small financial systems suffer from a structural comparative disadvantage with respect to those operating in larger systems.

Appendix: Definitions of Scale Economies

This appendix spells out the definition of the four measures of scale economies used.

Conventional Measure of Scale Economies in C_V

When a multiproduct cost function $[Q = (Q_1, Q_2, \ldots, Q_n)]$ is assumed, the conventional measure of scale economies is defined as

$$\varepsilon_V = \frac{1}{\displaystyle\sum_i^n \frac{\partial \ln C_V}{\partial \ln Q_i}}, \tag{A1}$$

which shows how cost changes in proportion to output variations.

Quality-Adjusted Measure of Scale Economies in C_V

By analogy with Hughes and Mester (1998), the quality-adjusted measure of scale economies is derived by holding relative asset quality constant—that is, by assuming that the adjusted ratio of nonperforming loans to total assets q ($npla = npl/AS$) increases in proportion to total assets Q—and is conditional on the level of financial capital k:

$$\varepsilon_V^q = \frac{1}{\displaystyle\sum_i^n \frac{\partial \ln C_V}{\partial \ln Q_i} + \left(\sum_i^n \frac{\partial \ln C_V}{\partial \ln k} \frac{\partial \ln k}{\partial \ln Q_i} + \frac{\partial \ln C_V}{\partial \ln q} + \frac{\partial \ln C_V}{\partial \ln k} \frac{\partial \ln k}{\partial \ln q} \right)}. \tag{A2}$$

By taking into account the endogeneity of risk and financial capital, this parametric measure will reflect the effect on cost of a proportionate variation in the levels of output and nonperforming loans over total assets taken as a proxy for risk-related asset quality. It therefore captures the full effect on cost of both output and risk changes. Estimating the individual components of the denominator of equation (A2) provides further insights on the differential impact of various sources of systemic scale externalities.

Economic Cost Scale Economies in C_T

Following Hughes, Mester, and Moon (2001), who use a shadow valuation of financial capital, the measure of the economic cost scale economies from a shadow total cost function is given by

$$
\varepsilon_T = \frac{1}{[\partial C_T(Q, w_p, w_d, w_k^*, q, \phi, t)/\partial Q] \cdot [Q/C_T(Q, w_p, w_d, w_k^*, q, \phi, t)]}
$$

$$
= \frac{1}{[\partial C_V(Q, w_p, w_d, k, q, \phi, t)/\partial Q] \cdot [Q/C_V(Q, w_p, w_d, k, q, \phi, t) + (-\partial C_V/\partial k)k)]}
$$

$$
= \frac{1 - \dfrac{\partial \ln C_V}{\partial \ln k}}{\sum_i \dfrac{\partial \ln C_V}{\partial \ln Q_i}} = \varepsilon_V \left(1 - \frac{\partial \ln C_V}{\partial \ln k}\right), \tag{A3}
$$

where C_T is the economic total cost function, defined as the sum of variable cost (C_V) and the shadow cost of financial capital $[(-\partial C_V/\partial k)k]$, as a substitute for its market price value. This specification allows the measurement of scale economies taking into account the economic impact of the demand for financial capital on variable cost.[21]

Economic Cost and Quality-Adjusted Scale Economies in C_T

Finally, combining equations (A2) and (A3) yields the new comprehensive measure of adjusted scale economies in total cost function,

$$
\varepsilon_T^q = \varepsilon_V^q \left(1 - \frac{\partial \ln C_V}{\partial \ln k}\right), \tag{A4}
$$

which incorporates the asset quality control feature into the total (economic) cost structure of bank production.

Notes

1. Scale economies and network externalities interact with and reinforce each other, as the increase in the number of network users may reduce the average cost of using the service, at least until countervailing factors—such as congestion—take over and reverse the effect.

2. Hypothetically, if the same technology development takes place in two network systems that only differ in size, the network externalities in the larger system are stronger, because the larger size attracts more users, and more users mean larger economies of scale and lower service charges, which in turn generate additional network economies. The reduction in production costs and service charges per time unit would be larger in the larger system.

3. This effect rests on the assumption that banks use capital markets like other nonbank investors. As stock markets aggregate and reflect the views of a wide range of different investors on prices, they provide multiple checks on individual firms and, therefore, are likely to be the best available indicators of the true value of the firms (Allen and Gale 1999).

4. Hughes and Mester (1998) and Hughes, Mester, and Moon (2001) refer to cash flow costs. Equation (3.1) can be thought of as a value-maximizing cost function conditioned on the level of financial capital and risk-related asset quality. For bank managers who are not risk neutral, maximizing value (as against profits) implies that they are willing to trade profit for reduced risk. They thus attribute a positive value to guarding against financial distress and the need to signal their bank's safety by choosing a level of capitalization that likely exceeds the cost-minimizing level.

5. As distinct from the market rental price of financial capital from which the shadow price may deviate in the short run.

6. Average total assets over 1995–97 were estimated at US$19.4 billion (adjusted for inflation).

7. For cross-country comparability we used inflation-adjusted values whenever applicable, which are also available in the Bankscope database.

8. As other operating expenses reported by Bankscope include other noninterest expenses, this may lead to an overestimation of the actual price of physical capital. However, the data seem to be relatively consistent across countries in that information disclosure and accounting standards are identical for all banks.

9. Although they include only banking variables, these indicators should also indirectly reflect the size of some of the main infrastructural components underpinning the financial system, for example, payment and clearing systems; legal, regulatory, and supervisory systems; information systems and services; liquidity facilities; and safety nets.

10. The small economies are Bahrain, Bangladesh, Costa Rica, Croatia, Cyprus, Dominican Republic, Ecuador, Estonia, Ethiopia, Iceland, Jamaica, Jordan, Malta, Mauritius, Nigeria, Oman, Peru, Qatar, Romania, Slovak Republic, Slovenia, Sri Lanka, Trinidad and Tobago, and Tunisia. The medium economies are Algeria, Argentina, Chile, Colombia, Czech Republic, Finland, Greece, Hungary, Indonesia, Ireland, Israel, Kuwait, Lebanon, Malaysia, New Zealand, Norway, Pakistan, the Philippines, Poland, Portugal, Saudi Arabia, South Africa, Turkey, the United Arab

Emirates, and the Republica Bolivariana de Venezúela. The large economies are Australia, Austria, Belgium, Brazil, Canada, Denmark, France, Germany, Hong Kong (China), India, Italy, Japan, the Republic of Korea, Luxembourg, the Netherlands, Singapore, Spain, Sweden, Switzerland, Taiwan (China), Thailand, the United Kingdom, and the United States.

11. Detailed parameter estimates are available on request from the authors.

12. R^2 is 0.972 for the variable cost equation, 0.392 for the labor cost-share equation, 0.405 for the deposit cost-share equation, and 0.176 for the shadow price of financial capital equation. The log of likelihood functions is computed as 6809.86 over 2,625 total sample observations.

13. In a broad sense, ε_T can be viewed as a sort of adjusted measure for ε_V but here it is regarded as a conventional measure in that no asset quality adjustment was made. Note that the presence of $npla$ ($NPL/Q/AS$) as an explanatory variable in the regression may induce the belief that ε_V implicitly adjusts for the quality of assets. In fact, given our definition of asset quality, adjusting for quality requires that $npla$ be kept constant with respect to changes in O. To the extent that ε_V is estimated without keeping the $npla/Q$ ratio constant, it does not adjust for quality and therefore can be considered as a conventional measure of scale economies. According to table 3.3, its mean values appeared to be extremely modest between small and large classes, ranging from 0.97 to 0.99. The reason for small differential performances may be due to the use of a shadow price for the quasi-fixed input (w^*_k), rather than the unobservable equilibrium price (w_k).

14. As a dominant domestic bank operating in a highly concentrated market has a lower demand for financial capital (see equation [3.6]), a positive relationship should be expected to hold between market concentration and scale economies as long as the marginal cost of financial capital, or the cost of signaling, is positive, as in Hughes and Mester (1998).

15. The basic model specification is $I_{ijt} = \alpha_0 + \beta_i B_{ijt} + \beta_j X_{jt} + \varepsilon_{ijt}$, where I_{ijt} is the dependent variable for domestic bank i in country j at time t; B_{ijt} are bank-specific financial variables for domestic bank i in country j at time t; and X_{jt} are country-specific variables for country j at time t. Here α_0 is a constant and β_i and β_j are coefficients, while ε_{ijt} is an error term.

16. We decided not to use fixed effects estimation because, in our setup, differences relating to country effects are captured by country-specific structural variables (FS, FSD, MS, CN).

17. The intuition behind this result is the same as that underpinning Honohan and Kinsella's (1982) proposal to measure bank concentration across countries by using a variant of the Herfindahl index, where the index is normalized by a minimum feasible value based on the size of the bank market in each country. Assuming increasing returns to scale in bank production, Honohan and Kinsella find that the maximum feasible number of

banks (that is, consistent with nonnegative profits) is roughly proportional to the square root of the bank market size.

18. $(\varepsilon_{CQ})^{-1} = \partial \ln C / \partial \ln Q = (\partial C / \partial Q)/(Q/C) = MC/AC$.

19. The reason for using a shadow total cost function here is that it is difficult to obtain a quality-adjusted AC and MC directly with the underlying variable cost function. Note that the indirect measure of scale economies, derived from the ratio of AC/MC in the bottom line of table 3.7, will be slightly different from that of other direct measures because of rounding and aggregations of errors of computation.

20. Parametric estimates of the marginal total cost $(\partial C_T / \partial Q)$ are directly obtained by differentiating the shadow total cost function with respect to Q.

21. This is because i (total) cost is minimized over the cash flow (variable) cost as well as the additional opportunity (or shadow) cost of financial capital.

References

The word *processed* describes informally produced works that may not be commonly available through libraries.

Allen, F., and D. Gale. 1999. *Comparing Financial Systems*. Cambridge, Mass.: Massachusetts Institute of Technology Press.

Beck, T., A. Demirgüç-Kunt, and R. Levine. 1999. "A New Database on Financial Development and Structure." Financial Sector Discussion Paper no. 2. World Bank, Washington, D.C.

Bossone, B., P. Honohan, and M. Long. 2001. "Policy for Small Financial Systems." Financial Sector Discussion Paper no.6. World Bank, Washington, D.C.

Claessens, S, and J. K. Lee. 2002. "Foreign Banks in Low-Income Countries: Recent Developments and Impacts." Background paper for *Global Development Finance 2002*. World Bank, Washington, D.C.

Claessens, S., A. Demirgüç-Kunt, and H. Huizinga. 2001. "How Does Foreign Entry Affect the Domestic Banking Market?" *Journal of Banking and Finance* 25(5): 891–911.

Demirgüç-Kunt, A., and H. Huizinga. 1999. "Determinants of Commercial Bank Interest Margins and Profitability: Some International Evidence." *World Bank Economic Review* 13(2): 379–408.

Honohan, P., and R. P. Kinsella. 1982. "Comparing Bank Concentration across Countries." *Journal of Banking and Finance* 6(2): 255–62.

Hughes, J. P. 1999. "Incorporating Risk into the Analysis of Production." *American Economic Journal* 27(1): 1–23.

Hughes, J. P., and L. J. Mester. 1998. "Bank Capitalization and Cost: Evidence of Scale Economies in Risk Management and Signaling." *Review of Economics and Statistics* 80(2): 314–25.

Hughes, J. P., L. J. Mester, and C. G. Moon. 2001. "Are Scale Economies in Banking Elusive or Illusive? Evidence Obtained by Incorporating Capital Structure and Risk Taking into Models of Bank Production." *Journal of Banking and Finance* 25(ER12): 2169–2208.

Hughes, J. P., W. Lang, L. J. Mester, and C. G. Moon. 2000. "Recovering Risky Technologies Using the Almost Ideal Demand System: An Application to U.S. Banking." Working Paper no. 00-5. Federal Reserve Bank of Philadelphia, Philadelphia.

La Porta, R., F. Lopez-de-Silanes, A. Shleifer, and R. Vishny. 1997. "Legal Determinants of External Finance." *Journal of Finance* 52(3): 1131–50.

———. 1998. "Law and Finance." *Journal of Political Economy* 106(6): 1113–55.

Levine, R., N. Loayza, and T. Beck. 2000. "Financial Intermediation and Growth: Causality and Causes." *Journal of Monetary Economics* 46(1): 31–77.

4

Are Small Countries "Underbanked"?

James A. Hanson

This chapter examines whether small countries are underbanked and the extent to which domestic underbanking is offset by the use of offshore banks. Some previous work has suggested that small countries may have smaller domestic financial systems than large countries (Bossone, Honohan, and Long 2002). This phenomenon may partly reflect higher bank margins in small countries (Bossone and Lee, chapter 3 in this volume; Bossone, Honohan, and Long 2002).

This chapter finds that small countries have a lower ratio of domestic bank deposits to gross domestic product (GDP) than large countries, even adjusting for differences in their per capita income and recent inflation rates.[1] However, this chapter also finds that residents of small countries rely more on offshore bank deposits than residents of large countries. In practice, small countries' combined onshore and offshore deposits (relative to GDP) do not differ from those of large countries in statistically significant terms. That is, deposits in offshore banks by residents of small countries appear to offset their smaller onshore deposits. As concerns loans,

The author would like to thank Gerard Caprio, Patrick Honohan, Giovanni Majnoni, and Jo Ann Paulson for their comments. Ying Lin provided helpful research assistance.

the differences in offshore borrowing by small and large countries, relative to GDP, were reduced substantially between 1996 and 1999. African countries, however, seem to have a lower ratio of bank deposits to GDP, onshore or offshore, than other countries.

This chapter discusses some possible explanations for these patterns in deposit behavior, namely, differences in economies' openness to international markets, in economies of scale, in competition, and in policies. Differences in corruption seem an unlikely explanation of the results, because the offshore deposit data are based on declarations of ownership and residence by depositors in Organisation for Economic Co-operation and Development (OECD) banks, declarations that are unlikely to be correct for deposits arising from gains from corruption. The chapter also discusses some possible implications of small countries' greater reliance on offshore banking.

Small Countries Have Smaller Domestic Banking Systems than Large Countries

Small countries have smaller banking systems than large countries, unless they are offshore financial centers. Fifty-nine countries have broad money stocks of less than US$1 billion, 118 have stocks of less than US$10 billion.[2]

To some extent the size of small countries' banking systems simply reflects their economic size. In the sample of 81 developing countries used in this chapter, the 61 countries with broad money of less than US$10 billion had an average GDP of about US$5 billion in 1996, while the 21 countries with broad money of more than US$10 billion had an average GDP of about $221 billion, over 40 times larger.[3]

Small countries' banking systems are, however, smaller than might be expected relative to their economic size. According to the International Monetary Fund's *International Financial Statistics,* at the end of 1996 the large countries' banking deposits averaged 38.3 percent of GDP, compared with 23.5 percent for the small countries.[4] By the end of 1999 the gap was even larger, with the large countries' banking deposits averaging 46.7 percent of GDP compared with 26.7 percent for the small countries.[5] However, these differences partly reflect the lower per capita GDP of the small countries in the sample, whose average per capita GDP was only about 40 percent of the figure for the large countries in the sample. As banking deposits tend to be positively correlated with per capita income, to some degree the difference in per capita income explains the difference in the size of the banking sector relative to GDP.[6] Differences in inflation might also explain the differences in deposits; however, about 40 percent of both large and small countries in the sample experienced average inflation of more than 15 percent per year in the five years prior to 1996.

Taking per capita GDP and inflation into account systematically, the small countries had about 10 percent of GDP less in deposits than large countries in 1996 and in 1999, on average. This is shown in table 4.1, which presents a regression of onshore deposits relative to GDP as a function of (a) the log of per capita GDP; (b) a high inflation variable that takes a value of 1 for countries with average inflation greater than 15 percent in the previous five years and for Argentina and Bolivia, two countries that had a history of high inflation that was reversed in the 1990s, and 0 for the other countries;[7] and (c) a small economy variable that takes on a value of 1 for the 61 countries in the sample with less than US$10 billion of broad money and 0 for the 20 countries with more than US$10 billion of broad money. In the regressions, the small country variable had a statistically significant coefficient of 9 percent in 1996 and 12 percent in 1999. The regressions also indicate a positive relationship between per capita income and deposits and a negative relationship between inflation and deposits, with both relationships being highly significant.

Table 4.1 Regressions of Onshore Deposits/GDP on GDP/ Population, Inflation, and Country Size, 1996 and 1999

Explanatory variable	Coefficient, 1996	t-statistic	Coefficient, 1999	t-statistic
Intercept	−0.33	(1.53)	−0.54	(1.93)
log(GDP/population)	0.38	(3.54)***	0.53	(3.89)***
High inflation (0,1) variable	−0.11	(3.30)***	−0.12	(2.86)***
Small country (0,1) variable	−0.09	(2.18)**	−0.12	(2.36)**
R^2adj	0.31		0.33	

** Indicates statistical significance at the 5% level.
*** Indicates statistical significance at the 1% level or greater.
Source: Author's calculations.

Small Countries Deposit Offshore More than Large Countries

To a large extent, the lower onshore deposits in small countries are offset by higher offshore deposits. The reported deposit to GDP ratio of the nonbank sector of small countries in OECD banks averaged roughly twice as much as for large countries (table 4.2). For small countries the average ratio of offshore deposits to onshore deposits was 48 percent in 1996 and 44 percent in 1999, compared with about 19 percent for large countries in both years. Thus about one-third of small countries' total bank deposits were offshore.

These data understate the size of offshore deposits in both large and small countries because they neglect (a) offshore deposits by nonbank OECD residents that report addresses in the OECD; and (b) deposits by the nonbank sector in non-OECD, offshore banking sectors such as the Caymans, Hong Kong (China), and Panama, which do not report the residency of deposit owners. However, there is no obvious reason why the unreported deposits should be larger for depositors in large countries than small countries. As with onshore deposits, large differences are apparent between countries. Kenya, the Seychelles, and Suriname (small financial systems) and the Republica Bolivariana de Venezúela (a large financial system) all had offshore deposits equal to more than 20 percent of GDP in both 1996 and 1999, the largest figures across countries. Indeed, Suriname, the Republica Bolivariana de Venezúela, and some of the African countries had more offshore deposits than onshore deposits.

Taking into account per capita GDP and inflation on a country by country basis, the small countries' nonbank sectors had about 5 percent of GDP more offshore deposits than the large countries.

Table 4.2 Offshore Deposits of Small and Large Countries, 1996 and 1999 (percentage of GDP and percentage of onshore deposits)

Countries	Offshore deposits/ GDP, 1996	Offshore deposits/ GDP, 1999	Offshore deposits/ onshore deposits, 1996	Offshore deposits/ onshore deposits, 1999
Small countries (61)	7.8	8.3	48	44
Large countries (20)	4.2	4.8	19	19

Source: Bank for International Settlements data.

This is shown in table 4.3 by regressions using the same format as those in table 4.1. These regressions are not as significant statistically as the regressions for onshore deposits, particularly in 1999. The lower significance mainly reflects the interesting result that GDP per capita does not seem to affect the volume of offshore deposits. High inflation and country size do affect the volume of offshore deposits, but with a lower statistical significance in 1999 than in 1996.[8]

Table 4.4 shows the key result: small countries effectively substituted offshore deposits for onshore deposits. Country size is not a

Table 4.3 Regressions of Offshore Deposits/GDP on per capita GDP, Inflation, and Country Size, 1996 and 1999

Explanatory variable	Coefficient, 1996	t-statistic	Coefficient, 1999	t-statistic
Intercept	−0.098	(1.07)	−0.135	(1.01)
log(GDP/ population)	0.063	(1.39)	0.083	(1.27)
Inflation (0,1) variable	0.032	(2.28)**	0.036	(1.74)*
Small country (0,1) variable	0.046	(2.64)**	0.049	(1.92)*
R²adj	0.10		0.04	

* Indicates statistical significance at the 10% level.
** Indicates statistical significance at the 5% level.
Source: Author's calculations.

Table 4.4 Regressions of Total Deposits/GDP on per capita GDP, Inflation, and Country Size, 1996 and 1999

Explanatory variable	Coefficient, 1996	t-statistic	Coefficient, 1999	t-statistic
Intercept	−0.44	(1.81)*	−0.672	(2.05)**
log(GDP/population)	0.44	(3.75)***	0.611	(3.82)***
High inflation variable	−0.08	(2.11)**	−0.086	(1.72)*
Small country variable	−0.04	(0.96)	−0.076	(1.21)
R²adj	0.22		0.23	

* Indicates statistical significance at the 10% level.
** Indicates statistical significance at the 5% level.
*** Indicates statistical significance at the 1% level or greater.

statistically significant determinant of total deposits, offshore plus onshore. Small countries are thus not underbanked in terms of deposits; they just tend to deposit more offshore.

Small and Large Countries' Offshore Borrowing Has Become Similar

Banking involves lending as well as deposit taking. In 1996, on average, the small countries' nonbank sectors borrowed much less offshore (as a percentage of GDP) than the large countries as shown in table 4.5.[9] However, by 1999 the average borrowing of both groups of countries was about the same percentage of GDP.

In terms of deposits, the small countries' debts to OECD banks were only about half of their deposits in OECD banks in 1996. In 1999 borrowings and deposits were about the same. In contrast, the large countries' debts to OECD banks were about 85 percent more than their offshore deposits in both 1996 and 1999.

The large countries' larger offshore debt stock (relative to deposits) probably reflects the greater percentage of large countries that are "rated" compared with small countries. Thus the large countries' nonbank sectors can borrow from international banks and issue bonds more easily than those of the small countries. Much of large countries' offshore debt is, of course, public sector borrowing, but private companies in large countries also borrow offshore. As small countries tend to lack ratings, both their public and private sectors may have less access to offshore capital markets and bank loans than those of large countries. Small countries may also have a relatively larger presence of multinational companies in relation to their GDP than large countries. To some extent, multinational companies may borrow through their home offices rather than through

Table 4.5 Offshore Borrowings of Small and Large Countries, 1996 and 1999, Percent of GDP and Percent of Offshore Deposits, 1996 and 1999

	Offshore debt/ GDP, 1996	Offshore debt/ GDP, 1999	Offshore debt/ deposits, 1996	Offshore debt/ deposits, 1999
Small countries (61)	4.9	8.0	0.62	0.96
Large countries (20)	7.8	8.9	1.86	1.85

Source: Bank for International Settlements data.

firms domiciled in the foreign countries. In effect, the foreign direct investors provide financial intermediary services. Hence offshore debt to banks of small countries may be smaller, relative to GDP, than offshore debt to banks of large countries. Finally, small countries' public sectors may also rely more on multilateral institutions for finance than large countries' public sectors, which would also explain their lower reliance on bank borrowings.

The rise in small countries' borrowings between 1996 and 1999 is partly explained by sharp increases in six countries (equivalent to more than 10 percent of GDP), but 47 of the 61 small countries received more foreign loans in 1999 than in 1996. Among the large countries only 11 of the 20 countries received more loans (relative to GDP), none received an increase of more than 7 percent of GDP, and some of the increases appear to be related to restructuring after the 1997 Asian financial crisis. This pattern of increased borrowings suggests that OECD banks were more willing to lend to a more diverse group of countries in 1999 (perhaps on the security of deposits) than in 1996, despite the crises in international capital markets in 1997 and 1998.

Nonetheless, one could argue that small countries were receiving fewer offshore loans than might be expected. Small developing countries, like large developing countries, should have higher productivity of capital than industrial countries, and should thus receive more offshore funds than are deposited offshore as the larger developing countries do. This argument is, of course, tempered by productivity and risk considerations. The productivity of investment may be lower in the small developing countries in the sample than in the large ones, because one can argue that capital productivity is correlated with their lower GDP per capita. Risk may also be greater: small countries are less diversified than large countries, experience more volatility, and more of them were experiencing or had just experienced wars or insurrections during this period. Nonetheless, one might still argue that offshore lending to small countries, like offshore lending to large countries, should exceed offshore deposits.

Africa Seems to Be Comparatively Underbanked

Many of the small countries in the sample are in Africa: 35 of 61 versus only 4 of the 21 large countries (Algeria, Morocco, Nigeria, and South Africa). Some observers argue that Africa is underbanked. The data certainly seem to support this statement.

Table 4.6 Regressions of Onshore Deposits/GDP on per capita GDP, Inflation, Country Size, and Africa Variable

Explanatory variable	Coefficient, 1996	t-statistic	Coefficient, 1999	t-statistic
Intercept	−0.14	(0.61)	−0.28	(0.95)
log(GDP/population)	0.29	(2.65)**	0.41	(2.90)**
High inflation variable	−0.11	(3.35)***	−0.13	(3.03)**
Small country variable	−0.07	(1.74)*	−0.10	(1.96)**
Africa (0,1) variable	−0.09	(2.57)**	−0.11	(2.35)**
R²adj	0.36		0.37	

 * Indicates statistical significance at the 10% level.
 ** Indicates statistical significance at the 5% level.
 *** Indicates statistical significance at the 1% level or greater.

Table 4.7 Regressions of Offshore Deposits/GDP on per capita GDP, Inflation, Country Size, and Africa Variable

Explanatory variable	Coefficient, 1996	t-statistic	Coefficient, 1999	t-statistic
Intercept	−0.12	(1.25)	−0.16	(1.05)
log(GDP/population)	0.08	(1.56)	0.09	(1.30)
High inflation variable	0.03	(2.25)**	0.04	(1.74)
Small country variable	0.04	(2.44)**	0.05	(1.82)*
Africa (0,1) variable	0.01	(0.75)	0.01	(0.32)
R²adj	0.10		0.03	

 * Indicates statistical significance at the 10% level.
 ** Indicates statistical significance at the 5% level.

In terms of domestic bank deposits, small African countries seem to have even lower ratios of deposits to GDP than small countries on average. This is shown in table 4.6, which repeats the regressions of table 4.1 with the addition of a separate variable for African countries, namely, 0 for non-African countries and 1 for African countries, which allows for a separate effect for African countries over and above the effect of being small. African countries' deposits average almost 10 percent of GDP less than those of small countries, after controlling for their per capita income and inflation.

The low level of deposits onshore in Africa is not, however, offset by a higher average level of deposits offshore. This is shown in table 4.7, which indicates that African countries do not appear to have especially large deposits in OECD banks compared with those of small countries. Thus Africa seems underbanked compared with other countries, even after taking offshore deposits into account.

Table 4.8 Regressions of Onshore plus Offshore Deposits/GDP on per capita GDP, Inflation, Country Size, and Africa Variable

Explanatory variable	Coefficient, 1996	t-statistic	Coefficient, 1999	t-statistic
Intercept	−0.26	(1.04)	−0.43	(1.23)
log(GDP/population)	0.36	(2.98)**	0.50	(2.97)**
High inflation variable	−0.08	(2.10)**	−0.09	(1.81)*
Small country variable	−0.03	(0.59)	−0.05	(0.87)
Africa (0,1) variable	−0.08	(2.00)**	−0.10	(1.83)*
R²adj		0.25		0.25

* Indicates statistical significance at the 10% level.
** Indicates statistical significance at the 5% level.

This is shown in table 4.8, which shows that African countries have statistically lower total deposits both onshore and offshore.

Some Possible Explanations

Why do small countries deposit offshore and why are deposits in Africa, onshore and offshore, lower than elsewhere? Explanations are probably best related to (a) the differences in return and risk (broadly defined to include physical security) between the small and large countries in the sample, and (b) the differences in residents' responses to these incentives. Viewing offshore deposits, sometimes called capital flight, as the product of rational economic choice has a long tradition (see, for example, Dooley 1988; Dooley and Isard 1980; Khan and Ul Haque 1985).

In this light, differences in the pattern of deposits can be related to the following four broad factors:

- Physical conditions
- Market behavior and conditions
- Government policies and the response to them
- Corruption.

Of course, the pattern of deposit holdings probably reflects a mix of the various explanations and not any single factor. Note again that the small country results reflect the small African countries to some degree, and that the African results reflect the degree to which African countries in the sample, both small and large, differ from the rest of the sample, taking into account whether they are small or large.

Physical security is an obvious factor that may affect the risk-adjusted rate of return and the pattern of deposit holdings. Many of the smaller countries have recently experienced civil war or insurrection. In such circumstances, onshore deposits are likely to be relatively low and offshore deposits relatively high.[10] Lack of infrastructure, in particular telecommunications, is likely to depress offshore deposits relative to onshore deposits, because poor telecommunications make accessing offshore deposits more difficult. These factors may partly explain the differences between the pattern of deposits in small and large countries and the lower level of onshore and offshore deposits by residents of African countries.

A market-related factor that could partly explain small countries' larger offshore deposits and smaller onshore deposits might be the greater importance of international activities in small countries' economies. Residents engaged in international trade may find that keeping funds both offshore and onshore is convenient.[11] Residents who work offshore may keep deposits both where they work and where they are citizens. Hence a larger share of offshore-related activities by residents of small countries than of large countries would be consistent with more offshore deposits.

A likely related explanation is the possibly greater importance of large companies in small countries' economies. Large companies, especially those engaged in trade, may bulk larger in small economies and may deposit offshore to receive services that they need for their businesses. Conversely, public sector corporations are often required to deposit domestically and, to the extent that public sector corporations bulk larger in large countries' economies, this would also help explain the difference in the pattern of deposits by large and small countries. The impact of multinational companies on the pattern of deposits is not clear. As noted earlier, their head offices may carry out some of their financial services, and thus such companies may economize on deposits, both onshore and offshore. Such behavior on the part of multinational companies would explain lower onshore deposits in smaller countries, but not larger offshore deposits. None of these observations regarding the role of trade and large companies help explain the low level of African deposits.

Differences in market behavior and the cost structure of banks in small and large countries might be a partial explanation of lower risk-adjusted rates on deposits in smaller countries and lower deposits. In particular, small countries' banks lack economies of scale or scope (have limited services) or may behave uncompetitively. Empirically, bank margins (the difference between interest earned and interest paid by banks) appear to be bigger in small countries' banking systems (Bossone and Lee, chapter 3 in this volume; Bossone, Honohan, and Long 2002). Much of these cross-country differences in banks' interest margins probably reflects differences in loan rates rather than in deposit rates, because competition for deposits with offshore banks is likely to be greater than for loans.[12] Nonetheless, banks in small, uncompetitive markets might try to pass on their higher costs to depositors, discriminate against some classes of depositors, or reduce service, as noted earlier. Any of these approaches would lower the banks' average effective interest rate on deposits and encourage the leakage of deposits into offshore banks. Low deposits in Africa, as well as in some of the transition economies, may reflect these phenomena, as well as concerns about the safety of bank deposits in local banks.[13]

Potential depositors may, of course, also substitute foreign currency holdings for deposits when banks try to hold down interest rates on deposits, especially when poor infrastructure makes access to offshore deposits difficult. This observation accords with both the low level of total deposits in Africa and the reported high levels of foreign currency holdings.[14]

Differences in government policies and the public's response to them represent another class of possible explanations for smaller onshore and larger offshore deposits by small countries. In analyzing the impact of policies on the pattern of deposits, what matters is the difference in the "average" policy in small countries compared with that in large countries, not whether a particular policy creates incentives for capital flight. For example, inflation combined with financial repression tends to create incentives for substituting offshore deposits and foreign currency holdings for onshore deposits, but to some extent the inflation variable captures the "average" degree of substitution across countries in the regressions.[15] The issue for the regression results is whether large or small countries repress real rates more. Perhaps more important, attempts to repress rates in smaller countries are more likely to be mitigated by the greater openness of these economies in both the current and capital account. Small country residents are likely to have easier access to offshore banking than large country residents and can probably evade capital controls more easily than residents of large countries.[16]

Thus one explanation of the larger offshore deposits of small countries is that to the extent that these countries attempt to repress domestic interest rates, more leakage into offshore deposits occurs than in large countries. Of course the governments of small countries, like banks in small countries, may attempt to take advantage of depositors who cannot move funds easily even if such policies result in a leakage of deposits. In other words, taxing bank deposits may be harder in small countries than in large countries, but this does not mean they will not be taxed, as demonstrated by the number of small countries that have relatively high inflation. Thus the difference in offshore deposits between large and small countries may partly reflect the greater effectiveness of capital controls in large countries.

A related explanation is that the deposit data for some of the large countries may reflect onshore "offshore" banking centers of one sort or another to keep deposits "onshore." One example is the Bangkok International Banking facility, where depositors were allowed to deposit "offshore" and make loans back to the domestic economy. Another example is Uruguay, which has a large volume of deposits from Argentine investors who sometimes also use Uruguayan addresses. While an attempt was made to remove small countries with "offshore" banking centers from the sample of small countries, this was not done for the large countries.

Differences in corruption are probably not a good explanation of the observed differences in deposit holding. Whether smaller countries suffer from greater corruption than large countries is not obvious, although examining this possibility would be an interesting extension of this chapter. Whether or not this is true, the proceeds of corruption are unlikely to be recorded in the Bank for International Settlements data as deposits coming from a particular country. Rather, such deposits are likely to be made through intermediaries domiciled in the country receiving the deposits, or they may not be made in OECD countries, at least initially, because deposits in OECD countries may be identified more easily or blocked more easily than in other financial centers. These problems in identifying deposits arising from corruption have been apparent in various countries' attempts to track down the deposits of their former chief executives. Thus corruption is unlikely to explain the difference between small and large countries' offshore deposits.

To summarize, openness is probably an important explanation for the small countries' lower ratio of onshore deposits and higher ratio of offshore deposits compared with the large countries. This openness means that residents of small countries not only want offshore deposits, but can more easily avoid any repression of deposit rates, either by the banks themselves or by policymakers, than residents of large countries. The low volumes of deposits by residents of African countries, both onshore and offshore, probably reflect residents' concerns about physical safety; weakness of local banks; and low levels of infrastructure, particularly telecommunications infrastructure, that limit their ease of access to offshore deposits.

These factors may also translate into larger (unobservable) holdings of foreign currency.

Implications of Reliance on Offshore Banking in Smaller Countries

If depositors in small countries do indeed go offshore because they consider that offshore deposits provide better risk-adjusted returns than onshore deposits, then offshore deposits represent a benefit for depositors and are desirable from that standpoint. Sometimes the use of offshore deposits to improve risk-adjusted returns, security, and service is called capital flight. The authorities may attempt to stop capital flight and keep deposits at home by imposing capital account controls of one sort or another. One useful way of thinking about such capital controls is that they are a tax that can be evaluated like any tax in terms of revenue, collection costs, and incidence. Such analyses must also consider the effectiveness of capital controls and the resulting impact on cost, benefits, and income distribution (Hanson 1994). For example, external traders and travelers abroad are likely to be able to evade the controls more easily than other residents, and their ability to do so not only shifts the income toward them, but may have the additional cost of decreasing respect for the legal system as a whole.[18]

In making such an analysis it is important to consider the approach to offshore lending and borrowing, as well as simply controls on offshore deposits. For example, limits on the offshore placement of funds by banks may mean that they are less able to offer attractive returns to depositors than offshore banks, or to hedge or "lay off" risks of foreign currency deposits, tending to reduce returns on and the attractiveness of onshore deposits. Offshore borrowing by the public sector and large companies reduces the domestic demand for credit and domestic interest rates, again tending to reduce the returns that can be paid on domestic deposits, and thus the attractiveness of domestic deposits. Finally, as this type of analysis suggests, the application of reserve requirements and taxes, including withholding taxes on interest, to offshore borrowing is not a capital control, but an equalization of taxation across onshore and offshore financial operations.[19]

More generally, offshore deposits mean a smaller domestic banking system, but is this a loss? If depositors are getting a higher risk-adjusted rate of return and better service, then offshore banks are a good substitute for domestic banks. All the arguments against protecting an inefficient industry in terms of the cost it poses to consumers hold for trying to use capital controls to increase the size of the domestic banking industry.

One could argue that offshore deposits and the corresponding reduction in the size and competitiveness of the domestic banking industry may particularly affect small depositors and small and medium borrowers. Small depositors may lack access to deposit facilities that pay reasonable rates of return if the domestic banking industry is small. Evidence suggests that higher ratios of deposits to GDP lead not only to more lending to the large borrowers, but to lending to new groups of borrowers, often small and medium enterprises (see, for example, Caprio, Atiyas, and Hanson 1994, and works cited therein).

Trying to keep deposits in the country to promote increased access to deposit-taking facilities and credit seems, however, to be a second-best policy. First-best policies would involve encouraging deposits to remain onshore by reducing the repression of deposit rates and by allowing foreign banks to enter and open branches that can provide service and security. The expansion of branch networks could be directly subsidized to provide access to deposit-taking facilities. Restrictions on lending offshore might also be eased to increase the incentive to offer deposit-taking facilities while meeting bankers' concerns that onshore lending is not profitable.

Of course many countries have attempted to keep deposits onshore to increase domestic lending, but these have generally have been unsuccessful in terms of either (a) the costs to depositors, particularly depositors that cannot easily avoid capital controls; (b) the incentives they create for corruption; or (c) the contribution they make to lending to small and medium borrowers and the rural sector, as the funds are often diverted to large borrowers or the state (see Caprio, Hanson, and Honohan 2001 and works cited therein). Hence the "obvious" solution of forcing deposits to remain onshore to increase lending to the rural sector and small and medium borrowers is probably not a good one.

Lending to small and medium enterprises can be directly stimulated by enhancing the security of property rights, improving titling, and upgrading the legal and judicial system for pledging and executing collateral. Developing credit information bureaus that generate information about borrowers' debt servicing history will also help and, as a by-product, help banks to improve their lending quality and stimulate creditors to service their debt promptly. Greater participation by foreign banks, particularly in the context of a better legal and judicial system, may lead to an expansion of small- and medium-scale lending and consumer lending.

Another issue is whether commercial banking is the best way to provide loans to the rural sector or to small and medium borrowers. Thus a desirable policy may be to encourage the growth of nonbank financial institutions to deal with these sectors of the population, while continuing to allow large clients to seek the best possible service and risk-adjusted returns, whether onshore or offshore.

Notes

1. The term small countries excludes small countries with offshore financial centers.

2. See Bossone, Honohan, and Long (2002), who define broad money as domestic currency plus bank deposits as reported in *International Financial Statistics,* lines 34 and 35.

3. The sample was based on the availability of data on offshore holdings, on GDP in 1999, and on inflation data. An attempt was made to exclude offshore financial centers.

4. The averages conceal substantial cross-country differences. China has far more deposits, relative to GDP, than any other country (92 percent of GDP in 1996) despite its relatively low per capita income. Other East Asian countries also tend to have relatively high ratios of deposits to GDP given their per capita GDP. In contrast, Sub-Saharan African countries and the large Latin American countries, with their history of inflation, tend to have low deposit to GDP ratios. Note also that there is much less difference in domestic currency holdings than deposit holdings across countries according to International Monetary Fund data. The Fund's currency data do not include foreign currency holdings, which are large in some countries.

5. The substantial increase in large country deposits between 1996 and 1999 almost wholly reflects increases in deposits in China, the Republic of Korea, Malaysia, and Thailand. In some of these countries part of the increase reflects a deposit shift from nonbank institutions to banks.

6. The relationship between deposits and per capita GDP is weak in the large countries, reflecting East Asia's larger deposits and lower per capita income than the other large countries in the sample.

7. The 0,1 inflation variable performed much better statistically than the actual average inflation rate over the previous five years, which was not statistically significant. The low correlation between the actual inflation rate and the relative size of deposits seems to reflect a lack of difference in deposit ratios between countries with very high inflation and those with high inflation. The limited difference between these two groups of countries may reflect differences in adjusting to inflation, for example, the very high inflation countries might have easier regulations on foreign currency deposits and more indexing. However, countries with high inflation or a history of high inflation do tend to have lower ratios of deposits to

GDP than other countries, as shown by the significance of the 0,1 variable. The choice of 15 percent inflation was arbitrary. Some exploration of a longer horizon was also made, but did not seem to make much difference, especially when Argentina and Bolivia were included among the inflationary countries.

8. The lower statistical significance of the income variable in 1999 may reflect the rise in deposits in the East Asian countries between 1996 and 1999, which occurred without a corresponding rise in these countries' per capita income.

9. The data on borrowing may be somewhat more representative than the data on deposits, because banks may have greater interest in reporting the correct addresses of borrowers than of depositors. Nonetheless the data understate borrowing, because some loans are made against the collateral of deposits (which do not report the correct domicile) and some loans are made outside the OECD from other banking centers.

10. For example, Olopoenia (2000) shows a strong positive relationship between capital flight and periods of political and economic instability in Uganda.

11. The lower level of loans to small countries than to large countries is not inconsistent with this view: as noted, many of the large countries' borrowings from commercial banks are public sector debts.

12. Banks in small countries may offer lower deposit rates because they lack economies of scale or do not face much competition and may try to take advantage of local depositors; however, effective competition for deposits between onshore and offshore banks is likely to be greater than for loans, unless capital account controls are effective. Thus differences in lending rates are likely to be much more important in determining margins, because the location of bank lending is more likely to reflect information asymmetries than the location of deposits. Moreover, lending rates may differ across countries because of differences in the required return on capital: smaller countries have lower per capita incomes, which may be an indicator of lower capital and higher returns on capital than in the large countries. Alternatively, lending rates may differ because of risk differences: small economies are subject to relatively greater shocks and face greater security risks than large economies, and thus banks in small countries would require higher interest rates on loans, on average, to allow them to provision properly and their owners to earn the same risk-adjusted rate of return on capital as in large countries. Countervailing balances by borrowers offshore are unlikely to explain the differences between offshore deposits of residents of large and small countries, because residents of small countries tend to borrow no more offshore than residents of large countries.

13. Banks in some African countries are reported to discourage small deposits because of their difficulties in using the funds to make loans and the cost of managing small deposits. These banks offer low deposit rates

and charge fees that represent a large proportion of the return on small deposits (I am grateful to Jo Ann Paulson for this observation). Of course, the fees might show up in the banks' accounts as noninterest income, and not affect reported margins. Brownbridge and Harvey (1998) cite concerns about the weakness of African banks as a factor limiting the growth of deposits in Africa and note foreign banks' unwillingness to increase deposit taking and domestic lending.

14. See Balino and others (1999, p. 6). As noted earlier, the International Monetary Fund figures on currency holdings do not include foreign currency.

15. Countries may allow onshore foreign currency deposits in an attempt to entice offshore deposits back, and some evidence indicates that this has occurred (Balino and others 1999; Hanson 2002; Honohan and Shi, chapter 2 this volume, and works cited therein). The inflation variable in the regression can be considered to take into account the policy that the "average" high inflation country adopts with respect to onshore foreign currency deposits.

16. If offshore deposits tend to face fewer legal barriers in small countries, then the residents of smaller countries might be more likely to use their own addresses when banking in OECD countries than residents of large countries. Hence, the data might be biased if capital controls are more prevalent in larger countries.

17. China, the country with the highest ratio of deposits to GDP, is often considered to have effective capital controls, although the large errors and omissions in China's balance of payments and the large volume of direct foreign investment have both been cited as evidence of leakages in the controls. India, another country with capital controls, also has a large ratio of deposits to GDP for its per capita income. However, Indonesia, Malaysia, and Thailand also have relatively high ratios of deposits to GDP and have maintained fairly open capital accounts with regard to offshore deposits.

18. Ajayi and Khan (2000, part II) indicate that overinvoicing of imports and underinvoicing of exports was a major factor in unrecorded capital outflows in Kenya, Nigeria, Tanzania, and Uganda.

19. For example, some countries have experienced a shift in deposits and borrowing offshore as resident companies and financial institutions try to avoid high reserve requirements.

References

Ajayi, S. I., and M. Khan, eds. 2000. *External Debt and Capital Flight in Sub-Saharan Africa.* Washington, D.C.: International Monetary Fund.

Balino, T., A. Bennet, E. Borensztein, and others. 1999. *Monetary Policy in Dollarized Economies.* Occasional Paper no. 171. Washington, D.C.: International Monetary Fund.

Bossone, B., P. Honohan, and M. Long. 2002. "Policy for Small Financial Systems." In G. Caprio, P. Honohan, and D. Vittas, eds., *Financial Sector Policy for Developing Countries—A Reader.* New York: Oxford University Press.

Brownbridge, M., and C. Harvey. 1998. *Banking in Africa.* Trenton, N.J.: Africa World Press.

Caprio, G., I. Atiyas, and J. A. Hanson. 1994. *Financial Reform: Theory and Experience.* Cambridge, U.K.: Cambridge University Press.

Caprio, G., J. Hanson, and P. Honohan. 2001. "Introduction and Overview: The Case for Liberalization and Some Drawbacks." In G. Caprio, P. Honohan, and J. Stiglitiz, eds., *Financial Liberalization: How Far, How Fast.* Cambridge, U.K.: Cambridge University Press.

Dooley, M. 1988. "Capital Flight: A Response to Differences in Financial Risks." *International Monetary Fund Staff Papers* 35(September): 422–36.

Dooley, M., and P. Isard. 1980. "Capital Controls, Political Risk, and Deviations from Interest-Rate Parity." *Journal of Political Economy* 88(April): 370–84.

Hanson, J. A. 1994. "An Open Capital Account: A Brief Survey of the Issues and the Results." In G. Caprio, I. Atiyas, and J. A. Hanson, eds., *Financial Reform: Theory and Experience.* Cambridge, U.K.: Cambridge University Press.

_____. 2002. "Dollarization, Private and Official: Issues, Benefits, and Costs." In G. Caprio, P. Honohan, and D. Vittas, eds., *Financial Sector Policy for Developing Countries—A Reader.* Oxford, U.K.: Oxford University Press.

Khan, M., and N. Ul Haque. 1985. "Foreign Borrowing and Capital Flight: A Formal Analysis." *International Monetary Fund Staff Papers* 32(4): 606–28.

Olopoenia, R. 2000. "Capital Flight from Uganda, 1987–94." In S. I. Ajayi and M. Khan, eds., *External Debt and Capital Flight in Sub-Saharan Africa.* Washington D.C.: International Monetary Fund.

5

Foreign Banks in Low-Income Countries: Recent Developments and Impacts

Stijn Claessens and Jong-Kun Lee

A good financial system is an essential ingredient for sustainable economic growth and reduced poverty (World Bank 2001a). Investigators have also shown that foreign participation can help develop a more efficient and robust financial system (see, for example, Claessens and Jansen 2000; IMF 2000, chapter VI). Across the globe, observers have found that increased foreign bank participation has generally improved the efficiency of and helped strengthen countries' financial systems, including by facilitating the privatization of state banks and broadening access to financial services.

Low-income countries have also benefited from this trend, although foreign participation in low-income countries is still less than that in many advanced emerging markets. Today about 18 percent of all banks in low-income countries are foreign owned, up from 5 percent in 1995. In terms of domestic assets in low-income countries, foreign-owned banks now account for some 7 percent, up from 3 percent in 1995. Empirical evidence shows that increased

The authors would like to thank James Hanson, Patrick Honohan, Giovanni Majnoni, Bill Shaw, and Aristomene Varoudakis for useful comments on earlier versions.

penetration has been correlated with lower financial intermediation costs and greater efficiency in financial service provision. It has also been associated with better quality balance sheets. At the same time, a higher foreign presence is associated with lower profitability.

While increased foreign bank participation has benefits, it does require concurrent measures to assure competitive financial services as well as broad access to financial services and financial sector stability. To assure that foreign bank participation remains a force for improvement, retaining a liberal entry regime will be important, including through commitments made in international agreements on financial services. Reaping all the benefits of foreign banks' technology and know-how in financial services provision requires adequate infrastructure, including good information, a proper framework for secured lending, and sufficient transparency. Foreign banks may introduce improved risk management practices and "import" supervision from their parent country regulators. At the same time, increased competition from foreign banks can lower the franchise value of incumbent financial institutions and lead to instability. Adequate regulatory and supervisory frameworks, including rules for dealing with weak banks, are thus called for.

This chapter analyzes the degree of financial participation of foreign banks in low-income countries, its motivation, and its effects. It starts by describing trends in foreign bank participation in low-income countries during 1995–2000. It then analyzes the motivating factors for foreign bank entry and the differences between domestic and foreign banks in some key balance sheet and performance measures. Finally, it presents detailed econometric evidence on the impact of foreign bank entry and presence on the competitiveness and performance of domestic banking systems.

Foreign Bank Entry in Low-Income Countries

Spurred by financial liberalization policies removing barriers to entry across geographic areas and markets and facing increased economic and financial incentives, the presence of foreign-owned banks in the form of branches and subsidiaries increased sharply in many countries during the 1990s. Most of this increased presence has come about as a result of mergers and acquisitions, although in some countries newly created establishments have been important. The total number of bank mergers increased from some 3,800 during 1978–89 to 11,500 during 1990–2001 (Buch and Delong 2001). In the United States the removal of intrastate banking and other restrictions has spurred mergers leading to the establishment of nationwide banks and a general consolidation in the banking industry. Cross-border mergers in particular have increased, rising from only 320 during 1978–89 to some 2,000 during 1990–2001.

Developing countries have participated in this trend. Entry through takeovers of existing, often state-owned or nationalized banks has been especially high in major emerging markets. Newly created establishments have arisen in new markets such as the transition economies. Low-income countries have also participated in this trend, although it started from lower averages and increased at a slower speed. The number of cross-border mergers between two financial institutions—not necessarily involving a bank—completed during 1978–89 in Africa was only 7, whereas during 1990–2001 96 cross-border mergers took place, and two-thirds of all mergers in the region were cross-border (Buch and Delong 2001).[1]

Table 5.1 shows the participation of foreign banks in 58 low-income countries.[2] It provides the number of foreign banks relative to the total number of banks in each country in 1995 and 2000 and also compares the share of assets of foreign-owned banks to total bank assets in those two years. Many low-income countries have had some foreign bank presence, partly as a result of colonial links, but this presence has increased in recent years. In terms of numbers, foreign banks now represent, on average, some 18 percent of the total number of banks in these low-income countries, up from 5 percent in 1995.[3] In terms of assets, foreign banks now account for some 7 percent, up from 3 percent in 1995. Increases have been sharp in some countries. In 1995 almost half of the countries had no reported foreign bank activity, while only 15 out of the 58 countries did not in 2000. In addition, 15 countries had foreign bank asset shares greater than 50 percent in 2000, sharply up from only 4 countries in 1995. However, large differences persist between the low-income countries in terms of foreign bank participation, with reported penetration rates varying between none and 100 percent (in case of the Solomon Islands) and having a standard deviation of 36 percent.

In total, the number of (reporting) foreign banks in these low-income countries more than tripled from 41 in 1995 to 140 in 2000. The number share and its increase during this period was typically larger than the asset share and its increase, indicating that many of the foreign banks have been relatively small, but this is not always the case, especially in Sub-Saharan Africa. In Tanzania, for example, the share of foreign-owned banks in total banks is 30 percent, while in terms of assets the share is 69 percent.

Table 5.1 Share of Foreign Banks in Domestic Banking Systems, Selected Low-Income Countries, 1995 and 2000

Country	1995			2000		
	Ratio of number of foreign banks to total number of banks	Ratio of foreign bank assets to total bank assets	Total number of foreign banks	Ratio of number of foreign banks to total number of banks	Ratio of foreign bank assets to total bank assets	Total number of foreign banks
Angola	0.00	0.00	0	0.00	0.00	0
Armenia	0.00	0.00	0	0.29	0.28	2
Azerbaijan	0.00	0.00	0	0.18	0.03	2
Bangladesh	0.00	0.00	0	0.00	0.00	0
Benin	0.20	0.37	1	0.60	0.53	3
Bhutan	—	—	—	0.00	0.00	0
Burkina Faso	0.00	0.00	0	0.75	0.95	3
Burundi	0.17	0.22	1	0.33	0.51	2
Cambodia	—	—	—	0.00	0.00	0
Cameroon	0.13	0.29	1	0.25	0.40	2
Central African Republic	0.00	0.00	0	0.50	0.46	1
Chad	—	—	—	0.00	0.00	0
Congo, Dem. Rep.	0.00	0.00	0	0.50	0.85	2
Congo, Rep.	0.00	0.00	0	—	—	—
Côte d'Ivoire	—	—	—	0.60	0.94	6
Ethiopia	0.00	0.00	0	0.00	0.00	0
Gambia, The	—	—	—	0.50	0.67	1
Georgia	—	—	—	0.22	0.15	2
Ghana	0.12	0.18	2	0.35	0.39	6
Guinea	0.00	0.00	0	0.00	0.00	0
Guinea-Bissau	0.00	0.00	0	—	—	—
Haiti	0.00	0.00	0	0.00	0.00	0
India	0.00	0.00	0	0.00	0.00	0
Indonesia	0.11	0.05	13	0.24	0.06	28
Kenya	0.06	0.12	3	0.16	0.33	8
Kyrgyz Republic	—	—	—	0.50	0.83	1
Lesotho	0.33	0.19	1	0.67	0.37	2

Liberia	0.00	0.00	0	0.00	0.00	0
Madagascar	0.50	0.56	2	0.75	0.79	3
Malawi	0.00	0.00	0	0.22	0.07	2
Mali	0.20	0.23	1	0.40	0.39	2
Mauritania	0.00	0.00	0	0.25	0.15	1
Moldova	0.11	0.19	0	0.11	0.04	1
Mongolia	0.00	0.00	1	0.00	0.00	0
Mozambique	0.20	0.14	0	0.60	0.34	3
Myanmar	0.00	0.00	0	—	—	—
Nepal	0.20	0.26	2	0.50	0.39	5
Nicaragua	0.00	0.00	0	0.13	0.12	2
Niger	—	—	—	1.00	1.00	4
Nigeria	—	—	—	0.05	0.01	4
Pakistan	0.00	0.00	0	0.08	0.02	3
Rwanda	0.20	0.36	1	0.20	0.34	1
São Tomé and Principe	0.00	0.00	0	0.50	0.63	1
Senegal	0.43	0.60	3	0.43	0.62	3
Sierra Leone	0.00	0.00	0	0.00	0.00	0
Solomon Islands	1.00	1.00	1	1.00	1.00	1
Sudan	0.13	0.71	1	0.13	0.76	1
Tajikistan	—	—	—	0.00	0.00	0
Tanzania	0.00	0.00	0	0.30	0.69	6
Togo	0.00	0.00	0	0.17	0.07	1
Turkmenistan	0.00	0.00	0	0.00	0.00	0
Uganda	0.05	0.11	1	0.42	0.46	8
Ukraine	0.00	0.00	0	0.10	0.03	5
Uzbekistan	0.00	0.00	0	0.25	0.00	2
Vietnam	0.05	0.01	1	0.15	0.03	3
Yemen	0.00	0.00	0	0.00	0.00	0
Zambia	0.15	0.35	2	0.62	0.58	8
Zimbabwe	0.10	0.34	3	0.10	0.42	3
Average	0.05	0.03	0.9	0.18	0.07	2.6

— Not available.

Note: A foreign bank is defined to have at least 50 percent foreign ownership.

Source: Bankscope.

Similarly, the asset share is larger than the number share in a number of other Sub-Saharan African countries: Burkina Faso, Burundi, Cameroon, Congo Democratic Republic, Côte d'Ivoire, The Gambia, Ghana, Kenya, Madagascar, Rwanda, São Tomé and Principe, Senegal, Sudan, Uganda, and Zimbabwe. In part this may reflect the availability of data to the extent that foreign banks report more frequently and more complete data to Bankscope than local banks do, but it also indicates that many of the largest banks in Sub-Saharan Africa are foreign owned. Six of the 11 largest banks in Sub-Saharan Africa are foreign owned (Ulgenerk 2001). In some other countries the entry of one or a few banks changed ownership structures significantly. In Armenia, for example, the entry of two foreign-owned banks raised the share of foreign ownership from 0 to 28 percent.

The entry of foreign-owned banks in low-income countries is, on average, much less than that in middle-income emerging markets. Mathieson and Roldòs (2001) show that the increase in the major emerging markets has been sharp. Specifically, they document that the foreign bank share in Central Europe rose from just 12 percent in 1994 to 57 percent in 1999. In several Central European countries the share of assets controlled by foreign-owned banks is now 60 percent or more, up from less than 10 percent in the Czech Republic and Poland and 40 percent in Hungary. A similar trend has occurred in Latin America, where by the end of the 1990s foreign banks accounted for nearly half or more of the banking systems of several countries (Argentina, Chile, Mexico, and Republica Bolivariana de Venezúela), up from shares of between 10 and 20 percent in 1994. Although the foreign bank share in the emerging markets in Asia doubled from 1994 to 1999, the foreign bank asset share remains relatively low at 13.2 percent. On average, the share of assets controlled by foreign-owned banks in 13 major emerging markets rose by some 23 percentage points between 1994 and 1999.

The differences in foreign bank penetration among countries can be further illustrated by grouping similar countries. A logical grouping of the low-income countries for which data are available is based on a combination of regional, language, and economic characteristics. Specifically, the sample of low-income countries is divided into 6 groups as follows: Asia and the Pacific (9 countries); transitional economies (11 countries); English-speaking Sub-Saharan Africa (15 countries); French-speaking Sub-Saharan Africa (16 countries); Portuguese-speaking Sub-Saharan Africa (4 countries); and others (3 countries). The detailed classification is shown in appendix 5.2.

Table 5.2 shows the breakdown of ownership by these groupings of countries, calculating foreign ownership by region as a simple average of individual countries' foreign ownership (country-based share) or as the total foreign ownership for the region as a share of total banking assets for the region for 1995 and 2000. Of the banks reporting, in 2000 French-speaking Africa had the relatively highest average share of foreign bank penetration, up significantly from 1995.[4] The English-speaking Africa group is next, with the figures also showing an increase from 1995. These numbers also show that, in contrast to the situation in other low-income countries, foreign banks in low-income Africa are larger than the average local bank, because the asset shares are larger than the number shares. During the period the shares of foreign bank ownership also increased sharply in the low-income countries of Portuguese-speaking Africa, somewhat in Asia and the Pacific, and significantly in the transition economies.

The shares calculated on a regional basis differ somewhat from the simple averages of the individual countries. Where, as in French-speaking Africa, for example, the region-based share of foreign banks is higher than the average for the individual country shares, this implies that it is in the larger countries of the region that the foreign banks are especially well represented. The opposite is true, for example, in the transition economies group, for example, the share of foreign banks in 1995–2000 is only 3 percent on a regional assets basis, compared with a country average in 2000 of 16 percent.

The distribution of markets by size is, of course, also affected by the size of the foreign banks entering the various markets. Using data for 1995–2000, foreign banks are, on average, the largest in English-speaking Africa and in the Asia-Pacific region with more than US$8 billion in asset size (figure 5.1). In the case of the Asia-Pacific region, this average is greatly influenced by a few extremely large foreign banks. In terms of size these two regions are followed by French-speaking Africa, where the average size of foreign banks is about US$3.7 billion, or about half that in the other two regions. Foreign banks in transition economies, Portuguese-speaking Africa, and other countries are all much smaller, averaging US$0.5 billion or less.

An analysis of the country of origin of the foreign banks highlights the still important historical, including colonial, and cultural links between countries, as well as the importance of regional proximity, in determining entry. Appendix 5.3 shows that the United Kingdom still accounts for a large share of foreign banks in English-speaking Africa: on average U.K. banks account for 19 percent of all banks' equity capital in English-speaking African countries, or

Table 5.2 Share of Foreign Banks in Domestic Banking by Region, 1995 and 2000

	Country based								Region based			
	1995				2000				1995		2000	
Region	No. of foreign banks in total	Foreign bank assets in total	No. of countries	No. of foreign banks	No. of foreign banks in total	Foreign bank assets in total	No. of countries	No. of foreign banks	No. of foreign banks in total	Foreign bank assets in total	No. of foreign banks in total	Foreign bank assets in total
Asia and Pacific	0.33 (0.46)	0.26 (0.43)	5	16	0.46 (0.40)	0.37 (0.45)	4	37	0.10	0.07	0.23	0.04
Transition economies	0.02 (0.04)	0.03 (0.07)	7	2	0.20 (0.14)	0.16 (0.27)	9	18	0.02	0.02	0.15	0.03
French-speaking Africa	0.14 (0.19)	0.22 (0.24)	9	8	0.53 (0.25)	0.60 (0.31)	11	31	0.14	0.77	0.50	0.30
English-speaking Africa	0.08 (0.14)	0.20 (0.22)	10	13	0.29 (0.22)	0.40 (0.26)	12	49	0.05	0.22	0.19	0.39
Portuguese-speaking Africa	0.10 (0.14)	0.05 (0.08)	3	1	0.55 (0.16)	0.49 (0.21)	2	4	0.14	0.22	0.57	0.43[a]
Other	0.00 (0.00)	0.00	1	0	0.13	0.12	1	2	0.00	0.14	0.13	0.14

Note: Averages are computed by excluding 19 countries, including 16 countries with civil unrest and 3 countries with missing data from 58 total sample countries. The figures within parentheses denote standard deviations. Country-based figures are simply averaged over n countries within a region, $(1/n) \sum_i [\mathrm{FB}_i/(\mathrm{DB}_i + \mathrm{FB}_i)]$ for country i whereas region-based figures are obtained from $\sum_{ij} \mathrm{FB}_{ij}/(\sum_{ij} \mathrm{DB}_{ij} + \sum_{ij} \mathrm{FB}_{ij})$ for country i and bank j within a region. FB and DB represent foreign bank and domestic bank, respectively.

a. Figures are for 1999 and 1995–99.

Source: Authors' calculations.

Figure 5.1 Asset Size of Foreign Banks by Region,
1995–2000

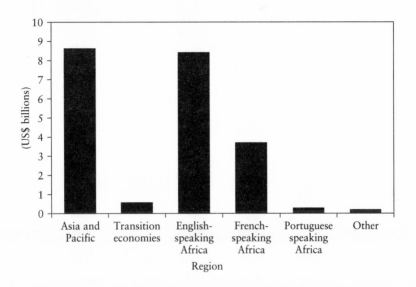

Source: Authors' calculations.

about one-third of all foreign banks' equity capital. Similarly in French-speaking Africa French banks account for about 11 percent of banking system equity in those countries, or 30 percent of all foreign banks' equity capital. The clearest indication of cultural links is for Portuguese-speaking Africa, where 24 percent of total banking system capital comes from Portuguese banks, or almost 80 percent of foreign capital.

The home countries of the foreign banks are more diverse in other low-income countries given the absence of cultural or other ties, and all of the foreign banks have been recent entrants, many after 1998. In some, but not all, Central Asian countries banks from Turkey are important. U.K. banks, for example, are quite important in Armenia, and especially in the Kyrgyz Republic. In low-income Latin America, Nicaragua has one large bank from the Cayman Islands and Haiti has no foreign bank reporting. Aside from countries such as France, Portugal, Turkey, and the United Kingdom there is no clear trend for other major home countries. Japanese banks tend not to establish branches abroad. Arab countries have only some indirect representation in Africa, with a large investment in the form of the Arab Bank for Economic Development in Africa in Sudan and some investment in Pakistan and Yemen. Banks from middle-income East Asian countries have established themselves to some degree in low-income East Asian countries. Finally, banks with participation by international financial organizations such as the International Finance Corporation and the European Bank for Reconstruction and Development have a presence in a diverse group of low-income countries.

The strong and long-standing historical links with a foreign bank presence in some countries may obscure the direct competitive effects of a foreign presence. In particular, incumbent foreign banks may have been protected from new entrants during the period under review, especially in the low-entry markets. Thus an increased foreign presence alone is insufficient to assure that domestic banking system markets are competitive, as the system needs to be contestable as well.

The rapid growth of foreign banks' operations raises questions about whether foreign banks behave differently from local banks in their funding and lending activities and whether their income, expenses, and profitability take different forms or whether they have similar portfolios and performance. Table 5.3 provides, on an aggregate basis, statistics on some key asset and funding variables for foreign and domestic banks for 2000 for those markets where there is some (but less than 100 percent) foreign presence. The table also reports the results of t-tests for any statistically significant differences between domestic and foreign banks.[5]

The table shows that foreign banks differ somewhat from domestic banks in terms of balance sheets. Foreign banks appear to have slightly higher shares of other and total earning assets and lower shares of fixed and noninterest-earning assets, with all four differences being statistically significant, but not very large. In terms of the liability mix, foreign banks appear to have a slightly higher share of non-interest-bearing liabilities, but the differences appear to be small overall.

Further analysis suggests that the balance sheets of domestic banks in high-entry markets do not differ much from those in low-entry markets in terms of capitalization (equity as a share of total assets) and asset and liability composition (share of other earning assets and customer and short-term funding as shares of total assets). When specifically studying the quality of loans, however, banking systems with a lower foreign presence have, in both absolute and relative terms, much more nonperforming loans. As a

Table 5.3 Difference between Domestic and Foreign Banks in Terms of Balance Sheets, 2000 (percentage of total)

	Assets					Liabilities and equity			
Origin	Loans	Other earning assets	Total earning assets	Fixed assets	Non-interest-earning asset	Customer and short-term funding	Other funding	Other (non-interest-bearing)	Loan loss reserves
Domestic	46.43	37.22	82.71	4.78	12.59	74.14	4.45	7.55	1.32
Foreign	46.03	39.73	85.53	3.57	10.95	74.00	4.64	7.77	1.40

Note: All ratios are averaged for 1995–2000 over 39 countries after excluding 16 countries suffering from civil unrest. Pairs of entries that are significantly different from each other at the 5 percent level of significance are in **bold.** In the case of asset-related variables, those pairs in bold are statistically different from each other at the 1 percent level of significance. The average of total earning assets is not necessarily equal to the column sum of each component's average as some banks do not report all balance sheet items.

Source: Authors' calculations based on Bankscope.

share of assets these amount to 5.79 percent for the foreign banks
versus 2.35 percent for the domestic banks, where the latter
excludes 1998 when many countries were affected by financial
crises. High-entry countries also have more loan loss provisions,
leading to significantly higher ratios of provisions to loans. Whereas
banks in low-entry countries provision less than 100 percent for
each nonperforming loan, banks in high-entry markets provision
150 percent. This suggests that the presence of foreign banks
encourages local banks to acknowledge their nonperforming loans
and provision more for these loans.

Determinants of Foreign Bank Entry in Low-Income Countries

The main driving force pushing industrial country banks into developing countries has been the search for profits. Banks have also followed their corporate customers that have started foreign operations. However, banks cannot expand abroad unless destination
countries let them in, which many developing countries have done.
Since the early 1990s many more developing countries have opened
up to foreign banking and removed rules that restricted foreign
ownership. Qian (2000) shows that between 1995 and 1997, years
in which an interim and final World Trade Organization agreements
on financial services were negotiated, countries generally opened up
further. Not all countries did so, however, and limits on foreign
entry tended to remain higher for low-income countries, including
countries that already had some foreign bank presence.

As Qian (2000) and Sorsa (1997) show, low-income countries
tend to have more restrictive entry regimes. They use an index,
devised by Sorsa and first developed for the 1995 financial services
negotiations, of the degree of permissible entry, as proxied by the
commitments the country had made under the 1995 negotiations,
and subsequently under the 1997 General Agreement on Trade in
Services financial services agreement. This index uses an average of
a number of dummies for specific policies with respect to the commercial presence of a foreign bank and ranges from 0 (closed) to 1
(completely open). Middle- to high-income countries scored, on
average, 0.768, while the average for all counties was 0.542. But it
is not only a country's income level that matters here. The openness
of its economy to trade in goods and the depth and competitiveness
of its financial sector are positively associated with opening up. On
the latter two indicators, low-income countries generally score

worse. Among the middle- to high-income countries, countries in Africa committed more to opening up than those in Asia and Latin America, with an average index value of 0.638 versus 0.463 and 0.452, respectively. This suggests that some countries with less developed financial systems viewed the potential gains from internationalization as so large that they wanted to open fully. Of course, they may not always have been able to attract foreign banks.

Countries have also welcomed foreign banks to help reduce the costs of resolving state-owned banks' financial problems. This has been important in emerging markets in Central Europe and Latin America, but has been less of a cause of entry in low-income countries, because bank privatizations have generally been slower in these countries. Accompanying reasons have included better financial and economic fundamentals in host countries; increased globalization and rising foreign trade; and more general financial liberalization, including the easing of restrictions on interest rates and directed credit requirements. Once again the low-income countries lagged behind many emerging markets in these areas.

As individual case studies for low-income and other countries show, the reasons for entry into specific markets have been varied (see, for example, Claessens, Demirgüç-Kunt, and Huizinga 2000; IMF 2000; Papi and Revoltella 2000; Ulgenerk 2001). Econometric analysis on the motivating factors for entry has found that the share of foreign banks is a function of some general factors, including banking net margins, profitability, country creditworthiness, and political stability. Papi and Revoltella (2000), for example, report evidence that political and economic stability, existing trade links, features of the host banking sector, and host country attitude toward foreign institutions play an important role in directing foreign direct investment toward countries in transition. In the case of low-income countries, as the raw data have already suggested, regional and historical links are probably also important.

To identify the determinants of foreign entry in low-income countries we specify a simple econometric model. We start with an accounting identity, equation (5.1), from the bank's income statement:

$$\text{net margin/ta} + \text{noninterest income/ta} =$$
$$\text{before tax profits/ta} + \text{overhead/ta} +$$
$$\text{loan loss provisioning/ta} + \text{other expenses/ta,} \qquad (5.1)$$

where *ta* stands for total assets.

We assume that foreign bank entry is exogenous to contemporaneous domestic banking variables, but determined by entry incentives in the country as of period *t-1*. This assumption also underlies

the work of Amel and Liang (1997), who investigate the determinants of entry and profits in local banking markets in the United
States. Specifically, we use the following equation for the presence
of foreign banks:

$$FS_{jt} = \alpha_o + \delta I_{jt-1} + \delta_j B_{jt-1} + \delta_j X_{jt-1} + \varepsilon_{jt}. \tag{5.2}$$

Equation (5.2) explains the foreign bank share in country j at time
t by averaged domestic bank variable I_{jt-1} for country j, averaged
bank control variables B_{jt-1} for country j, country variables X_{jt-1}, and
a random error term. The bank-specific variables can include interest income, noninterest income, overhead, taxes, loan loss expenses,
and net profits, all as ratios of total assets. Five specifications are
given, each with a different choice for the banking variable I_{t-1} from
the accounting equation (5.1).

Bank-level control variables are, on the profitability side, the
accounting value of a bank's net interest income over total assets
(*net margin/ta*), the net noninterest income over total assets (*noninterest income/ta*), and before tax profits (*before tax profits/ta*), and
on the cost side the variables are overhead costs over total assets
(*overhead/ta*) and provisions for loan losses over total assets (*loan
loss provisioning/ta*).

Regressions include country control variables, such as the rate of
growth of per capita gross domestic product (GDP), inflation, and
the real interest rate, which are all also lagged. To account for the
deterrent effects of civil unrest on entry or because countries were
essentially closed to foreign entry during such periods, we exclude a
number of countries from the regression.[6] We also explore the
extent to which differences in formal policies toward foreign presence can explain differences in entry. Specifically, the regressions
include the Sorsa index of entry liberalization mentioned earlier.

The regressions are conducted for the entire sample of countries
and all regressions are estimated over 1995–2000 with the White
correction for heteroskedasticity. The results of estimating entry
equation (5.2) are in table 5.4. The table indicates that foreign entry
is difficult to explain, as the R^2s are relatively low, less than 20 percent. Few of the banking variables are significant. Higher profitability seems to deter entry and is statistically significant; higher
margins and noninterest income also seem to deter entry but are not
statistically significant. Higher overhead and loan provisions are
positively associated with foreign bank presence, suggesting that
banking systems with high provisions for nonperforming loans are
more attractive. Higher-cost environments more generally seem to
be attractive to foreign banks, as the coefficient for overhead is positive, although not statistically significant. High banking costs may

Table 5.4 Determinants of Foreign Bank Presence
(dependent variable = the ratio of the number of foreign
banks to the total number of banks)

Variable	(1)	(2)	(3)	(4)	(5)
Net margin/ta$_{t-1}$	−0.108 (0.473)				
Noninterest income/ta$_{t-1}$		−0.446 (0.403)			
Before tax profits/ta$_{t-1}$			−0.529* (0.276)		
Overhead/ta$_{t-1}$				0.342 (0.431)	
Loan loss provision/ta$_{t-1}$					0.201 (0.265)
Equity/ta$_{t-1}$	0.095 (0.185)	0.101 (0.186)	0.176 (0.173)	0.089 (0.181)	0.143 (0.201)
Other earning asset/ta$_{t-1}$	−0.021 (0.096)	0.012 (0.101)	−0.018 (0.090)	−0.031 (0.106)	−0.002 (0.101)
Customer and short-term funding/ta$_{t-1}$	0.356* (0.189)	0.314* (0.168)	0.225 (0.183)	0.409** (0.180)	0.365 (0.226)
Index on degree of entry	0.095* (0.054)	0.085 (0.054)	0.113* (0.062)	0.117** (0.057)	0.110 (0.054)
Growth rate of GDP/cap$_{t-1}$	0.216 −(0.178)	−0.241 (0.163)	0.073 (0.234)	−0.155 (0.203)	−0.113 (0.241)
Inflation rate$_{t-1}$	-0.037 (0.025)	−0.036 (0.022)	−0.013 (0.024)	−0.041* (0.021)	−0.037 (0.023)
Real interest rate$_{t-1}$	−0.032 (0.060)	−0.035 (0.049)	0.017 (0.054)	−0.051 (0.051)	−0.033 (0.047)
Constant	−0.194 (0.185)	−0.157 (0.160)	−0.131 (0.173)	−0.269 (0.175)	−0.237 (0.214)
Adjusted R²	0.152	0.166	0.197	0.161	0.150
Number of observations	109	102	105	102	99

*Indicates significance at the 10 percent level.
**Indicates significance at the 5 percent level.
***Indicates significance at the 1 percent level.

Note: Regressions are estimated using weighted least squares pooling bank-level data across 39 countries for 1995–2000. Only domestic bank observations were used and averages were calculated over all domestic banks. The inverse of number of domestic banks in each period is used to weight the observations in the regressions to correct for varying numbers of bank observations in each country. Detailed variable definitions and data sources are given in appendix 5.1. Heteroskedasticity-corrected standard errors are given in parentheses.

Source: Authors' calculations.

also be an indicator of a less competitive banking environment, which may enhance entry possibilities for foreign banks. As expected, the financial liberalization index has a positive correlation with foreign bank presence. The control variables indicate that foreign banks are attracted to banking markets with low inflation and low real interest rates, although the results are mostly not statistically significant. Other control variables are not statistically significant, possibly because there is little variation among this group of all low-income countries.

These results can be compared with the results of Claessens, Demirgüç-Kunt, and Huizinga (2000), who investigated entry for a sample of 80 countries during 1988–95. In contrast to the results presented here, they found that low overhead costs are an important determinant of foreign bank presence. They also found that lower noninterest margins are associated with a greater foreign bank presence, although this result was less significant. They did not find a significant relationship between past profits and a current foreign bank presence. They did find a greater explanatory role for the control variables, possibly because they covered a wider distribution of countries and circumstances. Of the control variables they found that low taxes and a high level of per capita income, and in some specifications a lower concentration of the banking system, were significantly associated with greater foreign presence.

Impact of Foreign Banks on the Competitiveness of Domestic Banking Systems

Formal econometric evidence can provide a more complete picture of the effects of foreign bank entry and foreign presence on the operation of domestic banks. Specifically, we investigate how foreign bank entry affects each of the five variables in the accounting equation (5.1), including bank profitability.

We start by documenting the differences in performance between foreign and domestic banks. When discussing the relative performance of domestic and foreign banks we use all the items from the accounting identity (5.1) of the bank's income statement. Table 5.5 provides statistics on these key performance data for banks for 1995–2000, distinguishing foreign from domestic banks, averaged by the regional groupings as well as the overall averages. The table also reports on t-tests for statistically significant differences between foreign and domestic banks. Note that not all banks report all income items in all periods. As a result, averages are taken over samples that may differ for each variable and country and regional

Table 5.5 Bank Spreads and Profitability: Domestic Versus Foreign Banks, Selected Aggregates, 1995–2000 (percent)

Region	(1) Owner-ship	(2) Net margin/ total asset	(3) Noninterest income/ total asset	(4) Overhead/ total asset	(5) Tax/ total asset	(6) Loan loss provision/ total asset	(7) Other expense/ total asset	(8) Net profit/ total asset	No. of countries (banks) in 2000	Regional total
Asia and Pacific	Domestic	2.97	1.27	3.19	0.50	1.71	0.53	-0.31	3 (127)	4 (164)
	Foreign	5.45	2.48	2.98	1.81	3.65	1.66	1.83	4 (37)	
Transition economies	Domestic	8.20	5.84	6.86	1.46	2.77	-0.49	3.69	9 (103)	9 (121)
	Foreign	6.17	6.28	7.01	1.43	1.79	-0.64	2.95	8 (18)	
French-speaking Africa	Domestic	5.35	3.43	4.94	0.84	1.73	0.04	1.49	10 (28)	11 (57)
	Foreign	5.24	3.85	5.02	0.82	1.21	0.18	1.53	11 (29)	
English-speaking Africa	Domestic	6.36	5.31	7.16	1.05	1.45	0.52	2.26	12 (201)	12 (262)
	Foreign	7.53	5.35	7.18	1.59	1.38	-0.25	2.70	12 (51)	
Portuguese-speaking Africa	Domestic	4.94	2.54	7.35	0.18	5.96	3.66	-5.43	2 (3)	2 (7)
	Foreign	4.58	1.40	6.43	1.19	1.23	n.a.	-1.89	2 (4)	
Other	Domestic	5.45	1.82	6.70	0.15	4.68	0.25	-3.74	1 (14)	1 (16)
	Foreign	3.74	1.37	4.72	0.25	0.19	0.21	0.30	1 (2)	
Total	Domestic	5.72	4.09	5.88	0.94	1.93	0.30	1.60	37 (476)	39 (617)
	Foreign	6.17	4.21	5.52	1.45	2.02	0.55	2.10	38 (141)	

Note: Ratios are calculated for each bank in each country and then averaged for domestic and foreign banks separately within a region. Pairs of entries that are significantly different from each other are in **bold** and *italics* at the 1 percent and 10 percent level of significance, respectively.
Source: Authors' calculations.

averages themselves do not necessarily satisfy the accounting identity (5.1). Also some of the country and regional averages are for extremely small samples of banks, making some of the tests less meaningful.

For all the low-income countries combined net margins, noninterest income, taxes, loan loss expenses, and other expenses are slightly higher for foreign banks than for local banks, while overhead is lower for foreign banks. Most of these differences are not statistically significant at the 5 percent level. For the whole sample of low-income countries only in regard to taxes paid there is a statistically significant difference (higher for foreign banks) at the 5 percent level. The combination of these factors means that in low-income countries foreign banks perform somewhat better than domestic banks, that is, they have a higher net profitability of about 0.5 percentage points. This is consistent with Claessens, Demirgüç-Kunt, and Huizinga's (2001) finding that foreign banks have generally higher profitability in low-income countries than domestic banks.

To study the impact of foreign banks we next estimate the following equation:[7]

$$\Delta I_{ijt} = \alpha_o + \beta \Delta FS_{jt} + \beta_i \Delta B_{ijt} + \beta_j \Delta X_{jt} + \varepsilon_{ijt}, \tag{5.3}$$

where

Δ = the difference operator

I_{ijt} = the dependent variable (say, *before tax profits/ta*) for domestic bank i in country j at time t

FS_{jt} = the share of foreign banks in country j at time t (that is, the number of foreign banks divided by the total number of banks)

B_{ijt} = financial variables for domestic bank i in country j at time t

X_{jt} = country variables for country j at time t

α_o = a constant

$\beta, \beta_i,$ and β_j = coefficients

ε_{ijt} = an error term.

The regressions are specified in first differences for both left-hand-side and right-hand-side variables. This specification implies that we investigate the effect of changes in foreign bank presence, that is, new entry, on changes in the performance of individual domestic banks. The estimation is done by weighted least squares, with the weight being the inverse of the number of domestic banks in a country in a given year to correct for varying numbers of banks across countries. It excludes countries with limited entry because of civil unrest, reducing the sample to 39 countries.

Table 5.6 Changes in Foreign Bank Presence and Domestic Bank Performance

Variable	(1) ΔNet margin/ta	(2) ΔNoninterest income/ta	(3) ΔBefore tax profits/ta	(4) ΔOverhead/ta	(5) ΔLoan loss prov./ta
ΔForeign	−0.164***	0.044	0.037	0.037	−0.114
bank share	(0.052)	(0.044)	(0.107)	(0.034)	(0.113)
Index on degree	−0.032***	0.003	0.013	0.014*	−0.048
of entry	(0.012)	(0.010)	(0.032)	(0.008)	(0.033)
ΔEquity/ta	0.224***	0.060***	0.765***	−0.032*	−0.502***
	(0.040)	(0.013)	(0.101)	(0.019)	(0.093)
ΔOther earning	0.033*	0.012	0.066	−0.039***	−0.017
assets/ta	(0.039)	(0.013)	(0.042)	(0.010)	(0.043)
ΔCust. & short-	0.062**	0.031***	0.083	0.029**	−0.011
term funding/ta	(0.029)	(0.010)	(0.079)	(0.013)	(0.066)
ΔOverhead/ta	0.518***	0.353***	−0.203		0.477
	(0.147)	(0.084)	(0.296)		(0.417)
ΔGrowth rate	0.072	−0.069*	0.521***	−0.065*	−0.476***
of GDP/cap	(0.057)	(0.036)	(0.142)	(0.013)	(0.158)
ΔInflation rate	0.020***	0.002	0.023**	−0.001	0.008
	(0.007)	(0.005)	(0.011)	(0.006)	(0.008)
ΔReal interest rate	0.019	0.006	0.050*	0.015	−0.017
	(0.012)	(0.012)	(0.030)	(0.011)	(0.029)
Constant	0.024***	−0.002	−0.014	−0.011*	0.040*
	(0.008)	(0.007)	(0.022)	(0.006)	(0.023)
R^2adj.	0.429	0.380	0.704	0.148	0.632
No. of obs.	959	958	951	968	853

*Indicates significance at the 10 percent level.
**Indicates significance at the 5 percent level.
***Indicates significance at the 1 percent level.

Note: Regressions are estimated using weighted least squares pooling bank-level data across 39 countries for 1995–2000. Only domestic bank observations were used. The number of domestic banks in each period is used to weight the observations. In column (1) the dependent variable is the one period change in net margin/ta defined as interest income minus interest expense over total assets. In column (2) it is the one period change in net noninterest income/ta. In column (3) it is the change in before tax profits over total assets (before tax profits/ta). In column (4) one period change in overhead/ta is the dependent variable defined as personnel expenses and other noninterest expenses over total assets. In column (5) the dependent variable is the change in loan loss provisions divided by total assets. The foreign bank share is the ratio of the number of foreign banks to total number of banks. Detailed variable definitions and data sources are given in appendix 5.1. Heteroskedasticity-corrected standard errors are given in parentheses.

All independent variables except index of degree of entry are in first differences.

The estimation results, shown in table 5.6, indicate that foreign bank entry in low-income countries is associated with a statistically significant lowering of margins of domestic banks (column 1). Actual entry and the degree to which the domestic market is formally open to entry have complementary and similar effects on the performance of domestic banks. The statistically significant negative coefficient for the index on the degree of entry in the margin equation (column 1) indicates that the more contestable the domestic market, that is, the lower the degree of formal entry barriers, the lower the banking margins. The coefficients on the entry index for the other four variables pertaining to the performance of domestic banking systems also have the same signs as those for actual entry, although mostly lack significance.

Thus holding other factors constant, increased foreign presence and a more contestable system seem to put downward pressure on domestic banks' margins (column 1). The positive (but not statistically significant) coefficient for noninterest income (column 2) may indicate that domestic banks are also encouraged to broaden their income streams as a result of actual and possible entry. The fact that changes in profitability are positively (but not statistically significantly) related to actual foreign entry and the index of possible entry (column 3) may be because while the greater presence of foreign banks forces local banks to lower spreads on the one hand, on the other hand their greater actual and possible presence leads to a rationalization of cost structures, perhaps more than offsetting the first effect. The suggestion from the regressions (column 4) that foreign entry, actual and possible, may lead to higher overhead costs in domestic banks, which may reflect pressures for higher wages, even as foreign banks might encourage more efficient management and organizational structures. An increased foreign bank presence may therefore mean that domestic banks' costs increase while they assimilate more and newer banking techniques and the practices of foreign entrants.

The regression results also indicate the importance of using both bank and other country control variables and studying the effects of changes in foreign bank presence, that is, entry, on changes in local bank performance measures. Turning first to the bank-specific control variables, better capitalized banks increase their margins and noninterest income more, as well as having lower overheads and more loan loss provisioning. This leads to greater profitability for these banks, which in turn supports their better capitalization. This has been found for other markets as well (see Berger and others 2000). In addition, the degree to which banks' balance sheets carry other earning assets, that is, assets other than loans and non-interest-earning assets, increases their margins and lowers their overhead, leading to increased profitability. This probably indicates that banks that engage less in traditional banking activities and more in higher-value activities, such as providing advice and underwriting securities, see their profitability rise more. As banks upgrade their activities they may also become more efficient, thereby lowering their overheads. Greater reliance by a bank on customer and short-term funding seems similarly to raise margins, noninterest income, and overhead and lower loan loss provisions, with no statistically significant effects on income. Increases in the overhead expense ratio are associated with relatively higher margins and noninterest income and lower profits, although the latter is not statistically significant. In addition to confirming that banks that are less efficient are less profitable, this also suggests that higher overhead costs are being passed on to customers to a significant degree in the form of higher margins and higher other noninterest costs.

In terms of the country-specific control variables, increases in GDP per capita are associated with reduced costs and lower noninterest income and loan loss provisions, but with higher margins, although this is not statistically significant. The first relationship suggests that as the economy develops banks acquire better technology and know-how, lowering relative costs, or face a more competitive environment in general. The second relationship suggests that banks reduce their loan provisioning as economic prospects improve. The effect on margins may be that a growing economy allows banks to increase their margins. The change in inflation is statistically significant and positively related to net interest margin and profitability, and also positively related (but not statistically significantly) to noninterest income and loan loss provisions, and negatively related (but also not statistically significantly) to overhead. The signs are consistent with increasing inflation and higher real interest rates requiring higher bank margins and higher nominal profitability to maintain real bank capital.

The regression results so far are for all countries with both limited and greater foreign presence. To investigate whether the impact varies by degree of entry, we also split the sample into two groups, low and high presence, and reran the regressions (see Claessens and Lee 2001). The results are generally quite consistent: foreign entry lowers margins in both groups of countries (with the results being statistically significant). In high-presence markets entry is also associated with lower noninterest income, lower profits, lower overhead, and higher loan loss provisioning, although none are statistically significant. This is not the case for the low-presence markets, where entry is associated with higher noninterest income (statistically significant) higher profits, higher overhead, and lower loan loss provisioning, although the latter three coefficients are not statistically significant. The index of permissible entry is also significant much more often in high-entry countries than in low-entry countries.

The differences between the two groups suggest that foreign bank entry is more effective in markets with a higher foreign presence. This may be because the impact of entry on the domestic banking system has some threshold characteristics, with the effects of new entry being more important when there already is large presence. This could be because in low-presence countries foreign banks do not compete as much with local banks, but focus mostly on servicing foreign clients and other niche markets. This could easily be the case in many low-income countries where, because of barriers to entry in practice—including concerns about country risks, limited demand for more advanced financial services, and still incomplete financial reforms—foreign banks might not consider seriously committing themselves to the local markets, even when the governments have liberalized entry in theory. Put differently, in low-presence markets domestic banks face a less effective threat of entry. In higher-presence markets, faced with a threat of new entry, domestic bank managers are willing to give up their sheltered "quiet life" and to exert greater efforts to achieve cost efficiency.[8]

So far this chapter has investigated the effect of changes in foreign presence on changes in individual bank performance measures. We also examine whether the mere presence of foreign banks is associated with differences in performance among local banking systems by using the same regression results, but altering both the left-hand-side and right-hand-side variables to be level variables. This can be a correct approach provided that entry is based on past period banking system characteristics, and if it is the presence, rather than entry, which causes local banking systems to behave differently. Specifically, the foreign bank presence at time t should be determined by entry incentives as of period $t-1$. If the foreign bank share is only endogenous to lagged bank variables, an equation like (5.4) can be estimated separately using cross-country time series data:[9]

$$I_{ijt} = \alpha_o + \beta FS_{jt} + \beta_i B_{ijt} + \beta_j X_{jt} + \varepsilon_{ijt}. \tag{5.4}$$

Equation (5.4) explains the domestic banking variable I_{ijt} by the foreign bank share FS_{jt} in market j, and again the bank and country control variables and a random error term. The results are reported in table 5.7 for the whole sample. We also ran the regression separately for low- and high-presence markets, but do not report these results here (see Claessens and Lee 2001). In low-income countries a greater foreign bank presence is associated with significantly lower net interest margins, noninterest income, profitability, and overheads for domestic bank (columns 1–4). In addition, as the for-

Table 5.7 Foreign Bank Presence and Domestic Bank Performance

Variable	(1) Net margin/ta	(2) Noninterest income/ta	(3) Before tax profits/ta	(4) Overhead/ta	(5) Loan loss prov./ta
Foreign bank	−0.076***	−0.128***	−0.320***	−0.124***	0.166**
share$_t$	(0.026)	(0.021)	(0.063)	(0.020)	(0.065)
Index on degree	0.150	−0.046***	0.008	−0.097***	−0.037*
of entry	(0.010)	(0.010)	(0.023)	(0.010)	(0.020)
Equity/ta$_t$	0.129***	0.037***	0.365***	−0.025*	−0.210***
	(0.031)	(0.011)	(0.100)	(0.014)	(0.079)
Other earning	0.010	0.013**	0.096***	−0.012**	−0.081***
assets/ta$_t$	(0.010)	(0.007)	(0.022)	(0.006)	(0.021)
Cust. & short-	0.040**	0.001	0.020	0.004	0.010
term funding/ta$_t$	(0.020)	(0.012)	(0.058)	(0.009)	(0.048)
Overhead/ta$_t$	0.508***	0.444***	−0.168		0.222
	(0.084)	(0.059)	(0.247)		(0.273)
Growth rate	0.063	−0.049	0.670***	−0.150***	−0.690***
of GDP/cap$_t$	(0.059)	(0.035)	(0.155)	(0.029)	(0.142)
Inflation rate$_t$	0.027***	0.007	0.060***	0.008	−0.031***
	(0.009)	(0.007)	(0.011)	(0.008)	(0.009)
Real interest rate$_t$	0.069***	0.010	0.131***	0.029**	−0.073***
	(0.017)	(0.012)	(0.032)	(0.012)	(0.025)
Constant	−0.030	0.045***	−0.075	0.137***	0.084*
	(0.023)	(0.011)	(0.060)	(0.009)	(0.050)
R²adj.	0.368	0.429	0.503	0.233	0.423
No. of obs.	1349	1349	1342	1362	1213

*Indicates significance at the 10 percent level.
**Indicates significance at the 5 percent level.
***Indicates significance at the 1 percent level.

Note: Regressions are estimated using weighted least squares pooling bank-level data across 39 countries for the 1994–2000 time period. Only domestic bank observations were used. The number of domestic banks in each period is used to weight the observations. In column (1) the dependent variable is net margin/ta defined as interest income minus interest expense over total assets. In column (2) it is net noninterest income/ta. In column (3) it is before tax profits over total assets (before tax profits/ta). In column (4) overhead/ta is the dependent variable defined as personnel expenses and other noninterest expenses over total assets. In column (5) the dependent variable is loan loss provisions divided by total assets. The foreign bank share is the ratio of the number of foreign banks to the total number of banks. Detailed variable definitions and data sources are given in appendix 5.1. Heteroskedasticity-corrected standard errors are given in parentheses.

eign bank presence is higher, the degree of loan loss provisioning increases (column 5, statistically significant). A statistically significant negative impact of the degree of lack of formal barriers to entry on noninterest income, overheads, and the degree of loan loss provisioning (columns 2, 4, and 5) is also apparent.

Thus holding other factors constant, foreign presence puts pressure on domestic banks' profitability, reflecting more competition. The presence of foreign banks and the lack of barriers to entry also force local banks to have lower margins and other noninterest income sources. The evidence also indicates that a greater foreign presence and lower barriers to entry result in greater operational efficiency and lower overheads. The presence of foreign banks is also associated with higher loan loss provisioning, although the lack of barriers is associated with lower loan loss provisioning. This suggests that on one hand local banks increase their loan loss provisioning as foreign banks are present, and on the other hand a possible improvement in the quality of loans as systems become more open.

In terms of bank and country control variables, the results are very similar as for the regressions in first differences. Better capitalization is associated with higher profitability because of a combination of higher income and lower costs, both lower overhead and loan loss provisions. To a large extent overhead costs tend to be passed on in the form of higher margins and costs. The other control variables have similar signs. A positive coefficient for profitability and a negative one on provisioning indicate that banks in growing countries make more profits and can be less conservative in their provisioning policies. The negative coefficient for changes in per capita GDP on overhead suggests that banks in growing countries can reduce costs or face more competition and have better technology. Inflation is positively related to the net interest margins, profitability, and overheads, consistent with the notion that high inflation requires higher bank margins and profitability to maintain real bank capital, and that the cost of operating in those environments is also higher. Similar effects exist for the real interest rate.

When the sample is split into high- and low-presence countries the results are the same as for the regressions using first differences (not reported; see Claessens and Lee 2001): the effect of a foreign presence on domestic banks is stronger in higher-presence countries. Both the actual presence and the degree of permissible entry affect margins in a statistically significant negative way in high-presence countries. Overhead is also negatively affected and statistically significant in high-presence markets by the degree of permissible entry. This is not so for low-presence markets, where even opposite signs are found for the degree of permissible entry variable. Control variables are similarly signed and significant in both groups of countries, however. The differences between the two groups suggest again that the effectiveness of a foreign presence and the lack of barriers depends on the absence of other, actual barriers as reflected in the degree of actual presence.

The regression results of tables 5.6 and 5.7 combined suggest that it is the new entry of foreign banks that leads domestic banks to reduce their costs and lower their margins, while a greater presence by foreign banks lowers overall profitability in the domestic banking system, provided the system is contestable. This suggests a dynamic process whereby initial new entry forces adjustments in the cost structures of local banks, while over time a greater foreign presence leads to adjustments in the pricing structure of domestic banks. At the same time, the system needs to be effectively open to new entry that is contestable by having a combination of both low formal barriers as well as limited other barriers preventing foreign banks from being interested in entering.

Conclusions

The presence of foreign banks has increased in a number of low-income countries. Whereas in some countries, because of long-standing historical links, foreign banks have played a role in the domestic banking system for some time, there has been a trend toward opening up and an increased presence by foreign banks. This seems to have had benefits for local banking systems in terms of reducing financial intermediation costs and making systems more efficient and robust. The results also suggest that a foreign bank presence alone is not necessarily sufficient to achieve these gains. A combination of a high foreign presence and a commitment to continued open markets seems to lead to the greatest gains.

Foreign banks have also introduced improved risk management practices and imported supervision from parent country regulators, thereby helping to strengthen banking systems. At the same time increased competition may lower the franchise value of incumbent banks, leading to financial instability. While adequate regulation and supervision would be the natural policy response, many low-income countries have had great difficulty in establishing good legal and institutional frameworks. The answer might be to make greater use of the benefits of foreign entry, while focusing institutional development efforts on a few key aspects rather than attempting to build a broad regulation and supervision apparatus. In addition, the benefits of foreign banks' presence will have to be considered in light of technological advances that allow financial services to be delivered across borders without a physical presence (e-finance). Some low-income countries might be able to obtain some financial services directly from offshore sources, thereby reducing the need for domestic regulation and supervision.

Appendix 5.1. Variable Definitions and Sources

Net margin/ta = interest income minus interest expense over total assets

Noninterest income/ta = other operating income, such as trading costs, advisory fees, and so on over total assets

Before tax profits/ta = before tax profits over total assets

Overhead/ta = personnel expenses and other noninterest expenses over total assets

Other expenses/ta = nonoverhead, noninterest, and other expenses over total assets

Equity/ta = the book value of equity (assets minus liabilities) over total assets

Other earning assets/ta = assets other than loans and non-interest-earning assets such as cash and non-interest-earning deposits at other banks over total assets

Customer and short-term funding/ta = all short-term and long-term deposits plus other nondeposit short-term funding over total assets

Foreign bank share = the number of foreign banks to the total number of banks, with a bank defined as a foreign bank if it has at least 50 percent foreign ownership

GDP/cap = real GDP per capita in thousands of U.S. dollars

Inflation = the annual inflation of the GDP deflator

All individual bank-level variables were obtained from the International Bank Classification Agency's Bankscope database. The index of the degree of entry present and the degree of commercial presence in banking came from Qian (2000). Other data were drawn from standard international sources.

Appendix 5.2 Classification of Selected Low-Income Countries

Grouping	Number	Countries
Asia and Pacific	9	Bangladesh, Bhutan, Cambodia, India, Indonesia, Myanmar, Nepal, Pakistan, Solomon Islands
Transition economies	11	Armenia, Azerbaijan, Georgia, Kyrgyz Republic, Moldova, Mongolia, Tajikistan, Turkmenistan, Ukraine, Uzbekistan, Vietnam
Africa — French speaking	16	Benin, Burkina Faso, Burundi, Central African Republic, Chad, Congo (Dem. Rep.), Côte d'Ivoire, Guinea, Madagascar, Mali, Mauritania, Niger, Rwanda, Senegal, Togo
Africa — English speaking	15	Cameroon, Ethiopia, The Gambia, Ghana, Kenya, Lesotho, Liberia, Malawi, Nigeria, Sierra Leone, Sudan, Tanzania, Uganda, Zambia, Zimbabwe
Africa — Portuguese speaking	4	Angola, Guinea-Bissau, Mozambique, São Tomé and Principe
Other (Latin America and the Caribbean and the Middle East)	3	Haiti, Nicaragua, Yemen
Total number of countries	58	

Note: Following the *World Development Indicators*, the low-income group is defined as countries whose gross national income per capita in 2000 was less than US$755. Of the 63 low-income countries reporting, 5—Afghanistan, Comoros, the Democratic Republic of Korea, Lao PDR, and Somalia—are not included here because there was no bank reporting from these countries to the Bankscope database. Because of civil unrest probably deterring foreign entry a number of countries are excluded from some of the cross-country averages and regressions, including Angola, Bangladesh, Bhutan, Cambodia, Chad, Congo Democratic Republic, Ethiopia, Guinea, Haiti, India, Liberia, Rwanda, Sierra Leone, Tajikistan, Turkmenistan, and Yemen.

Sources: Language classification: CIA Factbook; income and region classifications: World Bank (2001b); *World Development Indicators.*

Appendix 5.3 Nationality of Foreign-Owned Banks: Details (percentage of equity capital)

Region/ Host country	Domestic	Foreign	Nationality of foreign-owned bank									
			Low-income country	United Kingdom	United States	France	Portugal	Other industrial	Arab	South Africa	Other countries	Remarks
Asia and Pacific												
Bangladesh	99.6	0.4						0.4				
Bhutan	74.5	25.5	14.7		5.2						5.5	India (14.7), II (5.5)
Cambodia	100.0	0.0										
India	99.5	0.5				0.1					0.4	
Indonesia	80.3	19.7	2.1	0.1	0.1	1.2		10.9			5.3	Singapore (2.0), Korea (1.4)
Myanmar	100.0	0.0										
Nepal	62.0	38.0	6.7			4.4		26.7			0.2	
Pakistan	93.6	6.4				0.1		0.6	3.1		2.8	
Solomon Islands	49.0	51.0			51.0							
Transition economies												
Armenia	58.9	41.1		30.6							10.4	Russia (5.4), Turkey (6.0)
Azerbaijan	86.1	13.9				0.7		1.9			11.4	Cyprus (5.6), Russia (3.9)
Georgia	86.9	13.1		0.2	2.0			3.3			7.5	II (5.0)
Kyrgyz Republic	12.6	87.4		87.4								
Moldova	95.5	4.5			0.9			1.8			1.8	
Mongolia	100.0	0.0										
Tajikistan	100.0	0.0										
Turkmenistan	100.0	0.0										
Ukraine	95.9	4.1		0.0		0.5		1.1			2.6	
Uzbekistan	99.6	0.4						0.1			0.3	
Vietnam	95.6	4.4						0.2			4.2	Korea (1.6), Malaysia (1.1)

English-speaking Africa

Cameroon	49.8	50.2		13.2	0.2	35.8	0.8			0.2
Ethiopia	100.0	0.0								
Gambia, The	61.5	38.5					38.5			
Ghana	74.2	25.8	4.7	8.3	0.2	0.2	8.4	0.3		3.6
Kenya	73.5	26.5	0.7	19.6			1.7		1.5	2.9
Lesotho	97.6	2.4							2.4	
Liberia	100.0	0.0								
Malawi	94.2	5.8		0.8		0.7	2.1		2.1	0.1
Nigeria	87.4	12.6	1.3	0.8	4.9	0.9	0.9		3.2	0.6
Sierra Leone	83.6	16.4		16.4				98.4		
Sudan	1.6	98.4		0.0	15.7		21.9	98.4		BADEA (98.4)
Tanzania	59.0	41.0	4.8	25.9			2.5		(1.4)	1.6
Uganda	64.8	35.2	3.0					1.4	0.8	
Zambia	27.8	72.2	2.1	47.4	15.8				6.9	Maurit. (6.9)
Zimbabwe	63.9	36.1		27.4			0.5		6.7	1.5

French-speaking Africa

Benin	79.9	20.1	5.3				12.9			2.0
Burkina Faso	43.9	56.1	4.6			17.6	14.5			19.3 II (19.3)
Burundi	50.0	50.0				2.1	32.1			15.8 Foreign Inv. (13.8)
Central African Rep.	55.9	44.1	4.6				44.1			
Chad	86.3	13.7				9.1				
Congo Democratic Rep.	34.0	66.0					0.4		65.7	
Côte d'Ivoire	46.4	53.6	2.9			32.9	17.2			0.6
Guinea	63.2	36.8				19.6	13.1			4.1
Madagascar	29.4	70.6				53.4	12.4			4.8
Mali	60.9	39.1	0.3			5.0	13.3			20.5 II (18.5)
Mauritania	75.7	24.3					8.3	14.6		1.4
Niger	45.5	54.5	11.3			2.1	20.9	16.1		4.1
Rwanda	75.4	24.6					24.6			
Senegal	60.2	39.8				29.1	8.6			2.1
Togo	90.8	9.2				1.9	5.6			1.7

Appendix 5.3 Continued

Region/ Host country	Domestic	Foreign	Low-income country	United Kingdom	United States	France	Portugal	Other industrial	Arab	South Africa	Other countries	Remarks
Portuguese-speaking Africa												
Angola	100.0	0.0										
Guinea-Bissau	100.0	0.0										
Mozambique	39.6	60.4					39.6			10.3	10.6	II(10.6)
São Tomé and Príncipe	45.4	54.6					54.6					
Other												
Haiti	100.0	0.0										
Nicaragua	77.0	23.0				0.1		2.2			20.7	Grand Cayman (20.4)
Yemen	95.0	5.0							5.0			
Average	73.8	26.2	4.6	18.5	9.6	10.4	47.1	10.4	19.8	10.2	5.4	
Total		69.1	278.1	96.0	217.4	94.2	354.4	138.9	91.4	177.5		

Nationality of foreign-owned bank

BADEA: Arab Bank for Economic Development in Africa. II: International organization.

Source: Authors' calculations.

Notes

1. The numbers Buch and Delong (2001) cite refer to mergers where at least one partner was a commercial bank. They therefore do not refer only to mergers involving two banks, but also where a foreign bank acquired a nonbank financial institution in a low-income country.

2. Not all low-income countries had any foreign or domestic banks reporting to Bankscope, the major source of data we used. In addition, in all the countries not all, or necessarily even most, banks reported data to Bankscope. We may thus misreport the presence of foreign banks. The data are described further in appendix 5.1.

3. The increase may be overstated to the extent that more foreign banks reported data to Bankscope in 2000 than in 1995. Of course another possibility is that more domestic banks reported data in 2000 than in 1995, in which case the increase is understated.

4. All data refer to reporting banks only. As noted earlier, as foreign banks are more likely to report, the asset shares and relative number of foreign banks presented may overstate the presence of foreign banks.

5. The data on asset and liability composition should be treated with care as data definitions and quality vary considerably across banks and countries. The available data also do not allow any meaningful further breakdown of lending or funding portfolios in, say, lending to governments, municipalities, corporations, and so on or of funding from deposits, commercial paper, money markets, and other sources.

6. These countries are Angola, Bangladesh, Bhutan, Cambodia, Chad, Congo Democratic Republic, Ethiopia, Guinea, Haiti, India, Liberia, Rwanda, Sierra Leone, Tajikistan, Turkmenistan, and Yemen.

7. Equation (5.3) can be seen as a reduced form equation that relates endogenous banking variables, such as profitability, to banking "inputs" like bank equity and non-interest-earning assets, and a set of controls, including the foreign bank share. DeYoung and Nolle (1996), among others, more explicitly derive a profit function that relates profitability to bank inputs and various controls.

8. Berger and Hannan (1998) estimate that the efficiency costs related to market power as explained by the quiet life hypothesis are substantial.

9. See Claessens, Demirgüç-Kunt, and Huizinga (2000). See also Amel and Liang (1997), who investigate the determinants of entry and profits in local banking markets in the United States. Specifically, they estimate two equations, one explaining the entry decision and the other explaining the impact of entry on contemporaneous local banking profits.

References

The word *processed* describes informally produced works that may not be commonly available through libraries.

Amel, Dean F., and J. Nellie Liang. 1997. "Determinants of Entry and Profits in Local Banking Markets." *Review of Industrial Organization* 12(1): 59–78.

Berger, Allen N., and Timothy H. Hannan. 1998. "The Efficiency Cost of Market Power in the Banking Industry: A Test of the 'Quiet Life' and Related Hypotheses." *Review of Economics and Statistics* 80(3): 454–65.

Berger, Allen N., Robert De Young, Hesna Genay, and Gregory F. Udell. 2000. "Globalization of Financial Institutions: Evidence from Cross-Border Banking Performance." *Brookings-Wharton Papers on Financial Services 2000:* pp. 23–120.

Buch, Claudia, and Gayle Delong. 2001. "Cross-Border Bank Mergers: What Lures the Rare Animal?" Baruch College, New York. Processed.

Claessens, Stijn, and Marion Jansen, eds. 2000. *The Internationalization of Financial Services.* The Hague: Kluwer Law International.

Claessens, Stijn, and Jong-Kun Lee. 2001. "Foreign Banks in Low-Income Countries: Recent Developments and Impacts." World Bank, Washington, D.C. Processed.

Claessens, Stijn, Asli Demirgüç-Kunt, and Harry Huizinga. 2000. "The Role of Foreign Banks in Domestic Banking Systems." In Stijn Claessens and Marion Jansen, eds., *The Internationalization of Financial Services.* The Hague: Kluwer Law International.

———. 2001. "How Does Foreign Entry Affect the Domestic Banking Market?" *Journal of Banking and Finance* 25(5): 891–911.

DeYoung, Robert, and Daniel E. Nolle. 1996. "Foreign-Owned Banks in the U.S.: Buying Market Share or Earning It?" *Journal of Money, Credit, and Banking* 28: 622–36.

IMF (International Monetary Fund). 2000. *International Capital Markets Report.* Washington, D.C.

Mathieson, Donald J., and Jorge Roldòs. 2001. "The Role of Foreign Banks in Emerging Markets." Paper presented at the World Bank, International Monetary Fund, and Brookings Institution Third Annual Financial Markets and Development Conference, May 19–21, New York.

Papi, Luca, and Debora Revoltella. 2000. "Foreign Direct Investment in the Banking Sector: A Transitional Economy Perspective." In Stijn Claessens and Marion Jansen, eds., *The Internationalization of Financial Services.* The Hague: Kluwer Law International.

Qian, Ying. 2000. "Financial Services Liberalization and GATS." In Stijn Claessens and Marion Jansen, eds., *The Internationalization of Financial Services*. The Hague: Kluwer Law International.

Sorsa, Piritta. 1997. "The GATS Agreement on Financial Services—A Modest Start to Multilateral Liberalization." Working Paper no. WP/97/55. International Monetary Fund, Washington, D.C.

Ulgenerk, Esen. 2001. "Foreign Banks in Low-Income Countries: Background Paper for *Global Development Finance 2002*." World Bank, Washington, D.C. Processed.

World Bank. 2001a. *Finance for Growth: Policy Choices in a Volatile World*. Washington, D.C.

_____. 2001b. *World Development Report 2002: Building Institutions for Markets*. New York: Oxford University Press.

Part III

Securities Markets

6

Securities Market Efficiency

Ajay Shah and Susan Thomas

From the 1960s onward, the industrial countries experienced an enormous increase in the importance of anonymous securities markets, as opposed to banks, for financial intermediation. During the 1980s policy debates in the developing countries started to display an awareness of the importance of developing securities markets as a vehicle for efficient utilization of capital. In the 1990s dozens of developing countries embarked on building stock markets, which they saw as a key ingredient of market-oriented economic policies.

These efforts have not been entirely successful. Today most stock markets appear to be highly illiquid, and annual equity trading volume exceeds 75 percent of equity market capitalization in only 16 countries. The promise of liquid, anonymous markets that would play a pivotal role in resource allocation appears to be out of reach in all but a handful of developing countries.

As a first approximation, market size appears to be an important factor at work. The smallest countries with active securities markets

We would like to thank Shantanu Bharadwaj for able research assistance. We are grateful to Tadashi Endo, James Hanson, Giovanni Majnoni, and Mathew Rudolph for comments and suggestions; to Tony Weeresinghe of Millennium Information Technologies and Satish Naralkar of NSE.IT for help in estimating the capital cost of securities infrastructure; and to Brett Tarleton of Elkins/McSherry in New York, which made its cross-country dataset on equity transactions costs available to us.

seem to have a gross domestic product (GDP) of at least US$20 billion. The apparent relationship between country size and trading volume raises a host of questions for economic policy analysis, for example:

- What are the channels through which increasing returns to scale might affect securities markets?
- What is the empirical evidence about the role of size in shaping successful securities markets?
- What can policymakers do to increase liquid markets in small countries?

This chapter seeks to shed some light on these questions. It starts by highlighting an identification problem: small countries often have small firms, and stocks of small firms tend to be illiquid everywhere in the world. This section also looks at the difficulties of measuring liquidity and tries to identify possible sources of increasing returns to scale in securities markets. The next section turns to an examination of the empirical evidence. This is followed by a section on normative economics followed by our conclusions.

Issues in Measuring Market Liquidity

Casual empiricism suggests that liquid and efficient equity markets are difficult to achieve with securities with low capitalization and in small countries. This section attempts to illuminate some aspects of this problem by highlighting an identification problem between illiquidity resulting from small firms versus illiquidity resulting from small markets. It looks at some measurement problems in liquidity and turnover ratios and then examines increasing returns to scale in markets.

Market Versus Firm Characteristics as Sources of Market Illiquidity

Understanding the problems of stock market liquidity in small countries is complicated by an identification problem between two possible explanations of low liquidity: the role of small firm size and the role of small country size.

Small firms are likely to be less liquid in markets. Small firms have lower capitalization, which in itself deters some institutional investors that have internal criteria requiring a minimum market capitalization in any firm that they will invest in. Hence small firms are likely to have a smaller investor base than larger firms. Small firms also are generally less diversified, which enhances their earnings volatility; tend to expend fewer resources on information disclosure; and are likely to have fewer investors and analysts following their performance. Thus small firms are likely to have high volatility and highly asymmetric information. An extensive literature, beginning with Benston and Hagerman (1974) and Stoll (1978), finds that these characteristics are associated with poor liquidity. These arguments hold regardless of the characteristics of the country where the firm is traded.

Small countries are likely to have a smaller pool of investors and a smaller financial sector than large countries, with fewer resources devoted to operating exchanges; less extensive legal and information infrastructure; and fewer people involved in analyzing firms and portfolios, trading, and so on. Small countries often have poor laws about disclosure and insider trading, which produces conditions of highly asymmetric information, and weak enforcement against market manipulation, which raises adverse selection costs. As a result, liquidity is likely to be less in small countries. Note that many of these features have characteristics of high fixed costs and low marginal costs. It is particularly difficult for countries with a small GDP to support the large expenses that may be involved in these various required infrastructures.

Small countries generally have small firms, which inherently are less liquid than larger firms. Thus the gains from policy proposals that enhance the quality of financial infrastructure (that is, of market characteristics) in small countries can be limited by the characteristics of firms, as well as by the countries' size.

This argument suggests that the most useful policy question that can be asked about improving market infrastructure in a small country is would product X become much more liquid if it were traded on greatly superior market infrastructure? In this question we hold the characteristics of product X constant and ask whether liquidity can be sharply altered using a substantially altered market infrastructure.[1] If the environment in terms of product characteristics is hostile, the gains that can be obtained by improving market infrastructure may be severely limited; however, the gains that can be made from market infrastructure are limited because of the inherent problems of small economies.

Difficulties in Measuring Liquidity

To analyze cross-country evidence about stock market liquidity we need to obtain metrics that are logically sound and are consistently measured across countries. Liquidity is defined as the transactions costs of undertaking trades. This reflects a combination of broker-age and other charges and the market impact cost incurred on the market when the trade is executed.

Unfortunately, measuring the bid-offer spread and comparing it across different trading rules present numerous difficulties. Consider, for example, a comparison of transactions costs between the NASDAQ in the United States and India's National Stock Exchange (NSE). NASDAQ uses a market lot of 100 and the NSE uses a market lot of 1. Hence the bid-offer spread at the NSE typi-cally pertains to small transaction sizes that could be as small as one share. Furthermore, the typical share price on the NSE is Rs 90 or US$2, while the typical share price on NASDAQ is US$50. Thus a casual comparison of the bid-offer spread on NASDAQ versus the NSE is misleading, because the NASDAQ spread pertains to a trans-action size of roughly US$5,000 while the NSE spread pertains to a transaction size of roughly US$2.[2]

The second problem pertains to missing data. At many points in time both buy and sell orders might not exist at either NASDAQ or the NSE. When this happens the bid-offer spread is not observed. This raises questions about how a measure of liquidity might be estimated. Such difficulties inhibit a direct comparison of liquidity across exchanges.

The turnover ratio, defined as the annualized trading volume per unit of market capitalization, is often used as a measure of liquidity. For example, if a stock has a market capitalization of US$100 on December 31, 2001, and if the trading volume over calendar 2001 was US$125, then the turnover ratio works out to 125 percent.

Using cross-sectional data for the firms listed on NASDAQ, the rank correlation between log spread and log turnover ratio works out to 0.087. Although the t-statistic is a significant 4.25, the small size of the correlation means that the turnover ratio is only a poor proxy for transactions costs; however it presents no difficulties in measurement and cross-country comparison.

Sources of Increasing Returns to Scale in Securities Markets

Consider a traditional purely domestic securities industry. The costs incurred by the securities markets are

- The costs of securities regulation
- The costs of operating the exchange, clearing corporation, and depository
- The costs incurred by a "sufficient" mass of financial inter-mediaries
- The costs of information dissemination and information processing.

Most of these costs are ultimately paid by households and firms in the form of listing fees and transaction costs.[3]

For many of these elements there are significant increasing returns to scale. If we focus on the marginal cost in the financial system when one new firm enters into an initial public offering, then increasing returns to scale are sharply visible in the market infrastructure. This marginal cost for one additional firm is almost zero when it comes to regulation, the stock exchange, the clearing corporation, the depository, and the fixed costs of financial intermediaries. Information dissemination also has economies of scale in terms of market size.

Economies of scale appear to be less apparent in only one area: accounting and analyst coverage per listing. If n accountants and analysts are required to track m firms, then roughly $2n$ accountants and analysts would be required to track $2m$ firms. Apart from this the incremental cost of handling one more firm is near zero for the bulk of market infrastructure.

In a small country the aggregate revenues from financial intermediation might not be large enough to support a sophisticated securities industry in all these respects. A small country could be trapped in an equilibrium in which the securities markets are illiquid, which deters listings, so that the minimum economies of scale continue to elude the domestic securities markets.

Empirical Evidence

This section seeks to obtain empirical evidence on some of these issues using large-scale datasets on firms and countries. It also takes a closer look at the cross-sectional variation of liquidity in two countries using case studies.

Liquidity of Small Capitalization Stocks

As a broad empirical regularity, small capitalization stocks have poor liquidity all over the world. As an empirical example we focus on the cross-sectional evidence offered by NASDAQ, which is arguably the most successful exchange internationally in terms of obtaining liquidity for small stocks. In the United States substantial resources are devoted to disclosure, information processing, regulation, valuation of securities, trading, and so on. This produces a favorable environment for market liquidity. From the standpoint of developing countries, the NASDAQ experience with the liquidity of small firms is probably a good example of the effect of firm rather than market characteristics on liquidity. In other words, the NASDAQ evidence can tell us something about the impact of size on liquidity when the fixed costs of securities market infrastructure are not a strong constraint.

Figure 6.1 depicts the cross-sectional relationship between firm size (that is, market capitalization) and the bid-offer spread on NASDAQ at one point in time. Firms for which either the bid or the offer was not observed were removed from the dataset, hence this evidence is biased toward the characteristics of more liquid firms. The scatter points are individual firms. The line that has been super-posed is a robust regression and the slope of the robust regression of log spread on log market capitalization is –0.18, with a t-statis-tic of –12.6. The figure suggests that firm capitalization is an impor-tant explanatory variable of liquidity and that larger stocks tend to have smaller spreads.

Of 4,596 firms traded on NASDAQ only 2,403 had observations of both bid and offer prices. Of these only 1,194 had bid-offer spreads of better than 10 percent. Thus most firms seem to have bid-offer spreads above 10 percent, which is 100 times worse than the spreads of the order of 0.1 percent that are found for the most liquid financial products. In absolute terms, this figure suggests that even on NASDAQ the liquidity of small stocks is quite low.

Figure 6.2 shows the relationship between firm size and the turnover ratio. This figure involves a larger number of firms,

Figure 6.1 Size and Liquidity: Cross-Sectional Evidence from NASDAQ, October 2, 2001

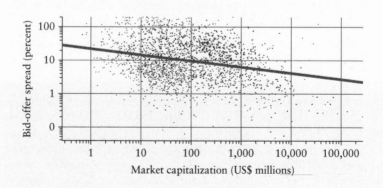

Source: NASDAQ data.

because the difficulty of unobserved bid or ask is absent. It suggests that size is a powerful explanatory variable of turnover: the larger stocks tend to have higher turnover ratios. The slope of the robust log regression shown in the figure is 0.42 with a t-statistic of 33.3.

Finally, table 6.1 re-expresses the turnover ratio for size deciles, broadly showing the same positive relationship between firm capitalization and turnover, particularly for the larger firms.

In sum, small stocks can apparently obtain liquidity ratios in the region of 100 percent given U.S.-style disclosure, U.S.-style regulation and enforcement, and given U.S.-quality securities markets infrastructure. Conversely, even under these benign conditions, unlike large stocks, small stocks are unlikely to obtain liquidity ratios much above 100 percent. In the typical small country firms (stocks) would seldom have a market capitalization in excess of US$100 million.

This hypothesis is supported by other evidence. Global experience with trading small stocks is dismal (Angel 1997). In the United States in 1992 the American Exchange tried to create the Emerging Companies Marketplace. This was closed down in 1995. In the United Kingdom the Unlisted Securities Market was closed down in

Figure 6.2 Firm Capitalization and Turnover Ratio from NASDAQ, October 2, 2001

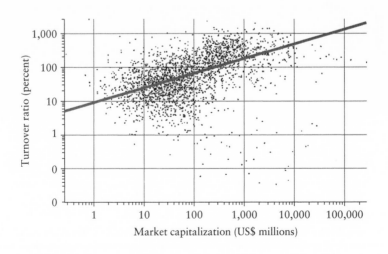

Source: NASDAQ data.

Table 6.1 Turnover Ratio by Size Decile on NASDAQ,
March 2001

Decile	Mean market capitalization (US$ millions)	Mean liquidity ratio (percent)
1	5.4	97.5
2	13.6	82.9
3	24.3	82.1
4	39.7	85.7
5	63.3	96.8
6	102.8	118.2
7	167.5	160.9
8	302.2	195.3
9	646.0	253.0
10	6,062.7	314.6

Source: NASDAQ data.

1996. Incubator segments for small stocks in Europe have uniformly failed.

A later section compares NASDAQ's turnover ratios with those
of two developing countries and finds that small firms on NASDAQ
generally have higher turnover ratios than the small firms in these
two countries. This is consistent with our interpretation of the
NASDAQ evidence as an upper bound for the turnover that firms
of a given size can obtain.

Market Size and Liquidity

In this section we analyze a unique dataset created by the firm
Elkins/McSherry, which monitors transaction costs incurred on real-
world trades by 1,600 brokerage firms on 208 exchanges in 42 countries (for more information see http://www.elkinsmcsherry.com). We
focus on the total transaction costs reported by Elkins/McSherry,
which include brokerage fees, charges, and market impact cost. This
would measure market liquidity from the point of view of the institutional investor.

Figure 6.3 shows a scatter plot of market capitalization of the
equity market and total transaction costs in the 42 countries covered by Elkins/McSherry. A robust regression is superposed on this
scatter plot. The coefficient (elasticity) is –0.156 with a t-statistic of
–3.87. These data suggest that countries with larger market capitalizations, which are generally larger countries, have a substantial
advantage in terms of obtaining greater stock market liquidity.

Figure 6.3 Market Size and Liquidity, Selected
Countries, 2001

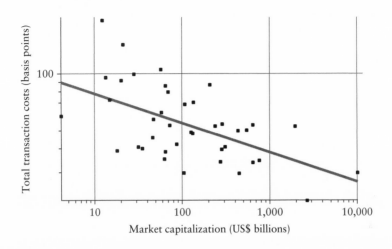

Source: Elkins/McSherry data.

Country Size and Turnover

Table 6.1 suggests that even the smallest firms on NASDAQ obtain
a turnover ratio of roughly 100 percent. The overall stock market
obtains a modest turnover ratio of above 75 percent in only 16 countries. This suggests that an active stock market is a rarity. It also
serves to highlight the difficulties that small countries face in obtaining liquid securities markets.

Table 6.2 shows the smallest five countries (by GDP) that obtain
turnover ratios above 75 percent. This suggests a rule of thumb of
around US$20 billion of GDP as a threshold for the smallest active
equity markets.

To obtain empirical evidence about the determinants of market
liquidity we created a dataset of all countries where information
about stock market turnover and stock market capitalization has
been observed along with other macroeconomic information. This
information is for 1999 and covers 87 countries. Table 6.3 summarizes this dataset.

As mentioned earlier, market liquidity is normally defined in
terms of transaction costs. As consistent measures of transaction

Table 6.2 Five Smallest Countries
with a Turnover Ratio above 75 Percent

Country	Aggregate GDP (US$ billions)
Swaziland	1.3
Oman	15.6
Slovak Republic	20.4
Kuwait	30.0
Hungary	45.7

Source: Elkins/McSherry data.

Table 6.3 Summary Statistics, Selected Countries, 1999

Statistic	Median	Mean	Standard deviation	N
Banking spread	6.35	8.92	7.71	64
Log GDP	9.91	10.34	2.02	87
Turnover ratio	0.12	0.38	0.62	87
Log turnover ratio	−2.06	−1.99	1.57	87

Source: Elkins/McSherry data.

costs across countries are not available, we fall back on the turnover ratio, that is, the trading volume divided by market capitalization, as a proxy for market liquidity.

At the level of casual examination, countries with large GDPs dominate the ranks of countries with high turnovers. The median GDP in the dataset in 1999 was US$20 billion and the median turnover ratio was 0.12. If we restrict ourselves to countries with a turnover ratio greater than 0.5, then the median GDP of this group is US$919 billion.

Table 6.4 shows simple ordinary least squares regressions explaining the log of the turnover ratio. The banking spread proves to be a useful proxy of financial sector development, and high values of the banking spread are associated with low stock market liquidity. In relation to country size, log GDP is a strong explanatory variable. The log-log specification allows us to interpret the coefficient as an elasticity. If we use a linear specification in log GDP the elasticity works out to roughly 0.3. If we use a linear spline with a break at the median value of log GDP (US$20 billion), the relationship is essentially flat below the median, and the positive

Table 6.4 Estimates of Models of the Turnover Ratio

	Model 1		Model 2	
Item	OLS	*Robust regression*	OLS	*Robust regression*
Banking spread	–0.058	–0.006	–0.056	–0.006
	(2.9)	(2.7)	(2.8)	(2.6)
Log GDP	0.299	0.554		
	(3.5)	(5.8)		
Linear spline in log GDP				
Below median			0.005	0.032
			(0.0)	(1.3)
Above median			0.433	0.064
			(3.3)	(4.6)
Intercept	–4.54	–0.349	–1.926	–0.150
	(4.7)	(3.2)	(0.9)	(0.6)
Number	62	62	62	62
R^2	0.327		0.348	
R^{2}adj.	0.304		0.314	

OLS Ordinary least squares.
Source: Authors' calculations.

impact of GDP comes strongly into play—with an elasticity of 0.43—above the median. The small countries' GDPs are generally below the median.

These regressions are vulnerable to outliers, hence we also show the same models estimated using Huber's robust regression.[4] The elasticities seen here are much smaller, however, the relationships are qualitatively similar.

Case Study of India

This section looks at cross-sectional evidence on the turnover ratio in India, a medium economy with aggregate GDP of US$460 billion. It focuses on the 924 most liquid stocks traded on the NSE, India's largest stock exchange. This is analogous to the set of 4,595 stocks on NASDAQ used for table 6.1. The variation of the turnover ratio by size decile is shown in table 6.5. This table supports the following four inferences:

• In deciles 1, 2, and 3 the stocks traded on the NSE are smaller than those observed in the smallest decile on NASDAQ. Thus while the turnover ratios appear to be low in absolute terms, whether these low turnover ratios are innately associated with size or whether they reflect inferior market characteristics in India is not clear.

• In deciles 4 through 7 the stocks traded on the NSE are comparable in size to the stocks traded on NASDAQ; however, their liquidity ratios are significantly inferior to those of their peers traded on NASDAQ.

• In deciles 8, 9, and 10 the turnover ratios observed on the NSE are comparable to those observed on NASDAQ.

• The top deciles on the NSE and on NASDAQ both have liquidity ratios of 350 percent or thereabouts; however the mean market capitalization seen in the top decile of the NSE is just US$847 million, which is much smaller than on NASDAQ (US$6 billion). In other words, stocks on the NSE obtain turnover ratios of about 350 percent at a much lower firm size than on NASDAQ.

This evidence suggests that India's NSE fares significantly worse than NASDAQ in terms of turnover for firms with market capitalization from US$6 million to US$24 million. Firms with market capitalization above US$24 million seem to fare well on the NSE. In particular, the NSE seems to obtain turnover ratios above 350 percent at a much lower firm size than NASDAQ. This could reflect (a) sound market infrastructure in terms of trading, clearing, and settlement, so that large firms trade extremely efficiently in India; or (b) poor disclosure and enforcement in India, which would affect the liquidity of small firms the most.

Table 6.5 Turnover Ratio by Size Deciles on India's NSE (January 2001)

Decile	Mean market capitalization (US$ millions)	Mean liquidity ratio (percent)
1	1.2	10.4
2	2.5	14.0
3	4.0	5.3
4	6.3	10.0
5	9.9	17.0
6	15.4	25.8
7	23.4	45.3
8	42.3	127.5
9	105.1	88.7
10	847.6	351.4

Source: NSE data.

Case Study of Mauritius

Mauritius is indisputably a small country. Table 6.6 summarizes the broad facts about the Mauritian equity market. The number of listed firms rose sharply till 1995, but has not grown since. The market's turnover ratio rose to roughly 5½ percent in 1994, went on to over 8 percent in 1997, but was back to roughly 5½ percent in 2000. The total market capitalization expressed as a percentage of GDP rose sharply from 4.3 percent in 1989 to 45.4 percent in 1994, but slipped to 31.3 percent in 2000.

The low base of the transaction volume in Mauritius has generated extremely high charges for exchange infrastructure. The exchange imposes a tariff of 0.25 percent of the value of a trade, the depository has a tariff of 0.2 percent, and the regulator has a tariff of 0.05 percent. Thus the basic charges for a transaction in Mauritius are 0.5 percent, which is one of the highest in the world.

Are these poor turnover ratio values in Mauritius inescapable? Specifically:

- Does the country's small GDP imply that the turnover ratio cannot be much higher?
- Does the small size of listed firms imply that the turnover ratio cannot be much higher?

Table 6.6 Basic Facts about the Mauritian Equity Market, 1989–2000

Year	Number of listed firms	Market capitalization (US$ millions)	Turnover (US$ millions)	Turnover ratio (percent)	GDP (US$ billions)	Market capitalization/ GDP (percent)
1989	6	93	0.9	1.0	2.2	4.3
1990	13	255	5.9	2.3	2.6	9.7
1991	19	310	5.2	1.7	2.8	11.0
1992	21	424	10.2	2.4	3.2	13.3
1993	29	842	39.1	4.6	3.2	26.4
1994	34	1,578	85.9	5.4	3.5	45.4
1995	39	1,563	69.2	4.4	3.9	40.3
1996	42	1,693	81.3	4.8	3.9	43.1
1997	42	1,755	142.0	8.1	4.1	42.9
1998	42	1,850	104.3	5.6	4.0	46.3
1999	43	1,643	77.9	4.7	4.2	39.2
2000	43	1,336	73.8	5.5	4.3	31.3

Source: Mauritius stock exchange data.

Table 6.7 Turnover Ratio in Countries with GDPs Similar
to That of Mauritius, 1997

Country	GDP (US$ billions)	Turnover ratio (percent)
Armenia	1.6	8.7
Fiji	2.1	2.3
Barbados	2.2	2.4
Namibia	3.2	4.1
Zambia	3.9	2.0
Mauritius	4.1	8.1
Honduras	4.7	67.3
Nepal	4.9	2.5
Botswana	5.1	12.1
Latvia	5.6	34.4
Trinidad and Tobago	5.9	6.0

Source: Elkins/McSherry data.

Table 6.7 shows the turnover ratio for 1997 in a selection of
countries with aggregate GDP close to that of Mauritius. While
none approached the 100 percent level of large countries, three
countries had turnover ratios significantly above those in
Mauritius and the figure for Mauritius was lower again by the
year 2000 (table 6.8).

Table 6.8 divides the listed firms in Mauritius into four quartiles by size. Market capitalization is strongly concentrated in the
10 companies that make up the top quartile. These companies
have an average liquidity ratio of 6.26 percent. The turnover ratio
drops off to 4 percent at the second and third quartiles and to
3.25 percent at the bottom quartile.

Table 6.9 compares the turnover of firms listed in Mauritius with
that of firms of similar size listed on India's NSE and NASDAQ in
the United States. The mean market capitalization of firms in the
quartiles of the Mauritius market works out to US$105 million,
US$18 million, US$9 million, and US$3 million. In all quartiles the
turnover ratios on the NSE and NASDAQ are far higher than those
found on the Mauritian market.

There are numerous caveats in the interpretation of this evidence.
Liquidity at the firm level is influenced by firm size; however, it also
varies by stock volatility, ownership patterns, disclosure quality,
enforcement against insider trading, design of the equity market,
and so on. The tables here only deal with the variation using one
explanatory variable (size). In reality all these other explanatory

Table 6.8 Variation of Turnover Ratio by Size Quartiles,
Mauritius, 2000

Quartile	Total market capitalization (Mau Rs millions)	Turnover ratio (percent)
1	29,624	6.3
2	4,995	3.9
3	2,397	4.0
4	834	3.3

Source: Mauritius stock exchange data.

Table 6.9 Mean Turnover Ratio on the NSE and NASDAQ
for Quartiles of Firms of the Same Size as in Mauritius,
2000

Quartile	Mean market capitalization (US$ millions)	Predicted turnover ratio (percent)	
		NSE	NASDAQ
1	105	89	118
2	18	35	83
3	9	17	90
4	3	15	0

Source: Authors' calculations.

variables do vary significantly across India, Mauritius, and the
United States. Specifically, this evidence does not imply that if top-
quartile firms from Mauritius listed on the NSE they would obtain
a turnover ratio of 89 percent. What this evidence does suggest is
that in well-developed financial markets much higher turnover
ratios are obtained for firms of a comparable size than those found
in Mauritius. This suggests that the poor turnover ratio observed in
Mauritius is significantly related to the market and country size and
is not inexorably a consequence of the small size of firms found in
Mauritius.

   Conversely, these estimates give us upper bounds for the gains in
turnover ratios that can be obtained by improving the securities markets infrastructure. For example, this evidence suggests that for the
bottom quartile by firm size, and neglecting country size, if Mauritius
could provide market infrastructure comparable with India's NSE it
might only yield a turnover ratio of 15 percent compared with the

value of 3.3 percent currently found in Mauritius. This would be a significant gain; however, for the bottom-quartile firms turnover ratio outcomes much beyond 15 percent require building a securities market infrastructure that is better than that found in India.

Policy Issues

Given this conceptual and empirical backdrop this section now turns to normative economics. What can policymakers in small countries do to improve stock market liquidity? An obvious answer is to encourage foreign investors, which will depend partly on better transparency and regulation. The following paragraphs discuss some additional options.

Making a Diagnosis

The first question that policymakers in small countries need to address is the extent to which their securities markets have inferior liquidity in a way that is inconsistent with their product characteristics. The broad strategy here is based on cross-sectional models that predict bid-offer spreads and turnover ratios in well-developed markets as a function of explanatory variables like size, volatility, and shareholding structure. The predicted outcomes from these models would be compared against the observed values for the bid-offer spread and the turnover ratio. If there is a gap in liquidity, these predicted outcomes show the maximal gains that could possibly be obtained from policy initiatives designed to obtain superior market infrastructure.

Considering a Role for E-Finance

In the last 40 years revolutionary advances have occurred in information technology (IT). Computer hardware has grown enormously in power and dropped in price. In addition, the computer industry has moved away from the proprietary technology where firms like Stratus, Tandem, IBM, or Microsoft earned rents to open standards based on Unix and Internet protocols where these rents have been eliminated. End users of technology have benefited from these two changes.

In the United States the bond market, the equity market, and the derivatives exchanges continue to use inefficient, labor-intensive methods; however, financial trading elsewhere in the world has undergone radical changes in terms of redesigning market mechanisms to move away from labor-intensive methods toward more technology-intensive modes of functioning. The Internet is the last and most visible part of this transformation, but the impact of technology on all aspects of securities trading is profound and pervasive. Many aspects of financial sector policy need to be reexamined bearing these new technological opportunities, which are collectively referred to as e-finance, in mind (Claessens, Glaessner, and Klingebiel 2001).

From the perspective of obtaining securities market liquidity in small countries, two aspects of e-finance are important: reducing the fixed costs of securities infrastructure and processing small-value transactions.

Reducing Fixed Costs. The fixed costs of core securities industry infrastructure have all dropped sharply because of the gains in IT. It is now possible to use a computer-intensive market design and obtain substantially lower costs than with traditional labor-intensive methods of functioning.

The impact of modern IT on fixed costs is apparent across the securities industry as follows:

• The cost of establishing a securities exchange with the ability to process, say, 10,000 trades per day in 2000 was roughly 100th of what it was in 1980.

• The risk management functions of the clearing corporation can be completely automated and implemented using low-cost software and hardware.

• The first implementation of a securities depository (in 1974 in the United States) was based on a warehouse for storing physical securities. In the 1980s the idea of "dematerialization" came about, whereby physical securities were eliminated and only a computer database existed. In the 1990s the fixed cost of establishing a depository fell from the cost of mainframe computers to that of small Unix servers.

• A variety of costs are incurred in the process of capturing information disclosure and news about one company and communicating this to investors and speculators across the economy. The fixed costs of establishing information networks are sharply lower when they are designed using modern IT.[5]

Credit rating firms incur a fixed cost in producing one credit rating and securities firms incur a fixed cost in producing one analyst's report. Both these fixed costs are substantially lowered in a world where information capture and processing exploit modern IT. In the field of credit risk in the West databases and models were a way to obtain low-cost credit analyses of individuals, where the human costs of credit analysis were larger than the costs of relatively inaccurate computer models. This argument applies in the developing world for small firms.

In the pretechnological world the overheads of intermediation were large for small and medium enterprises in OECD countries, and such firms consequently faced financing constraints. The IT revolution sharply cut the fixed costs of information capture, distribution, and processing. In the OECD this is merely useful, because it gives small and medium enterprises greater access to capital. In the developing world this is enormously more important, because most firms are small and medium enterprises by OECD standards.

Estimating the Costs of Core Securities Infrastructure for a Small Country. Today the exchange, clearing corporation, and depository can be purely computer-driven operations. For purposes of this chapter two Indian software firms were asked to offer price quotations for a complete exchange system (order matching, brokerage front office, brokerage back office, clearing corporation, and depository).[6]

The price quotations included hardware and software and the costs of installation, local training, and the minimal amount of customization required. Both firms were asked to cater to the needs of a small country with a modest peak capacity of 100 trades a minute. For a frame of reference the peak load observed at India's NSE in February 2001 was 2,500 trades per minute, and development efforts are under way to increase the trading system's capacity to 10,000 trades per minute.

The two price quotations imply that the fixed costs of establishing such a facility work out to roughly US$1 million. This number is vastly smaller than it would have been a decade ago and is not a large capital cost by the standards of even the smallest countries. This suggests that the capital costs of the core exchange infrastructure are no longer an important bottleneck for small countries. Thus many small countries, which may have opted for less sophisticated market designs in the past, can now build a full set of securities institutions at low cost. This could yield some gains in liquidity.

Processing Small-Value Transactions at Low Cost. A central feature of small countries and poor countries is small transactions and small portfolios. These are found in all aspects of the financial sector; for example:

- An individual can buy into a mutual fund in India for US$10, which would not be an acceptable transaction elsewhere in the world. In India's pension system a central goal for policymakers is to cater to the needs of individuals who have monthly contributions of US$6.
- The mean transaction size on the New York Stock Exchange is US$6,000, while the mean transaction size on India's NSE is US$500.
- The minimum balance at a typical retail bank in the United States is US$500 to US$1,000. Banks in the developing world use minimum balances as low as US$5.
- The share depository in India is unique by world standards because it features individual accounts, has 4.2 million accounts, and the mean account balance is US$25,000.

Maintaining low overheads while having small-value accounts and small-value transactions is a major challenge of process engineering in the financial sectors of poor countries. The fixed costs of the transaction loom large for such small transactions. This is particularly important in regard to international competition, which is increasingly prevalent in the securities industry. When an exchange in a country with a mean transaction size of US$500 competes with an exchange in a country with a mean transaction size of US$5,000 there is greater pressure on the former exchange to have a low tariff per transaction.

Many elements of financial sector design that are conventionally used in the Western world require large transaction sizes to cover transaction overheads. These elements do not scale to the developing world. In a pretechnological financial sector the marginal cost of processing a transaction in the developing world is lower because of cheap labor. This may appear to offset the small transaction values; however, many financial firms are characterized by large fixed costs and relatively low per transaction marginal costs, and these fixed costs would be distributed over a smaller base of transaction values in the developing world. In addition, in a focus on marginal cost there is a subtle contest between the ratio of transaction sizes versus the ratio of wages. Whether these ratios work out in favor of intermediation efficiency in the developing world is not clear.

E-finance offers opportunities for sharply reducing the costs per transaction. By using modern IT the marginal cost of processing a transaction can drop to near zero levels. The average trade value at

India's NSE is one-tenth of that on the New York Stock Exchange because the NSE uses computers for matching orders, while the New York Stock Exchange uses human beings. In the industrial countries e-finance is merely beneficial, insofar as it reduces costs. In the developing world e-finance is vitally important, because it makes possible transactions that were previously infeasible.

Avoiding Fragmentation

A central feature of the securities industry is economies of scale. Once a securities markets infrastructure is working, the marginal cost of trading one more security or conducting one more trade is close to zero until the industry reaches a point at which it requires infrastructure of a much larger capacity. In addition, as noted earlier, expansions of infrastructure capacity require less than linear cost increases.

Given these realities small countries could usefully take stock of all traded financial instruments and integrate their trading under a unified single securities market. These instruments would include shares, corporate bonds, government bonds, some commodities, and some derivatives. Trading in these products currently tends to be scattered across disparate, small markets. Moreover, regulations frequently conflict, often creating problems of regulatory arbitrage. For example, government bonds are typically traded using a non-transparent over-the-counter market, with poor post-trade arrangements. In large countries the market size supports such inefficiencies and unification is merely desirable, but small countries should make every attempt to bring the local securities markets up to a critical mass, and unification is essential. For example, there is no reason for having a stock depository and a bond depository as distinct institutional mechanisms requiring different procedures. The ownership records for all securities can easily be maintained using one depository. In many countries the stock market alone is small compared with the size thresholds described in this chapter (US$3 billion to US$6 billion of market capitalization or 8,000 to 12,000 trades per day). However, moving closer to these size thresholds may be possible by bringing bonds and some other traded products into a unified securities infrastructure.

Establishing International Linkages

In recent years securities exchanges across the world have attempted a plethora of different mechanisms for cooperation (Lee 1998). The policy positions that a country could choose can be classified into three types as follows:

- A country can have a complete set of markets domestically, which is the typical solution.
- A country can have domestic securities market institutions while avoiding the fixed costs of the core market infrastructure by outsourcing some or all of these functions. This outsourcing can be done to the market infrastructure in another country or to a neutral facility shared by a group of countries.
- A country can have domestic investors interacting with domestic firms on securities markets offshore.

This section will focus on the strengths and weaknesses of the second and third strategies.[7]

Outsourcing Core Market Infrastructure. Using the outsourcing strategy the small country embarks on the full complexity of regulation and institutional design of the securities markets, but it reduces costs by outsourcing the IT infrastructure. It can do so in two ways. One way, shown in figure 6.4, consists of outsourcing to securities infrastructure in another country. In the figure the exchange in country L matches orders for stocks in country L and for stocks in country S. Alternatively, a group of countries could work together to build a central, shared IT facility.

The cost savings obtained through this strategy are valuable; however, they are relatively limited. The costs of the IT infrastructure—which comprises the exchange, the clearing corporation, and the depository—are no longer the dominant part of the overall costs of the securities industry, but the case for outsourcing is stronger than a simple cost-saving argument. If a small country S is able to outsource its IT to a large country L, then it is likely to be able to harness the research and development that is taking place in L. The securities industry is characterized by a high pace of innovation in traded products, trading mechanisms, methods of harnessing information technology, and so on. Securities exchanges in small countries typically underinvest in research and development because of their resource constraints. Hence the dynamic argument in favor of such outsourcing is stronger than a simple static, cost-saving argument.

One example of an outsourcing opportunity is between India, Mauritius, and Sri Lanka. India's depository is designed for 10 million accounts and 5 million transactions per day and imposes a tariff of roughly 0.005 percent on transactions. By comparison, the depositories in Mauritius and Sri Lanka have a tiny base of users

Figure 6.4 Outsourcing IT Facilities

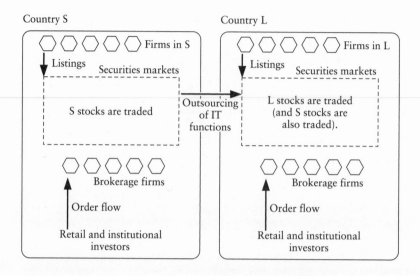

Source: Authors.

and transactions and impose extremely large charges; for example, the depository in Mauritius imposes a tariff of 0.2 percent. Both Mauritius and Sri Lanka could realize major cost savings by outsourcing a dematerialized depository function to India's National Securities Depository Limited.

Outsourcing core securities industry infrastructure is easy insofar as it does not involve complex legal and institutional difficulties. Mauritius would continue to have a depository governed by Mauritius law. Only the internal IT implementation of the depository would be performed by a foreign contractor.

Using Markets in Another Country. Some small countries are endowed with neighbors that have well-developed securities markets. In such circumstances harnessing these markets is often the simplest path for local products to achieve liquidity and market efficiency.

The mechanism that would be employed would be as follows (see figure 6.5):

- Firms in country S would be listed on exchanges in country L.
- Firms would use not only the physical infrastructure of the exchange, clearing corporation, and depository, but also the regulatory framework in country L.

Figure 6.5 Harnessing the Securities Markets
of Another Country

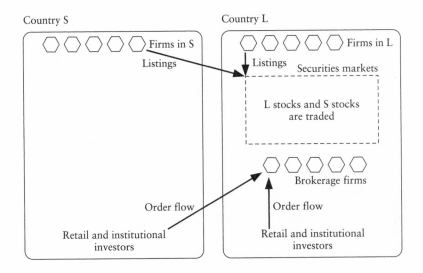

Source: Stoll (1978).

- These securities would trade alongside local securities in L.
- Retail or institutional investors that could access intermediaries in L would be able to trade these stocks exactly as they could access other stocks in L.
- Citizens of S would purchase intermediation services from brokerage firms or mutual funds in L when they wanted to undertake transactions or investments in these stocks.

Examples of possible relationships of this type include Ireland, which could use the United Kingdom; Malaysia, which could harness Singapore; Mexico, which could use the United States; and Sri Lanka, which could harness India. Geographical proximity is convenient for aligning time zones and reducing the transaction costs of travel when required. However, the core activity on financial markets—traders watching screens and placing orders—is now quite implementable between any desktop in the world and any exchange in the world, regardless of geographical distance, by using the Internet.

In the case of Mexico, U.S. securities markets are the dominant venue for trading Mexican products. This has provided Mexico with liquidity and market efficiency without requiring the development of local securities markets. This phenomenon fuels factor payments to labor and capital employed in the U.S. financial sector as opposed to the Mexican financial sector. While this should be a minor issue compared with the importance of liquid securities markets in obtaining allocative efficiency, it can become a political stumbling block when it triggers protectionist responses by the domestic financial industry. In a typical small country, the domestic financial industry is politically more effective at obtaining protectionist government policies than many other industries; hence policymakers who seek to adopt such a course as suggested here should anticipate and plan for such pressures.

If developing domestic capital markets is a goal, then a firm's decision to list abroad has negative externalities insofar as it reduces the mass of financial transactions that are taking place through the domestic capital markets. If a domestic securities industry is in an intermediate stage of liquidity, defections by a few key firms to offshore listings can have a significant impact on the viability of domestic securities markets.

A prerequisite for such working arrangements is an open capital account on the part of both countries. For example, Sri Lanka once asked India to trade Sri Lankan government bonds in India. While this would fuel factor payments into India's financial industry while simultaneously offering improved liquidity to Sri Lankan bonds, it proved to be inconsistent with India's repressed capital account. Similarly, Malaysian capital controls may impede the trading of Malaysian products in Singapore.

Finally, such relationships can only come about in an environment of political stability. A small country has to feel comfortable in abandoning its financial sector development and trust that access to the securities markets in a large neighboring country will be reliable. In numerous cases political friction between two countries prevents the exploitation of such opportunities.

A variation of this strategy is the concept of a financial free trade zone, whereby a group of countries seek to obtain scale efficiencies by pooling their financial sectors. Thus the group of countries would have a single regulator, a single exchange, and one set of brokerage firms without regard for nationality. This is also a viable approach; however, it does demand the full complexity of financial sector institutional development, of obtaining cooperation across countries, and so on.

Case Study of the Middle East Financial Network

From the late 1950s onward, the Union of Arab Stock Exchanges has debated mechanisms for greater cooperation between Middle

Eastern stock exchanges. The notion of a single, unified Arab stock exchange has been discussed periodically, without any progress in implementation. Such unification is considered desirable from the perspectives of economic policy and furthering the larger political goal of unification in the Arab world.

In the meantime, individual countries set about building separate stock exchanges. These stock exchanges typically started out as trading floors in the 1980s and migrated into electronic trading in the 1990s. Countries that embarked on launching stock markets in the 1990s adopted electronic trading from the outset. The Middle East has also succeeded in obtaining a high degree of capital mobility. The existing regime can be summarized as follows: citizens of the Gulf Cooperation Council countries can own shares in any country, but only citizens of Gulf Cooperation Council countries are allowed to own shares of Gulf Cooperation Council companies.

In 1999 the union conceived a mechanism for cooperation known as the Middle East Financial Network (MEFN) (see http://www. alshabaca.com). The design of the MEFN was as follows. The MEFN would be a central order routing facility. It would obtain an information feed from each participating exchange, which would continue to perform existing order matching functions. The MEFN would produce an integrated screen that would show bids and offers for every stock on the MEFN. This screen would be available over the Internet to every brokerage firm that had a membership on any exchange that participated in the MEFN. This screen would also be available to any institutional or retail investor in the Middle East or elsewhere over the Internet. Each brokerage firm would establish links with respondent brokerage firms in exchanges on the MEFN where it did not have memberships. The central MEFN systems would be told of these relationships. When investors in a particular country wanted to place orders for any stock visible on the MEFN, they would approach their local brokers in exactly the same fashion as they would for trading a local stock. The broker would place such orders on the MEFN screen, which would route them to a respondent broker in the appropriate country.

The information flows on the MEFN may be summarized as follows:

- Information feeds will originate from each participating exchange and come to the central MEFN facility over the Internet.
- This information will be broadcast to all MEFN terminals and go to brokerage firms and investors all over the world over the Internet.
- When an investor wants to place an order with a brokerage firm that is a member of an exchange participating in MEFN, this

order will be placed on the MEFN screen and routed by the central MEFN facility to that brokerage firm.

- If the brokerage firm does not have a membership on the exchange where the order is destined, the order will be routed on to a respondent firm through the central MEFN facility.
- Order confirmations will be sent back through the MEFN.

The key concept of this design is to harness the latent order flow that could emanate from countries in the region where regional capital account convertibility is already in place. The MEFN design would only increase the order flow that any one exchange could obtain and the transactions that any one brokerage firm could process. Hence it is in brokerage firms' and exchanges' self-interest to support the MEFN. This was a key feature in overcoming the political mistrust that a cross-country financial network would normally attract from entrenched players in each country.

The major vulnerability of such an architecture lies in dispute resolution and incompatible regulations. If a transaction fails or encounters malpractice in one country, what are the rules of the game whereby the dispute will be resolved? Differences in enforcement principles and practice between different countries could also throw up hurdles for the MEFN, which is merely an order routing system and has no legal powers over participating exchanges and brokerage firms.

The question of disclosure and accounting is another important bottleneck. The MEFN will act like a single market offering a large number of homogeneous traded securities if, and only if, all participating firms and countries have similar accounting and disclosure norms.

The MEFN is being implemented by a private firm, QTes, which has been contracted by the Federation of Arab Stock Exchanges for this purpose. QTes will build, own, and operate the central facility where feeds from exchanges and orders will flow, to be routed on to MEFN terminals or respondent brokers over the Internet.

The implementers of the MEFN were highly conscious of the problem presented by low transaction intensity, at least at the outset. For the MEFN to be a low-cost system was therefore essential, so that the transaction charges it would impose per trade would not be onerous.[8]

Conclusion

Small countries do appear to have a limited ability to support a modern securities industry. An aggregate GDP of US$20 billion seems to be the threshold below which active stock markets do not occur. However, when examining this issue distinguishing between product characteristics and market characteristics is important. Small countries typically trade small securities, and these securities would have inferior liquidity even if they were traded on the best possible securities markets. Undertaking benchmarking exercises through which the maximal gains from policy reforms could be measured for a given country is possible.

The constraints small countries face are less binding today than ever before because of sharp cost reductions in IT costs for both hardware and software. The remarkable feature of the specific IT cost estimates cited in this chapter is their low magnitudes. A pervasive adoption of e-finance brings modern financial systems within reach of smaller countries.

One element of a policy platform that small countries should evaluate is unifying all organized financial trading into a single securities market. This would avoid fragmentation across stock markets, bond markets, commodity markets, and so on and harness economies of scale.

The other path that small countries could evaluate is exploiting international linkages. This can be done at two levels: outsourcing the IT functions of core exchange institutions or listing on markets outside the country. Both these approaches have strengths and weaknesses and could be relevant in certain circumstances.

The arguments and case studies presented in this chapter suggest that there are innovative policy options that small countries could consider that could significantly enhance the functioning of their securities markets. The key engine of change in this context is e-finance given the falling prices of computer hardware, the availability of telecommunications links (particularly via the Internet, which is now the global public data network), and the development of custom software.

Notes

1. Mexican stocks trading in the United States are a natural experiment with such a phenomenon. The United States has superior securities markets infrastructure compared with Mexico, so the gains in liquidity accruing to Mexican stocks when trading in the United States began as a response to improved market infrastructure. At the same time the Mexican stocks are small in absolute terms, and their liquidity in the United States is poor in absolute terms.

2. "Snapshots" of the complete limit order book are observed on the NSE. Thus any market order can be simulated and the impact cost measured

accurately. If a transaction of say US$5,000 is of interest, it can be simulated and the market impact cost measured. However, few electronic markets in the world put out datasets of the complete limit order book. Hence this approach would work at India's NSE, but it does not apply to other countries.

3. The costs of regulation may be borne by the government, and thus by taxpayers in general, and not solely by participants in the market.

4. The robust regression approach used here consists of first rejecting observations where Cook's $D > 1$, and then using an iterative procedure where regressions are recalculated using weights based on absolute residuals (Huber 1964).

5. The Center for Monitoring Indian Economy (http://www.cmie.com) has applied technology to its information processing system over the last decade, resulting in a 1,000-fold increase in the number of firms in its database while increasing its labor force only 10-fold. This has allowed it to market a CD-ROM with basic financial information about 200,000 firms in India for a sales price of roughly US$700.

6. The two firms were Millennium Information Technology in Sri Lanka (http://www.millenniumit.com) and NSE.IT, the IT firm created by the NSE (http://www.nse-india.com). Both firms are leading providers of software solutions to the global securities industry.

7. Other, more radical, alternatives are also possible. One proposal involves the establishment of a stock market in the Seychelles, which has a population of less than 100,000 people, whereby a single Western financial firm would provide all trading, listing, and brokerage services.

8. Three elements were central in the MEFN's strategy to realize low costs: (a) use of the Internet as a public wide-area network, (b) use of open protocols to help ensure that every component had multiple competing vendors, and (c) use of an Indian software company to develop the information dissemination and order routing system.

References

The word *processed* describes informally produced works that may not be commonly available through libraries.

Angel, J. J. 1997. "How Best to Supply Liquidity to a Small-Capitalization Securities Market." Technical report. Georgetown University, Washington, D.C. Processed.

Benston, G. J., and R. L. Hagerman. 1974. "Determinants of Bid-Asked Spreads in the Over-the-Counter Market." *Journal of Financial Economics* 1(4): 353–64.

Claessens, S., T. Glaessner, and D. Klingebiel. 2001. *E-Finance in Emerging Markets: Is Leapfrogging Possible?* Financial Sector Discussion Paper no. 7. Washington, D.C.: World Bank.

Huber, P. J. 1964. "Robust Estimation of a Location Parameter." *Annals of Mathematical Statistics* 35(1): 73–101.

Lee, R. 1998. *What Is an Exchange? The Automation, Management, and Regulation of Financial Markets.* New York: Oxford University Press.

Stoll, H. R. 1978. "The Pricing of Security Dealer Services: An Empirical Study of NASDAQ Stocks." *Journal of Finance* 33(5): 1153–72.

7

The Value of International Portfolio Diversification

Joost Driessen and Luc Laeven

Domestic investors in small countries are often prohibited from investing in financial assets outside their home country (IMF 2001). Such restrictions typically apply to institutional investors, but can also apply to households. These investment restrictions are potentially costly for such investors, because they reduce their portfolio diversification possibilities (Black 1974; Stulz 1981). In other words, investors in such countries are forced to assume more risk for the same level of expected return on their investments than investors in countries that permit portfolio diversification abroad.

However, even in countries without investment restrictions, such as the United States, most investors still invest largely at home (Baxter and Jermann 1997; French and Poterba 1991; Lewis 1996). This so-called home-bias of financial assets is puzzling, because observers generally believe that the gains from international diversification are large. For instance, Harvey (1995) shows that from a U.S. perspective, investors can realize large benefits from investing in emerging markets, where stock returns are driven to a larger extent by local factors.

We are grateful to Gerard Caprio, Frank de Jong, Jim Hanson, Patrick Honohan, Giovanni Majnoni, Roberto Rocha, Haluk Unal, Dimitri Vittas, and seminar participants at the World Bank Small Financial Systems Conference for helpful comments and suggestions.

Others argue that the gains from international diversification can largely be achieved indirectly, in domestic markets, by investing in stocks of multinational firms (Rowland and Tesar 1998) or in country funds and depository receipts (Errunza, Hogan, and Hung 1999).

Most of the literature on international portfolio diversification takes a U.S. perspective. This chapter investigates whether adding international stock investment opportunities leads to diversification benefits for a domestic investor compared with investing in local stocks only for a large cross-section of countries with both large and small stock markets. It also measures the size of these diversification benefits and compares the international diversification benefits across economies. In particular, it looks at the size of international diversification benefits in industrial versus developing economies.

Thus our contribution to the literature is an estimation of the benefits of international portfolio diversification from the perspective of a local investor for a large number of economies. This chapter therefore extends the analyses in Bekaert and Urias (1996); De Roon, Nijman, and Werker (2001); and Huberman and Kandel (1987), which analyze international diversification benefits from the perspective of a U.S. investor. We estimate global portfolio diversification benefits for an investor that currently invests in the local equity index by allowing the investor to invest in equity indexes for the United States, Europe, and the Far East.

Specifically, our empirical analysis uses monthly data on stock index returns for 62 economies for 1996–2000. We apply the regression framework developed by De Roon, Nijman, and Werker (2001) and Huberman and Kandel (1987) to test statistically whether there are diversification benefits for domestic investors with mean-variance utility that currently only invest in the local stock index (a spanning test). We also calculate the economic size of the diversification benefits using Sharpe ratios. For any asset or portfolio of assets, the Sharpe ratio is defined as the mean excess return divided by the standard deviation of return. We calculate diversification benefits for investors that are interested in the local currency returns and investors that care about U.S. dollar returns.

Our results reveal economically large and statistically significant diversification benefits for investors in almost all economies. The gains from international portfolio diversification are larger for developing economies relative to industrial economies. This is consistent with the finding that developing countries are, on average, less integrated in world financial markets (Bekaert, Harvey, and Lumsdaine 2002).

The next section explains how we measure the benefits of international diversification for domestic investors. This is followed by the data. We then report our estimates of these potential gains from international diversification before concluding.

Measuring International Portfolio Diversification Benefits

To measure the benefits of international diversification for domestic investors we use Markowitz's (1952) standard mean-variance framework.[1] We measure the diversification benefits for an investor that currently only invests in the local equity index and a risk-free asset by analyzing whether the risk-return tradeoff of the domestic index portfolio can be improved by investing in three global indexes: the Morgan Stanley Capital International (MSCI) indexes for the United States, Europe, and the Far East. We calculate returns in terms of both local currency and U.S. dollars. For simplicity we assume frictionless markets with no transaction costs and no short-selling constraints. In contrast to the existing empirical work on diversification benefits (Bekaert and Urias 1996; De Roon, Nijman, and Werker 2001; Huberman and Kandel 1987), which typically looks at global diversification benefits for a U.S. investor, we take the viewpoints of domestic investors in 62 economies.

We calculate both the statistical significance of the diversification possibilities as well as the economic significance of these possibilities. To calculate the statistical significance, we use the regression tests for mean-variance spanning developed by Huberman and Kandel (1987). In this case we examine whether adding the three MSCI (international) asset indexes to the domestic asset index leads to a significant shift in the mean-variance frontier. In other words, we test whether the domestic asset index alone can replicate (span) the return-variance frontier for the domestic plus international indexes. In the case of frictionless markets this test of spanning can be performed using the following multiple regression:

$$r_{t+1} = \alpha + \beta R_{t+1} + \varepsilon_{t+1}, \tag{7.1}$$

where

r_{t+1} = an N-dimensional vector with N returns on the additional assets

R_{t+1} = the K-dimensional return vector for the K benchmark assets

ε_t = a stochastic error term

t denotes time at t.

We impose the usual distributional assumptions on the error term, that is, $E[\varepsilon_{t+1}] = 0$ and $E[\varepsilon_{t+1}R'_{t+1}] = 0$. Then the null hypothesis that the K benchmark assets span the entire market of all $K + N$ assets is equivalent to the restrictions:[2]

$$\alpha = 0, \; \beta\iota_K = \iota_N. \tag{7.2}$$

In this case the return on each additional asset can be decomposed into the return on a portfolio of benchmark assets plus a zero expectation error term that is uncorrelated with the benchmark portfolio return. Thus in the case of mean-variance spanning, such an additional asset can only add to the variance of the portfolio return and not to the expected return, and investors would not want to include the additional asset in their portfolios. This implies that, if the spanning hypothesis holds, the optimal mean-variance portfolio only consists of the K benchmark assets.

Using data on stock returns, equation (7.1) can be estimated using ordinary least squares and the $2N$ restrictions in equation (7.2) can easily be tested using, for example, a Wald test. Under the null hypothesis of spanning the Wald test statistic will have a chi-square distribution. In this case the spanning test investigates whether the local stock market index spans a portfolio that also includes the stock market indexes of the United States, Europe, and the Far East. A lower value of the Wald test statistic indicates lower diversification benefits from investing abroad, and therefore suggests that the stock market is better integrated with world financial markets. Note that for these spanning tests no information about a risk-free rate is needed.

The economic significance of the diversification benefits of investing in the new N assets can be measured by calculating the maximum change in the Sharpe ratio when adding the new N assets to the K benchmark assets. More precisely, the Sharpe ratio for the mean-variance efficient portfolio based on the K benchmark assets (and a risk-free asset) and on all $K + N$ assets (and a risk-free asset) can be calculated. A difference between these two Sharpe ratios indicates that investors could increase their risk-return tradeoff by investing in the additional N assets.

Data

We use stock market data from several sources. Data on stock market capitalization come from MSCI in the case of developed markets and from Standard & Poor's in the case of developing markets. The most developed developing markets are part of the Global index series of Standard & Poor's and the least developed developing markets are part of the Frontier index series. Appendix 7.1 provides more details about data sources.

For the stock index return data we use the period 1996–2000. A longer history of reliable stock return data is difficult to obtain for stock markets in developing countries. For example, the base year of the Standard & Poor's Frontier index series is 1996. In addition, as the characteristics of developing countries typically change structurally over time, using a longer data period would make the stationarity assumptions that are needed for the spanning tests less reasonable.

We collected monthly stock market returns calculated in both local currency and U.S. dollars (unhedged). We dropped a number of countries because of the lack of data. Our final dataset includes monthly data on stock index returns for 62 economies for 1996–2000 (see appendix 7.2 for a list of the sampled economies). We also took into account three regional MSCI stock market indexes for the United States, Europe, and the Far East (see appendix 7.1 for a list of the countries included in each index).

As a proxy for the risk-free rate we used the economy's Treasury bill rate reported by the International Monetary Fund. For those economies where this information was unavailable we assumed a risk-free interest rate of 5 percentage points. Note that this assumption only influences the Sharpe ratios and not the spanning test results, as the latter do not depend on the risk-free rate.[3]

Estimates of the Benefits of International Portfolio Diversification

This section starts with the case of investors that are concerned about local currency returns and considers their potential for global portfolio diversification. Local currency investors are defined as those investors that care about local currency returns, that is, they convert the returns to their investments, whether denominated in local or foreign currency, into local currency. As global investment opportunities we consider investments in the MSCI stock market indexes for the United States, Europe, and the Far East. Table 7.1 reports the results for the spanning tests by region: for each economy we tested whether the local stock index (mean-variance) spans the three global MSCI indexes. Table 7.2 presents the average increase in the Sharpe ratio by region when allowing for these global investments: for each economy

Table 7.1 Results by Region (share of countries rejected)

Returns	North America	Latin America	Western Europe	Eastern Europe	Asia-Pacific	Other Asia	Middle East and Africa
Local currency returns	2 out of 2	9 out of 9	14 out of 15	8 out of 8	5 out of 5	11 out of 11	12 out of 12
U.S. dollar returns	2 out of 2	9 out of 9	14 out of 15	8 out of 8	5 out of 5	11 out of 11	12 out of 12

Note: The table reports the share of countries per region for which the test leads to a rejection at the 5 percent level, both for local currency and U.S. returns. Latin America includes Argentina, Brazil, Chile, Colombia, Ecuador, Jamaica, Mexico, Peru, and Venezuela. Asia includes Bangladesh, China, India, Indonesia, Korea, Malaysia, Pakistan, Philippines, Sri Lanka, Taiwan, and Thailand. Eastern Europe includes Czech Republic, Hungary, Lithuania, Poland, Russia, Slovakia, Slovenia, and Turkey. Middle East and Africa includes Botswana, Côte d'Ivoire, Egypt, Ghana, Jordan, Kenya, Mauritius, Morocco, Nigeria, South Africa, Tunisia, and Zimbabwe. Western Europe includes Austria, Belgium, Denmark, Finland, France, Germany, Greece, Ireland, Italy, Netherlands, Norway, Spain, Sweden, Switzerland, and United Kingdom. Asia-Pacific includes Australia, Hong Kong, Japan, New Zealand, and Singapore. North America includes Canada and United States. The regional division for the developing countries follows the definitions of S&P/IFC. For the developed countries we use regional MSCI indices.

Source: Authors' calculations.

Table 7.2 Global Diversification Benefits by Region (increase in Sharpe ratio)

Returns	North America	Latin America	Western Europe	Eastern Europe	Asia-Pacific	Other Asia	Middle East and Africa
Local currency returns	0.188	0.444	0.210	0.388	0.417	0.442	0.431
U.S. dollar returns	0.193	0.421	0.272	0.385	0.465	0.469	0.430

Note: We calculate for each country the maximum increase in Sharpe ratio when the three global MSCI indices are added to a local stock index portfolio. These increases in Sharpe ratios per country are averaged within region and these averages are reported in the table. The Sharpe ratios are calculated both for local currency returns and U.S. dollar returns. For list of countries and regions, see note to table 7.1.

Source: Authors' calculations.

we tested the maximum increase in the Sharpe ratio when the three global MSCI indexes are added to a local stock index portfolio. The results in tables 7.1 and 7.2 are summarized by averaging results within each region.

The spanning hypothesis is rejected for all countries except the United Kingdom at the 1 percent confidence level, which shows that there are statistically significant global diversification benefits for domestic investors around the world. In most cases, the p-values associated with the Wald test are so small that the spanning hypothesis would be rejected for all reasonable confidence levels. The economic size of the diversification possibilities is also large for most economies, as the increase in the Sharpe ratio indicates. Averaged over all economies the increase in the Sharpe ratio is about 0.37 on a yearly basis, which is substantial. The increase in the Sharpe ratio ranges from an average of 0.19 for countries in North America to an average of 0.44 for countries in Latin America.

Figure 7.1 shows the increase in Sharpe ratio per economy. In addition to the large increase in the Sharpe ratios, averaged over economies, this figure also shows that the size of the diversification benefits varies substantially across countries. The increase in the Sharpe ratio for local currency investors ranges from 0.11 for France to 0.84 for Ghana.

U.S. dollar investors are defined as those investors that care about the U.S. dollar returns of their investments, that is, they convert the returns to their investments, whether denominated in local or foreign currency, into U.S. dollars. Again, as global investment opportunities we consider investments in the MSCI stock market indexes for the United States, Europe, and the Far East. The U.S. dollar results for the spanning tests by region are presented in the second row of table 7.1, and the second row of table 7.2 reports the increase in the Sharpe ratio for U.S. dollar investors. Figure 7.2 shows the increase in the Sharpe ratio for U.S. dollar investors per country. The increase in the Sharpe ratio for U.S. dollar investors ranges from 0.14 in Finland to 0.71 in Slovakia and averages 0.39 on an annual basis.

It follows from tables 7.1 and 7.2 and figures 7.1 and 7.2 that the diversification benefits for U.S. dollar investors are, in general, somewhat smaller than those for local currency investors. This is because by not converting the returns to their investments into local currency, U.S. dollar investors did not profit from favorable movements of the U.S. dollar relative to most other currencies during 1996–2000. In other words, part of the international diversification benefits for local currency investors are due to currency effects rather than stock

182

Figure 7.1 Foreign Diversification in Local Currency

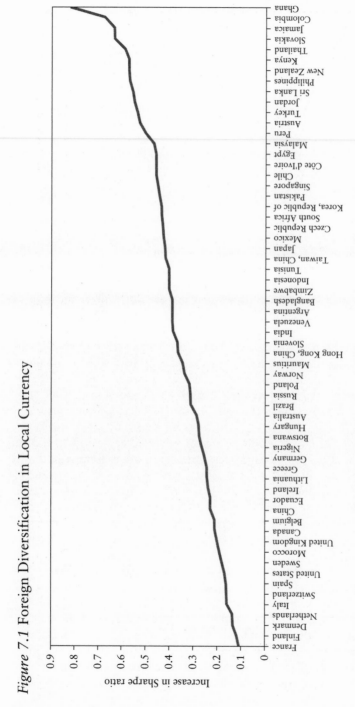

Note: This figure shows the difference between the Sharpe ratio of the portfolio that includes the local stock market index and the world portfolio (consisting of the local portfolio plus the stock market indexes of the United States, Europe, and Asia-Pacific as measured by MSCI) or the regional index, and the Sharpe ratio of the local stock market index for each economy in our sample. The Sharpe ratios are estimated using local currency returns for 1996–2000.

Source: Authors' calculations.

Figure 7.2 Foreign Diversification in U.S. Dollars

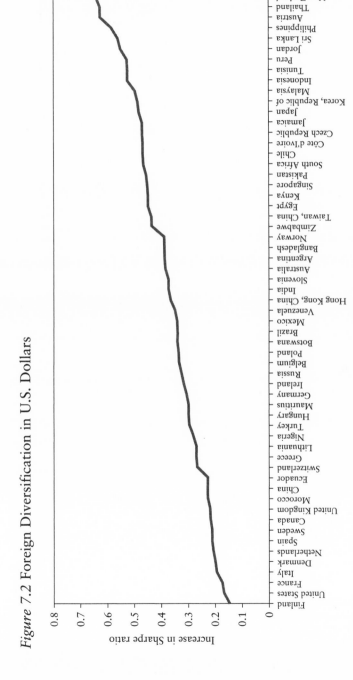

Note: This figure shows the difference between the Sharpe ratio of the portfolio that includes the local stock market index and the world portfolio (consisting of the local portfolio plus the stock market indices of United States, Europe and Asia-Pacific as measured by MSCI), and the Sharpe ratio of the local stock market index for each country in our sample. The Sharpe ratios are estimated using U.S. dollar returns for the period 1996–2000.
Source: Authors' calculations.

returns in the foreign indexes. Note that as these currency effects are based on historical experience they may not be good predictors of currency-related diversification benefits in the future.

The test statistics of the spanning tests and Sharpe ratios indicate that the benefits of international portfolio diversification vary considerably across countries, or in other words, the degree of risk diversification that can be attained by investing in home country equities varies from country to country. At first sight the diversification benefits appear to be the largest for the developing countries. Previous research has shown that many developing countries are not well integrated with world capital markets (see, for example, Harvey 1995). This suggests that investors in developing countries could realize significant benefits from international portfolio diversification. To test whether this is indeed the case we compare the increase in the Sharpe ratios between developing economies and industrial economies. The results are reported in table 7.3.

Our dataset includes 62 economies, of which 41 are developing and 21 are industrial economies. When comparing the increase in Sharpe ratios caused by international diversification for the different groups of economies the results indicate that the global diversi-

Table 7.3 t-Test of Mean Differences

	Increase in Sharpe ratios			Industrial versus developing economies (t-statistic)
Returns	All economies	Industrial economies	Developing economies	
Local currency returns	0.367	0.256	0.424	(−4.570)*
U.S. dollar returns	0.386	0.310	0.425	(−3.039)*

* Indicates significance at the 1 percent level.

Note: This table presents the average increase in Sharpe ratios caused by adding the global index portfolio to the local portfolio. Figures are averages for 1996–2000. We use the World Bank's 1995 classification for developing countries. The last column reports the t-statistic of the test of mean differences in the variables in the industrial economies and developing economies columns.

Source: Authors' calculations.

fication benefits tend to be larger for developing economies than for industrial economies. In local currency terms the increase in the Sharpe ratio averages 0.42 for developing economies and only 0.26 for industrial economies. This difference of 0.16 between developing and industrial economies in the increase in Sharpe ratios is large. A t-test of mean differences suggests that this difference is also statistically significant, when measured both in local currency and in U.S. dollars.

Several extensions to our analysis are possible. For example, many investors face market friction, such as transaction costs and short-sales constraints, in which case such restrictions have to be incorporated in the analysis. Investigating how the benefits of investing in regional indexes compare with the benefits of global diversification would also be interesting. Some of these topics are explored in Driessen and Laeven (2002), who also find that the benefits of investing abroad are largest for investors in developing countries, but show that a large part of the diversification benefits disappears when controlling for short-sales constraints, even for developing countries.

Conclusions

This chapter presents two main findings. First, by analyzing 62 different economies it shows that domestic investors in both industrial and developing economies can realize substantial benefits from global diversification. These benefits are both statistically and economically significant. Second, it shows that the benefits of international portfolio diversification are statistically significantly larger for developing economies relative to industrial economies. Unfortunately, investors in small countries often face restrictions on investing abroad, which underscores the importance of further liberalization of international financial markets.

The policy message is therefore for countries to lift their investment restrictions and allow investors to realize the diversification benefits of investing abroad. As the potential benefits from investing abroad are largest for developing countries, such policies would yield more benefits for residents in developing countries than in industrial countries. As a result of such financial liberalization stock markets will become more integrated and the allocation of capital could improve.

Appendixes

Appendix 7.1 Definitions of Variables Data Sources

Variable	Definition and source
MSCI	Stock market index for industrial countries. *Source:* Morgan Stanley Capital International (MSCI).
MSCI Europe index	Regional stock market index for industrial countries in Europe. The index includes the following countries: Austria, Belgium, Denmark, Finland, France, Germany, Greece, Ireland, Italy, the Netherlands, Norway, Portugal, Spain, Sweden, Switzerland, and the United Kingdom.
MSCI Far East index	Regional stock market index for industrial countries in the Far East. The index includes the following economies: Hong Kong (China), Japan, and Singapore.
S&P/IFC Global index	Stock market index for developing countries with relatively large stock markets. *Source:* EMDB.[1]
S&P/IFC Frontier index	Stock market index for developing countries with relatively small stock markets. *Source:* EMDB.[1]
Risk-free interest rate	Treasury bill rate. *Source: International Financial Statistics.*

[1]In January 2000 Standard & Poor's acquired the Emerging Markets Data Base (EMDB) from the International Finance Corporation and it is now known as the Standard & Poor's Emerging Markets Data Base.

Appendix 7.2 List of Sampled Economies

Asia-Pacific	Slovak Republic	Peru
Australia	Slovenia	Venezúela
Hong Kong, China	Turkey	
Japan		*Middle East and Africa*
New Zealand	*Latin America*	Botswana
Singapore	Argentina	Côte d'Ivoire
	Brazil	Egypt
Eastern Europe	Chile	Ghana
Czech Republic	Colombia	Jordan
Hungary	Ecuador	Kenya
Lithuania	Jamaica	Mauritius
Poland	Mexico	Morocco
Russian Federation		

Appendix 7.2 *Continued*

Nigeria	Indonesia	Finland
South Africa	Korea, Republic of	France
Tunisia	Malaysia	Germany
Zimbabwe	Pakistan	Greece
	Philippines	Ireland
North America	Sri Lanka	Italy
Canada	Taiwan, China	Netherlands
United States	Thailand	Norway
		Spain
Other Asia	*Western Europe*	Sweden
Bangladesh	Austria	Switzerland
China	Belgium	United Kingdom
India	Denmark	

Notes

1. We therefore assume either a mean-variance utility function for the investor or normally distributed asset returns.

2. See Bekaert and Urias (1996) and Huberman and Kandel (1987) for a derivation of equation (7.2).

3. In the case of U.S. dollar returns, the risk-free rate in the Sharpe ratio is the U.S. dollar Treasury bill rate for all countries.

References

The word *processed* describes informally produced works that may not be commonly available through libraries.

Baxter, Marianne, and Urban J. Jermann. 1997. "The International Diversification Puzzle Is Worse Than You Think." *American Economic Review* 87(1): 170–80.

Bekaert, Geert, and Michael S. Urias. 1996. "Diversification, Integration, and Emerging Market Closed-End Funds." *Journal of Finance* 51(3): 835–69.

Bekaert, Geert, Campbell Harvey, and Robin Lumsdaine. 2002. "Dating the Integration of World Equity Markets." *Journal of Financial Economics* 65(2): 203–49.

Black, Fischer. 1974. "International Capital Market Equilibrium with Investment Barriers." *Journal of Financial Economics* 1(4): 337–52.

De Roon, Frans A., Theo E. Nijman, and Bas J. M. Werker. 2001. "Testing for Mean-Variance Spanning with Short Sales Constraints and Transaction Costs: The Case of Emerging Markets." *Journal of Finance* 56(2): 721–42.

Driessen, Joost, and Luc Laeven. 2002. "International Portfolio Diversification Benefits: Cross-Country Evidence." World Bank, Washington, D.C. Processed.

Errunza, Vihang, Ked Hogan, and Mao-Wei Hung. 1999. "Can the Gains from International Diversification Be Achieved without Trading Abroad?" *Journal of Finance* 54(6): 2075–2107.

French, Kenneth R., and James M. Poterba. 1991. "Investor Diversification and International Equity Markets." *American Economic Review* 81(2): 222–26.

Harvey, Campbell R. 1995. "Predictable Risk and Returns in Emerging Markets." *Review of Financial Studies* 8(3): 773–816.

Huberman, Gur, and Shmuel Kandel. 1987. "Mean-Variance Spanning." *Journal of Finance* 42(4): 873–88.

IMF (International Monetary Fund). 2001. *Annual Report on Exchange Restrictions and Exchange Arrangements.* Washington, D.C.

Lewis, Karin K. 1996. "What Can Explain the Apparent Lack of International Consumption Risk Sharing?" *Journal of Political Economy* 104(2): 267–97.

Markowitz, Harry. 1952. "Portfolio Selection." *Journal of Finance* 7(1): 77–91.

Rowland, Patrick F., and Linda L. Tesar. 1998. "Multinationals and the Gains from International Diversification." Working Paper no. 6733. National Bureau of Economic Research, Cambridge, Mass.

Stulz, René M. 1981. "On the Effects of Barriers to International Investment." *Journal of Finance* 36(4): 923–34.

Part IV

Pension Issues

8

Pension Reform and Pension Service Efficiencies

Thomas C. Glaessner
and Salvador Valdés-Prieto

This chapter explores the proper respective roles of the private sector and the state in relation to pension policy, especially in small economies, defined in this chapter as those where employment in the formal sector is less than 1 million people. Small populations result in a less than minimum efficient scale in the provision of some pension services. This leads us to conclude that small countries should expose themselves to greater international competition in the provision of pension services.

As well as having fewer workers, many small countries exhibit high international mobility of labor and capital; are subject to a greater scarcity of human capital specialized in financial supervision and tax administration; and have far fewer independent financial and political interests, relatively less independent civil services, and less political stability over the long time horizons involved in mandatory pension systems.

We would like to thank Robert Lacey for his continued support in the development of this paper, Roberto Panzardi and Miguel Navarro for excellent research assistance, and participants at a seminar at Catholic University for their helpful comments on an earlier version of this chapter.

In small countries relatively more attention should be paid to designing pension systems that ensure adequate competition or, more formally, contestability, in the provision of pension services. Because small countries often experience greater labor mobility than large countries, their total mandatory contribution rates will not be as high as elsewhere. Thus small countries have to forgo the potential benefits (for improvident workers) of a high replacement rate funded by high mandated contributions. In this setting an increase in administrative charges cannot be absorbed by increasing the total contribution rate, as it could be in larger countries. Rather, the net contribution rate and the final average replacement rate must be reduced.

Perhaps the most robust overall policy implication of this chapter is that the case for opening the economy to permit greater trade in financial services is much stronger in small countries than in large countries. This is so because

• The infrastructure needed to support pension services can be radically reduced by importing key services, which would allow the small country to rely on the financial supervision, financial sector laws, and, in the extreme, even the civil law framework of larger, more developed trading partners.

• The relative lack of competition in the provision of key pension services in small countries resulting from the small contribution base and the absence of independent interests can be mitigated through greater international trade in the provision of these services, for instance, data processing, investment management, and longevity insurance, combined with actions to mandate the unbundling of collection services from other pension services.

• The free trade in financial services should enable residents of small countries to contract for the provision of investments in foreign currencies, implying the need for explicit convertibility guarantees over long time horizons.

• The securities markets in many small countries are not liquid and are often characterized by a lack of independent interests. Mandating offshore investments may be necessary in addition to permitting greater foreign competition in the provision of investment management services.

The chapter is organized as follows. It begins with a brief statement of the three main objectives of pension policy, noting the importance of income redistribution (though that is not a main focus of the chapter). The following section analyzes how pension provision can be analytically decomposed into nine distinct services, discusses how the costs of these services might be related to whether or not they are disintegrated, and discusses how these costs might also depend on type and quality of other infrastructures in place. Pension fund reform and institutional strengthening are thus closely related. Then comes a section which focuses on the provision of trustee services. Policy design here is crucial, particularly in avoiding monopoly. The section following assesses the degree to which the various pension services are prone to being monopolized. Before concluding, a penultimate section examines investor protection as well as funding and investment policy.

Pension Services and Institutional Infrastructure

Objectives of Pension Policy

National pension policy has three well-established objectives: (a) to alleviate the market failures that limit the efficiency and reliability of private capital markets for voluntary saving and insurance; (b) to help improvident individuals by ensuring that they save and insure prudently, including preventing individuals who rely on support from their family, community, or state from exploiting that support by failing to save adequately; and (c) to help the elderly poor who could not save enough during their working lives for survival in old age (World Bank 1994).

Other objectives, such as capital accumulation and the redistribution of wealth between generations, can be achieved with tools other than pension policy, such as fiscal policy and national debt policy. Thus pension policy should focus on the three objectives mentioned previously, where it is indispensable. The use of pension policy for these other objectives (for which other adequate policy tools exist) is inefficient if this implies sacrificing these three objectives.

While the third objective of pension policy, income redistribution toward the long-term poor, is not the focus of this chapter, it merits discussion. The income distribution effects of a pension system can be both intended and unintended. Two examples of intended redistribution are a minimum pension and a benefit formula that includes a fixed amount of benefits plus some proportion of past wages. Unintended redistribution in favor of high-income workers occurs for many reasons. One is that high-income workers naturally take more advantage of fiscal incentives. Defined benefit schemes are more prone to unintended redistribution, because the benefit formula is not adjusted for the higher life expectancy of richer people. Similarly, defined benefit schemes that rely on the average earnings of the last few years of work do not adjust for high-income workers' steeper age-earnings profile.

Intended income redistribution through the pension system finds a tough competitor in tax and transfer systems. In most countries the pension system only covers formal sector workers, which means middle and high-income workers. In this setting redistribution among covered workers omits the really poor, who work in the informal sector or do not have employers to act as collection agents, as in developing countries' subsistence and communal sectors. In most countries granting pensions to the elderly poor requires the use of institutional vehicles different from formal social security, such as municipal networks to distribute transfers financed by the national government. Collecting revenue from independent workers is possible, as proposed for Latvia (Holzmann 1994), but requires an administrative effort.

Income redistribution is more difficult to pursue in small countries, because they are generally subject to greater international labor mobility than large countries. This reduces the efficiency of all policies and institutions for redistribution, including the pension system. For example, citizens may work abroad for frequent and extended periods, while many foreigners may work in the domestic economy for years. This may imply that a citizen who contributed for only a few years could still obtain full support when returning to the country at age 65. Conversely, elderly poor who arrived in the country to work at age 55 may be considered ineligible for support. Income distribution through pensions may imply undesired redistribution between foreign residents and local emigrants who return, increasing the economic inefficiency and the political problems associated with these policies.

This chapter focuses on the other two objectives of pension policy, namely, helping improvident individuals and alleviating the market failures of the capital markets that provide savings and insurance products.

Primary Pension Services

Pension provision comprises the following services: (a) collecting contributions, wherein employers acting as retention agents are contacted periodically by a collection agency that receives payment and raw data about each worker's contributions; (b) processing data on contribution information, with processing oriented toward eliminating errors from the raw data; (c) providing accounting support to mark investments to market prices, to calculate net asset values for each fund on a daily or weekly basis, and to ensure that investment diversification guidelines and other regulations are met; (d) bringing together the information generated in the previous steps and processing individual accounts to obtain new balances; (e) providing client services to contributors and pensioners (members), such as sending account statements and answering inquiries; (f) managing portfolios, including analyzing investment opportunities and financial risk; (g) managing insurance and related benefits, including calculating benefits and purchasing disability, survivorship, and longevity insurance (in the form of annuities); (h) making pension payments and distributing lump sum payments to permit the purchase of annuities; and (i) processing transfers of individual account balances among authorized pension management trustees.

Theoretical considerations suggest that legislating the unbundling of those pension services characterized by a natural monopoly and sunk costs may facilitate entry into other markets for pension services.

Disintegration also facilitates the regulation of those pension services in which there is a natural monopoly. More effective regulation can help place downward pressure on charges. The alternatives for such services are competitive bidding for the right to operate a franchise (Demsetz 1968), price regulation, and self-regulation.

Lack of contestability is not always due to natural monopoly and sunk costs. Entry may also be blocked by legislation. One of the most common legal barriers found in small countries is the prohibition against cross-border provision of services. Thus, an effective strategy to prevent small market size from resulting in a monopoly is to allow the buyer to obtain the service from an offshore provider. In many cases the policy approach must go beyond the removal of barriers, for example, by reducing any special taxes on cross-border provision and by dismantling nontariff barriers such as nonacceptance of foreign formats for the services involved.

A reduction in concentration associated with mandatory disintegration may also be socially valuable for a nonstandard reason: atomistic trustees have less political power. Concentration creates a special type of externality, because an increase in the market share of the largest trustees reduces the quality of service other providers offer. This is because an increase in the overall concentration of trustees increases the political risk of all pensions a mandatory system offers. Because of this externality, interventions that limit concentration in the trustee market may be justified—a point returned to below.

Institutional Infrastructure and the Costs of Primary Pension Services

The costs of providing each of the primary pension services are not independent of the infrastructure present in a specific country. For example, inadequately functioning registries (contributor and employer identification systems) can make the imposition of a mandatory contribution system based on individualized accounts significantly more costly, if not impossible, to implement. In Peru, for example, the new pension system was forced to create its own identification numbers for members, and high costs could not be avoided even though the Peruvian Superintendency of Pensions coordinated procedures. These identification numbers are now being used by other services not related to pensions.

Cost-effective provision of pension services also requires the existence of basic infrastructure in the areas of clearing and settlement of payments and custody of securities, which are often not well developed in small countries. The financial information needed for efficient provision of insurance and fund management services requires actuarial, auditing, accounting, valuation, and securities rating services, some of which can be imported. Finally, adequate supervisory, legal, and regulatory frameworks are needed, which may be more difficult to import.

Although the institutional infrastructure required to support a low-cost pension system may appear daunting, the minimum local requirements are well within the capability of small countries, particularly if reforms are implemented to permit the free importation of a large number of the services. Evidence from some Central American countries suggests that this is already occurring in the case of a number of services; for example, Costa Rica has subcontracted certain securities pricing and trading functions to Chile's electronic stock exchange.

Pension Reform Design and Institutional Infrastructure

The extent of institutional infrastructure needed to support a pension system depends on the specific design adopted. For example, a mandatory occupational pension scheme like that in Switzerland, which places the burden of pension management on the employer, avoids the collection stage, and so the associated infrastructure is not needed. However, the duplication of accounts and account transfer can be extremely costly in such a setting, because there may be tens of thousands of pension managers. Similarly, a pension design wherein the government is the sole issuer of securities that can be bought by a fully funded scheme does not require much of the infrastructure associated with domestic securities markets, such as valuation and risk rating services or complex laws and regulations relating to conflicts of interest and corporate governance. Finally, to the extent that the management of a large portion of pension funds is contracted out to a single, major firm that manages international funds and that domestic investment by the pension funds is limited, there is less need for extensive supervision and infrastructure of the domestic securities market.

The effectiveness of some types of institutional infrastructure is also a function of the specific forms of infrastructure that can be provided together in one bundle. For example, if the pension supervisory body performs some operating functions, as it does in Peru, it loses some of the authority and incentives needed for effective supervision of that function. This is because the administrators of such a supervisory body are subject to a conflict of interest, because many of them may find it difficult to criticize their own performance. In addition, a supervisory authority in that role becomes hostage to its own personnel, because no alternate supplier is available to provide the operating functions it has centralized and nationalized. Information about the efficiency with which those functions could be performed elsewhere is also lost, which may further hamper the cost-effectiveness of nationalizing the provision of certain infrastructure services.

One type of pension reform option that can vastly reduce the infrastructure needed is one in which the government mandates contributions, creates a collection system, sets certain minimum standards for a pension contract, and then simply licenses international companies to offer that contract to local contributors. In this case the small developing country is importing supervision services and avoiding all the infrastructure needed for domestic securities markets except for registries to identify contributors and pensioners. In a less extreme case, some proportion of the assets could be invested in domestic financial markets.

Although such international licensing of providers can reduce the infrastructure needed, it introduces other risks and costs to pensioners. If, for example, under this setup each contributor could switch to a different international pension fund manger once a year, then each worker could have dozens of different suppliers through retirement. The cumulative costs of administering each pension would increase with each change. In addition, legal recourse by pensioners under laws in the country where the foreign investment management firm is domiciled would need to be carefully analyzed.

International trade of pension services in small countries also depends critically on the availability and prices of enabling infrastructure, particularly in the areas of telecommunications and computers. Lack of competition in these services can greatly increase the cost of cross-border provision of pension services.

Influencing Trustees' Role and Performance

In considering the concentration and governance issues surrounding the supply of trustee services distinguishing between services rendered to stocks and services rendered to flows is convenient. Services to stocks include pension fund management, custody, and transaction execution. Services to flows include collecting contributions, processing individual accounts, and paying pensions.

Although concentration and market power in processing accounts may result in large fees, this is unlikely to be on a scale that would significantly erode the funds (by comparison with poor investment yields), because in typical cases close to 70 percent of a pension is financed by past and future interest earned, and only 30 percent is a recouping of contributions (with no interest). To understand why administrative costs tend to be less important than investment yield for pensions, consider a case where administrative fees of 1 percent of wages are added to a contribution rate of 10 percent, which yields a gross pension equal to 70 percent of gross earnings. If achieving an increase in the rate of return on the invested funds from 4 to 5 percent per year were to require that administrative fees be increased from 1 to 2 percent of wages, then the same pension could be obtained while reducing the total contribution rate from 11 to 9.22 percent.[1]

However, concentration in pension fund management brings the prospect of fiduciary fraud and, more important, it allows financial power to be concentrated in a few hands. This in turn may induce politicians to attempt to gain access to that financial power and exploit it for their own purposes. The extent of political risk is a critical issue. The possibility of political intervention to direct the use of the pension funds is an important source of financial risk over the long term. This risk tends to be greatest when the government designates the boards of trustees.

Functions of Pension Trustees

Efficient investment management distinguishes between portfolio managers, who are experts in financial investments, and pension trustees, who hold residual or prudential oversight powers. Trustees are critical in determining financial performance, because they have the power to fire and hire portfolio managers and set guidelines for their financial strategy. In addition, trustees are also empowered to select auditors that value illiquid assets and to select custodians. When pension funds hold equity in corporations, trustees issue voting instructions at shareholders' meetings.[2]

The critical question is who performs the function of trustee.[3] This question has two aspects: (a) who designates the board of trustees, and (b) what is the minimum number of "independent" boards of trustees needed in the pension system. This should not be confused with the issues of how many providers of pension services should be hired and how vertically integrated they should be.

Independent Boards of Trustees

The number of distinct trustees should be greater than five, because a smaller number would create a monopoly or oligopoly that could control the domestic financial system (with the capacity, for example, to move the exchange rate) and domestic corporations if significant pension fund resources are to be invested domestically. A mandatory pension system is expected to accumulate assets that are 200 percent of gross national product if the coverage of workers is 100 percent, that is, two to four times the assets of the banking system of most countries. Sooner or later an oligopoly would use its power to attempt to control these assets.

If the country is willing to require the pension system to permanently invest at least 95 percent of its funds in international capital markets, a single or very few trustees or boards of directors could be considered. Requiring the pension system to invest a large proportion of its assets internationally could, however, mean forgoing some opportunities for developing the domestic economy, depending on the degree of international capital mobility.

The option of requiring the pension system to invest in debt instruments alone would eliminate the problems related to voting in shareholders' meetings of nonfinancial companies, but does not justify a monopoly trustee. The Swedish experience with this option in 1959 shows that the trustees can still wield enormous financial power by refusing to buy corporate or bank bonds until required covenants are accepted (Pontusson 1984).

The only case where a single or a few trustees are feasible is in an extremely small country that has an open capital account and enjoys such a high degree of access to foreign capital markets that even small and medium firms would not become dependent on the single trustee. These conditions are not met in most small developing countries; however, they are met by municipalities, and even state governments, in extremely large countries such as the United States. For all other cases there should be at least six trustees or separate boards, and coordination among them should be prohibited, despite the not insignificant difficulties of enforcing such a provision.

Aside from ensuring a certain number of trustees and limiting how they are related across separate pension funds, the issue of trustees' independence is multifaceted. First, they must be independent from affiliated investment managers to ensure that they are acting in the interests of pension fund contributors. Second, independence must also extend to trustees' dealings with related parties within the financial group and with nonfinancial companies if the pension fund can invest in equities. In small countries finding independent trustees may require using foreign nationals of sufficient standing and making them subject to adequate criminal and civil liability if they do not discharge their fiduciary obligations properly.

In sum, ensuring a certain number of trustees or separate boards of directors is a necessary, but insufficient, condition for small countries to realize the benefits of private investment management in such areas as corporate governance of nonfinancial companies. In many of these countries independent trustees or outside directors must be precisely defined in law and regulation and be subject to credible enforcement by supervisory agencies.

Trustee Selection and Political Risk

There are many ways to designate trustees. One is for the government to designate them at either the national or regional level. Another is for employers or unions to be assigned by law to designate the trustees. A third is for individual workers to choose among available trustee services offered by pension management firms.

Any approach to designating pension fund boards of trustees gains from insulating investment decisions from political influences, because the rate of return is by far the most important determinant of benefit levels. By contrast, nationalization of trustee designation involves none of the gains Willig (1994) mentions, because there is no need to respond to a social interest different from an individual interest, with the social interest narrowly defined as striving for secure and substantial pensions for the improvident. In addition, most trustee actions needed to achieve that purpose can be specified in advance or can be verified after the fact. Nevertheless, other gains can be realized by nationalizing the designation of trustees. These gains are related to the avoidance of costs that arise naturally with multiple providers of pension services under the non-nationalization option. Specifically, nationalization avoids the marketing costs associated with individual selection from among several pension management trustees and the potential for breach of trust by private trustees, whether they are designated by individuals, employers, or unions. However, nationalization often increases political risks to contributors, because the trustees have little insulation from political manipulation.

Options

The optimal design for the number and selection method of trustees and for the related regulatory supervisory framework turns on the relative size of the foregoing costs. The risk of fraud by employers and unions can increase the risk to pensions significantly, and this risk is higher in smaller countries because of the lower number of independent financial interests. This risk depends in part on the quality of supervision, but creating an adequate supervisory framework similar to the Employee Retirement Income Security Act in the United States or the Federal Pensions Law in Switzerland may be impossible for many small developing countries, which lack the specialized human capital needed to enforce such laws. In addition, to the extent that these laws create entities such as government guarantee funds, for example, the Pension Guarantee Fund in the case of the Employee Retirement Income Security Act, experience in small Latin American countries suggests that this is a dangerous policy given the moral hazard problems engendered. The establishment of guarantee funds for occupational pension plans creates distorted incentives even in large countries.

The high marketing costs observed in Argentina, Chile, and Peru are due in part to excessive government regulation of the fee structure. For example, the marketing costs, which run up to 30 percent of fee income in Chilean pension fund administrators, are only 18 percent of fees in Chilean health insurance companies, which also collect mandatory contributions, but are free to set their own prices, and are therefore free to offer group plans to each member (Valdés-Prieto 1995). High administrative fees may be warranted, but only if the reduction in the risk to the value of the pension is large enough.

The expected costs of political interference associated with government-designated boards of trustees depend on the extent of a country's political development. If the country can create government-designated boards and associated governance processes that are sufficiently insulated from politics and are able to perform their prudential role efficiently, this would be the best option. However, many small developing countries are not politically developed enough for this option. Consider, for example, the case of a military government that could replace the board of trustees with no opposition. If a single party has dominated the political spectrum for decades, as in certain Asian,

East European, and Latin American countries, boards of trustees in those countries could not be insulated from political pressures. What is more, a small country that depends on an imperialist power for more than 80 percent of its international trade may be forced to change its board of trustees because of pressures from that power.

There are many subtle ways to politically influence government-designated boards of trustees, and these are more prevalent in small countries because of a smaller number of independent political interests. If political parties compete mostly on the basis of promises to their immediate followers (patronage), or on the basis of promising benefits for the majority of current voters (populism), or if the parties or elected representatives can easily be bribed by pressure groups, then government-designated boards of trustees have few chances to succeed in their duties over the long term. Once politicians capture a regional or national board of trustees the board can threaten not to renew the contracts of the managers it hires unless they buy over-priced bonds from private firms that contribute to the politicians' campaigns; risky bonds issued by municipalities controlled by the dominating party; bonds that yield below-market rates issued by the treasury or by state-owned enterprises (Tiglao 1990); or if they do not buy overpriced mortgage bonds, as was required to support the official housing policy in Sweden (Pontusson 1984).

In countries that exhibit this type of political behavior, a pension system based on competitive selection of pension management companies by individual members can insulate trustees from many of these pressures. As each pension management company must compete for clients, this competitive process punishes those companies that concede to politicians. For example, if powerful politicians request that pension management companies buy a low-yielding debt from a state-owned enterprise, the company that resists this pressure will exhibit higher returns and will be rewarded with more customers and higher profits, as seen in a recent Chilean episode (Godoy and Valdés-Prieto 1994). Note that these benefits will obtain with more certainty if the supervision agencies help support the political independence of members of boards of trustees.

Therefore in all cases where the political development of a small country has not reached a stage where vulnerability to such pressure can be confidently ruled out, and where human capital is too scarce to supervise thousands of employer and union-run boards of trustees, the best option is individual selection of pension management companies. This proposition has received empirical support. A recent study by Mitchell and Hsin (1996) of the financial performance of 130 occupational pension plans for public employees at the state and county levels in the United States, where the sponsor is a political entity, finds that the presence of elected pensioner representatives, usually linked to unions, on the boards of trustees reduces the pension fund's rate of return.

The World Bank (1994) reports that the rate of return obtained by each of 14 provident funds (single, government-managed pension funds) was worse than that of privately managed pension fund management companies, and many had returns below negative 10 percent per year for five years. Mesa-Lago (1991) compares the financial returns of the funds invested by half-funded conventional social security systems in eight Latin American countries and comes to similar conclusions.

In light of this experience, small developing countries may wish to opt for privately owned, competing pension trustee companies supervised by a specialized government agency or superintendency. The exceptions where other trustee arrangements might be better would be countries that have enough human capital to supervise tens of thousands of employers and unions and have a high degree of political development and stability. However, the arrangement with privately owned, competing pension trustee companies may be rendered suboptimal if this market turns out to be concentrated. This is because a tight oligopoly of pension trustee companies would have too much power in the domestic securities markets, where international capital mobility is not significant, thereby increasing the risk that politicians would misuse these firms.

Potential for Monopoly in Different Pension Services

This section assesses the degree to which each pension service is characterized by monopoly. In each case specific options for the provision of that service are discussed.

Collecting and Processing Contributions

The collection and processing phase involves economies of scope as well as fixed costs; which raise issues of design important for policy.

Economies of Scope. The collection process is characterized by economies of scope that derive from three sources. First, each employer has to fill out a form for each provider of collection services, with each form listing the employees within the company who have chosen pension management companies that in turn have hired a particular collection provider. Completing these forms involves a fixed cost; therefore a collection service serving pension companies that represent a larger share of the workers can spread that fixed cost over that larger number. The differential between the average cost of collection for a large versus a small number of workers per form favors a particular organization of supply: a single provider of collection services per employer. This organization minimizes the number of forms per employer.

Second, the cost the employer bears clearly falls as the number of collection agencies falls, because many assignment errors are avoided and the remaining mistakes can be corrected at a smaller cost. The cost of correcting mistakes when the employer distributes 60 employees among 6 forms is much larger than the cost when all 60 employees are on a single form. This means that employers also favor an organization of supply of pension services in which there is a single collection agent.

In a competitive environment these two sources of economies of scope do not imply a natural monopoly in collection, because many collector firms can compete to act as the single collection agent for any given employer. However, in a regulatory setting in which employers are not allowed to express their preference for a single collector and where collectors are not allowed to pass on the lower costs of collecting all the contributions paid by a given employer, these economies of scope cannot be expressed in prices. This is precisely what happens in Chile, where regulations prevent both types of responses. Employers are not allowed to choose one collector because of the belief that the employer would obtain help to evade the obligation to contribute. A similar barrier to passing on economies of scope also seems to have prevailed in the Mexican retirement savings account system set up during 1992–94.

Restrictive regulations of these types do not necessarily result automatically in a monopoly, however, because the other side of the market, namely, collectors, would be willing to compete by offering discounts to groups of workers employed by a single employer. In the absence of price regulations, a small pension fund management company could start life with just a dozen contracts with 10 or 20 medium-sized employee groups that pass the savings from acting in a group on to their members and enjoy small collection costs. Thus no natural monopoly would originate in scope economies.

The restriction in Chile is that collectors are banned by law from offering discounts. As the cost savings remain but are not expressed in discounts, they benefit the collectors, which come closer to acting as a single collector for each employer. The pension management companies with a larger share of the worker market, assuming that those workers are evenly distributed across employers, enjoy a lower average collection cost per worker. This type of economy from larger market share is due largely to the regulations that prevent employers and collectors from expressing their savings in lower prices.

Discussing whether allowing discounts for worker groups employed by a single employer is a good idea is important. One possibility is that an employer would offer incentives to its workers to choose a particular pension management company to save on administrative costs and that the employer's influence could be tainted by a conflict of interest. This danger can be managed by imposing an obligation on employers not to influence their employees to favor a particular pension management company, but allow them to encourage the selection of a single pension management company.

A third type of economy of scope may be realized by consolidating the forms employers use to pay taxes, pension contributions, unemployment insurance, workers' compensation, and mandatory health insurance into a single form, or at least into a unique collection process. However, this approach may also entail diseconomies of scope, because a mistake in processing one service may affect the others. In any case, this source of economies does not favor concentration of supply, but rather a larger scope of the service.

Fixed and Sunk Costs. Collection services also exhibit costs that are both fixed and sunk. This is because collecting contributions is a specialized activity quite different from, say, banking. The design of operations in countries where few employers use computers must deal with the fact that 5 to 10 percent of the raw data (incoming forms) contain errors, a much higher error rate than the one that banks can manage at low cost. The contribution processing system should detect and directly solve some of these errors and allow for consultations with employers to reconcile the rest. In this setting specialization pays off handsomely.

A specialized processing system can take advantage of the fact that the error can be reconciled within a few months without major damage, which is not true of banking. In large Chilean pension management companies, a major part of the error reconciliation and correction occurs later on during the massive processing stage. Further specialization gains can be realized by building a network of contacts with the subset of employers that use computers to connect to their accounting systems.

Large savings can also be realized by moving collection offices out of expensive financial districts into areas with lower rents, and by designing the tasks to be able to employ inexpensive personnel and avoiding the complex training needed by bank clerks, who must master a much larger variety of tasks. This know-how may reduce collection costs per form to less than one-third of the collection costs of a commercial bank.

Specialized collection technology exhibits two properties. First, most of the specialized know-how needed to reduce average costs is lost upon exit. This means that this is a sunk cost, the first condition for a natural monopoly. Second, there are economies of scale in developing the specialized know-how needed to reduce average costs. An investment in specialized error correction procedures is justified only when the system serves a large number of employers of similar size.

Given that the specialized technology has been developed in a particular country, its use in another region or country may occur at constant average cost. In other words, the economies of scale may be dynamic, not static, in the sense that they are present at the birth of the new technology, but disappear as more suppliers surpass the threshold of scale and invest in adapting the new technology. Once the specialized know-how becomes diffused, additional units of service can be rendered at constant average cost. Current experience in a variety of countries suggests that decreasing costs resulting from scale economies in collections continue up to 300,000 workers or some 30,000 employers, but this may represent just the past of the pension industry, not the future. For a small country there is a crucial difference between dynamic and static scale economies, because the former can be tapped by allowing competition among firms that have already made the investment in the specialized technology through their association with international firms. In contrast, static scale economies are out of reach for small countries.

The available information does not allow us to discard the hypothesis that there also exist significant scale economies in collection over the number of contributors and employers observed in small countries. For example, even though none of the Chilean pension fund administrators with fewer than 100,000 members decided to diversify into collection (because of the fixed cost of the specialized technology), this does not settle the issue of whether static or dynamic scale economies are present. This evidence may be representative of the past, when Chile was the only country with competitive pension management companies, or it may demonstrate the importance of static scale economies. Evidence of these scale economies may be seen in the fact that SERVIPAG, a specialized Chilean collection company that services financial companies, utilities, and small pension fund management companies, has not been challenged by large-scale entry of other firms into this market. However, this same evidence may be viewed as the result of restrictions on the entry of banks and pension fund administrators into this specialized business.

Economies of scale do obtain in a small country. Given such economies of scale both conditions for natural monopoly (sunk and fixed costs) would be present. If the relative size of these economies of scale were substantial, competition among pension management companies that are vertically integrated into collections would favor the largest ones at the local level. In a small country this process would lead to a concentrated market structure and higher charges and to concentration of the trustee function. Given the negative impact of this latter outcome on the political risk affecting pensions, there may be a case for the government to intervene in collections.

The required intervention would be to prohibit the vertical integration of collection and processing of contributions with the other functions. The gain from prohibiting vertical integration is that it prevents concentration of the trustee function; however, forced disintegration does impose costs. For example, looking in the membership archives held by the account manager allows a cheap solution to some types of errors while avoiding contact with the employer. Some of these savings can also be realized by a monopoly collector arranging to be in contact with the processing center of each pension management company.

Policy Options in Collecting and Raw Processing of Contributions. This subsection considers several options for organizing the provision of collections services given mandated disintegration of this service. The first policy option is a nationalized monopoly. This appears attractive in small countries that have a well-functioning system for collecting personal income taxes, because collections related to pensions can piggyback on that infrastructure. This has been tried in Argentina through the Income Tax Office (DGI), a government-run entity, and could be attempted in small countries such as Costa Rica that have a fairly well-functioning system for collecting personal income taxes. DGI charges US$4 per form for collections, and each employer receives just a single invoice. An important problem with this option is that a government collection agency may not have incentives to adopt the most cost-efficient technologies for collections, but rather may wish to offer more employment to relatives and political supporters. For example, DGI uses a lot of manual labor and has yet to adopt the new technologies. A second important problem is that the nationalized monopoly may charge a large monopoly margin not subject to regulation, which acts as a hidden, unlegislated tax on labor. These factors may explain why the price for DGI charges for collections is 4 times what Chilean banks charge and at least 12 times the cost of large, vertically integrated pension fund administrators.

A second option is to periodically auction off the collection service to the one or several providers that offer the lowest charge per form. However, this is vulnerable to renegotiation, because of the large sunk costs involved.

A third option is for a private monopoly subject to tariff regulation to provide collection services. Such an option presents substantial problems, because regulation is difficult to implement effectively when the costs of providing collection services are sensitive to technical change. In addition, contrary to the situation in electricity and telecommunications, expertise in regulating these entities is scanty.

A fourth option is for collection to be provided by a self-regulated, open, capital company, whose shareholders include the entities buying collection services, including the private pension management companies. The government's role would be reduced to imposing the obligation to allow entry on an equitable basis to new pension fund management companies and the obligation of charging all pension fund management companies for collection services on the same basis. The government would also have to prevent this self-regulating organization from serving as a cartel for its members by charging prices far in excess of its costs. On the positive side, the government could impose an obligation of confidentiality about contributors and pensioners, as well as corporate governance regulations that create incentives for efficient self-regulation by the collection company.

This last option appears to be the best for small countries that have no infrastructure in place for collecting personal income taxes. Sometimes a mixed approach may be attractive. Some of the activities included in collecting and processing contributions may be run separately. For example, the Peruvian Superintendency of Pensions runs the processing functions related to error management. Although currently the private pension management companies in Peru collect forms, they could do so through a cooperative.

Paying Benefits

If traditional banking technology is used, payment services are subject to total costs proportional to the number of beneficiaries, although the existence of infrastructure such as a network of automated teller machines can have a significant impact on these costs. Significant scale economies seem to exist in benefit payments within the range observed in small countries, for example, 100,000 pensioners in Bolivia. In addition, the gains from specialization in such services seem to be large because of widespread geographic coverage, few service hours per month, and the relatively small number of pensioners. Again, specialized know-how gives rise to sunk costs, which, combined with scale economies, create a kind of natural monopoly in smaller countries. The options discussed earlier for data collection would also apply to the payments function.

Capturing Data

Data processing in relation to contributions includes a specific activity called data capture, in which each individual line of a form is typed into a computer. This is generally considered a variable cost, because it is proportional to the number of contributors being processed. Each pension fund management entity can provide this type of service at similar cost regardless of the scale of operations; however, the cost does depend substantially on unit labor costs, so subcontracting this function to the lowest-cost provider, or even to an offshore provider, may be attractive. Contracting with firms abroad is now standard practice for processing credit card debits. Regulations should allow free subcontracting of this activity, particularly in small countries.

Administering and Processing Accounts

Account administration and processing includes investment accounting and the recalculation of individual account balances. This function is subject to substantial economies of scale in relation to the number of accounts administered and processed. The main fixed costs are specialized computer programming personnel, software, and equipment. In large pension management companies in Chile a major part of error correction and checking occurs at this stage. Accounting cost evidence from the Chilean market suggests that average processing costs may fall to a third of initial costs when the number of members rises from 200,000 to 1 million. Further evidence of economies of scale in processing is that small pension management companies in Argentina and Chile purchase processing services from a few major computer systems companies, such as IBM and the Chilean software company SONDA, that do not experience much competition.

IBM and SONDA also provide a number of pension-related services in a single standardized package, so a relatively small trustee company can obtain access to attractive average costs with little effort. These packages include most of the services present in the master trust arrangements used in Australia and the United States with two exceptions: custody and selection and control of portfolio managers.

The economies of scale in account administration and processing may seem problematic in small countries. For example, in Bolivia, where perhaps no more than 200,000 members are served and at least six different trustees must compete to limit political risk, private providers of processing services would be unable to realize the scale economies noted earlier if each pension fund administrator undertook these services in-house. More important, even contracting out account processing within Bolivia would not achieve these economies of scale.

These problems in account administration and processing in Bolivia could be solved by allowing trustees to subcontract account administration and processing abroad. For international trade to be effective, regulations must not impose special requirements on the types of reports or other uses of the information or define a specific processing method that creates fixed costs that will have to be shared throughout the country. In the Bolivian case, the key role for the government is to harmonize standards to permit international firms to offer processing services onshore or offshore. This will allow account processing functions not only to be privately supplied, but to be competitive in terms of cost. International companies specializing in information processing (EDS, IBM, SONDA) will compete to provide the service much more efficiently and at lower cost, passing along the economies of scale to Bolivian consumers.

Adopting New Technologies

The new electronic technologies, such as electronic data interchange, offer small countries a substantial reduction in the administrative costs of pension systems by permitting complete integration and dematerialization of many different pension services at once. Cost reductions can result from decreased documentation requirements and security checks needed to effect transfers of funds, transfers among entities managing pension fund investments, collections, benefit payments, and reporting to members about the status of their accounts. Such a system can also reduce costs by dematerializing these functions, which can be performed through direct computer entries at every stage of pension service provision. By means of electronic data interchange many of the processing functions can be transferred abroad, where economies of scale may be available at low cost.

This promise will materialize in a small country only if free trade in new computer technology is allowed and if a good telecommunications infrastructure is available. For many small countries this expectation may be premature. However, an important policy implication is that multilateral and other donors should actively seek to help small developing countries acquire this infrastructure.

Providing Client Services

The costs of providing client services depend on the quality of the service, including the variety and frequency of the services that must be provided. These costs generally do not exhibit scale economies. Quality of service varies with the frequency with which account statements must be sent to clients, the way in which returns must be calculated, and the degree to which the service provider is required to address individual consumers' requests in relation to their account. Achieving a specified quality of service does not require vertical integration of other functions. For example, SONDA offers an on-line connection to small Chilean pension fund administrators so that its customers can obtain details about their accounts from SONDA's computers in real time.

The problem with client services is that regulators may require an excessive quality of service. To allow costs to remain low, supervisory agencies should not require pension fund administrators to provide their clients with on-line facilities to answer their questions about statements of account, especially in small countries where telecommunications are expensive or unreliable.

Reporting and Regulatory Compliance

The costs of reporting to the supervisory agency depend on the frequency, quantity, and complexity of the reports required with respect to benefits, the investment portfolio, and financial statements and accounts. Real-time systems of control and off-site supervision of investment portfolios are also expensive. Thus reporting standards will determine some of the administrative work required of a pension management company. As this is a fixed cost, it generates economies of scale. Given the implications of scale economies in small countries, supervisory agencies in small countries should be particularly careful to justify the need for each required report.

In small countries, where imperfections in the domestic equity market are more likely than in large countries, regulations relating to minimum capital are more likely to generate a fixed cost. The conventional justification for requiring minimum capital from trustee pension management companies is to ensure their commitment to the market. However, the minimum capital that is justified may be much smaller if collection is separate and processing is subcontracted than if pension services are vertically integrated. Thus this aspect of prudential regulation design deserves special attention in small countries and is not independent of other aspects of pension reform.

The scale economies of many types of costs also depend on the type of regulation to which the pension management companies are subject. In Chile observers think that replacing the detailed regulation imposed by the superintendency with modem supervisory approaches, such as focusing on the quality of the internal control system rather than on each operation, reduced personnel needs by more than 60 percent. Hence the impact on scale economies is clear.

Managing Investment Portfolios

Unlike many of the services discussed so far, portfolio investment management services are not characterized by large sunk costs, with the possible exception of advertising costs associated with market penetration. In addition, investment management does not involve large economies of scale. This is why so many small firms have emerged in the United States and Europe to service the large market of portfolio investment management services for occupational pension funds.

For small countries separating the discussion of domestic and international portfolio management is useful. Regarding domestic portfolios, if the lack of independent interests is coupled with a small number of portfolio management firms, this could create the potential for price manipulation or conflicts of interest in domestic asset markets. The lack of liquidity in small countries' securities markets can permit irregularities in the valuation of domestic securities portfolios and create incentives for manipulation among market participants. This can increase the risk of fraud and insolvency for contributors to pension schemes. These problems can be tackled in three ways: (a) improve supervision of the domestic market, which is costly in terms of specialized human capital; (b) stimulate trading of domestic securities by domestic investors in foreign stock and bond markets to take advantage of their supervision; and (c) require that 40 to 50 percent of the investment portfolio be invested offshore in investment-grade securities.

Trustees in small countries must hire foreign managers to take care of their international portfolios. Direct cross-border provision of these services must be permitted. To reduce the burden on domestic regulators that wish to ensure that foreign managers are trustworthy, cross-border agreements between supervision authorities should make provisions for certification, and regulatory accounting principles should be harmonized.

Another problem in countries that want to copy the Chilean regulation requiring portfolio managers to post a performance bond of 1 percent of the assets under management is that the performance bond requirement is difficult to pass on to foreign portfolio managers. This problem results from a difference in format: if international managers do not perform, their contract is not renewed. Therefore a simple way to facilitate the subcontracting of international managers is to redefine the performance bond to be more easily understandable, such as "30 percent of the income of the pension management company, net of collection, processing, insurance, and administrative costs." An arrangement along these lines is needed in small countries because they rely heavily on subcontracted foreign portfolio managers.

A related problem appears when the regulations define a benchmark portfolio made up of domestic securities and then impose it on the international portfolio. To avoid delaying or blocking investment abroad, two options may be considered: (a) defining a different benchmark for each part of the total portfolio, and (b) defining a global benchmark that includes both domestic and international investments.

Providing Insurance

Insurance can be of two types: (a) short-term coverage, such as disability and survivorship or life coverage, which the trustee pension management company usually purchases on behalf of members; and (b) long-term coverage for longevity risk provided through annuities at the time of retirement. Small countries largely reinsure the short-term type of coverage abroad because of worldwide economies of scale in reinsurance. The second, longer-term insurance service is sold to individuals and is not characterized by large scale or scope economies, even in small countries.

In the provision of longevity insurance, advertising and information (established relationships with customers and reputation) can create important barriers to entry, which tend to increase concentration, political risk, and average charges. In small countries these problems are best solved by allowing cross-border provision of annuity insurance by certified insurance companies with a suitably supervised home office. To this end small countries should eliminate regulatory and legal barriers and harmonize insurance regulations to allow the local use of at least a few foreign insurance providers of annuities.

The lack of specialized human capital in small countries may justify changes to some aspects of the pension system. First, mandatory disability insurance requires establishing specialized medical commissions to assess disability claims. An option is to make this form of coverage available on a voluntary basis only via employers or individually. Second, technical information about mortality, expressed in life tables, will be less reliable in small countries because of their relatively greater international labor mobility. This problem raises the risk that life tables are wrong, which will induce life insurance companies to increase the price of annuities.[4]

Assessing Entry, Market Size, and Wage Levels

In small countries the privatization of pension service provision cannot be considered independently from the size of the market to be served (the number of individual accounts) or the level of wages of contributors. Market size can affect the desire of major foreign investors to compete through direct entry, especially when a vertically integrated industrial structure provides pension services. This kind of problem is best illustrated by the case of Bolivia. If no more than 200,000 active workers are contributing to individualized pension accounts and their monthly wages are about US$200 each, the annual flow of resources into privately managed accounts would be of the order of US$50 million. If a typical company obtains 25 percent of this market and commissions are 1.5 percent just for pension services (excluding insurance), the gross income before any costs would be US$2 million for a single company. The annual income for the whole industry would be of the order of US$10 million. Therefore the fixed and variable costs of competing against vertically integrated entities will make direct entry by foreign pension fund administrators unlikely, given the high sunk costs and scale economies noted earlier.

Under these circumstances, inducing competition in a small economy will require that pension services be unbundled (vertically disintegrated) so that entry can occur within each level of pension services or be provided through international subcontracting. What is clear is that the small size of the market will hinder foreign investment less in the provision of some aspects of pension services (for example, fund investment management services) than in others (for instance, collections).

Other Pension Policy Considerations

Preconditions for Successful Pension Policy

Financial supervision that improves the reliability and efficiency of voluntary saving and insurance by attacking market failures is a key element of successful pension policy. Countries that do not have the human capital or institutional infrastructure in place to deliver effective supervision should not have a national pension policy. If a developing country attempts to adopt a pension policy when it cannot develop the tools of pension policy or cannot expect them to be minimally effective, the social cost will be larger than the social benefit. In this case not having a national pension policy is a better option.

While this is an unfortunate outcome from the point of view of old-age security, it is certainly not detrimental to economic development. To understand this recall that the United States adopted its social security program as late as 1939, the Republic of Korea as late as 1988, and Australia as late as 1986–92, after each had become industrial countries. The United Kingdom did not mandate contributions for old-age pensions until 1908, well after the second industrial revolution. When the preconditions for a national pension policy are absent, a workable alternative is for the country to provide for old age through family support, community support, and occupational pension plans for some government employees (armed forces, police, judges). Such arrangements already exist in many small countries.

In a second group of small countries just a few of the tools of national pension policy operate efficiently, while the other tools cannot operate. A pension policy can still exist under such circumstances.

Protection for the Pension Saver

The conclusion derived from the previous subsection is that the identification of policy tools that can be used reliably in a given country is the critical input in support of a specific pension policy recommendation. The following paragraphs outline the preconditions for using the tools of pension policy.

Legal Framework. Policy governing the legal framework and supervision seeks to prevent fraud and abuse and minimize the risk of insolvency on the part of institutions providing voluntary saving and insurance products. This objective must be attained while creating adequate incentives for the efficient provision of financial services. A first precondition for using the tools of financial supervision is that the government must supply a reliable body of civil and commercial law to make enforcement effective. This must include a judicial system of reasonable quality to adjudicate conflicts between consumers and financial firms.

A second precondition is for the government to supply specialized financial sector laws and effective ongoing supervision of financial intermediaries such as banks, insurance companies, and securities markets. Many small countries find performing this function difficult, because it requires a substantial amount of specialized human capital.

As small countries may have difficulty meeting these two preconditions for effective supervision, an attractive option could be to allow international trade in these services, thereby relying on the financial supervision, financial sector laws, and even civil laws of larger countries. For example, financial contracts may be signed under the jurisdiction of another country, and financial firms may be required to be branches of licensed suppliers in well-supervised countries. In this way the residents of small countries would still have access to efficient, voluntary saving and insurance mechanisms. In the case of retail financial products where consumer protection is an issue, such as life insurance, the small country should require that the supplier be subject to the consumer protection of the larger country's laws for its domestic sales.

Voluntary Saving and Supervision. In cases where small countries allow domestic financial intermediaries to develop new financial instruments for voluntary saving for old age, the government should devote substantial effort to supervising these instruments, because foreign supervision will not apply. This is the case with the Costa Rican voluntary, individualized, defined contribution plans that both onshore and offshore banks offer to residents of other Central American countries, and with the Paraguayan pension plans.

The case of voluntary saving and insurance benefits offered by employers raises important consumer protection questions. In a setting with no fiscal incentives, employers may offer occupational plans to unsophisticated workers who do not realize the potential for fraud that such arrangements entail. For example, in defined benefit plans the employer may fail to build a fund, either directly by manipulation of the actuarial assumptions, or by failing to diversify investments away from the firm itself. The employer may also choose to reduce wage increases for those who are about to receive a pension and may dissolve the firm when the benefit expense becomes large. In defined contribution occupational plans the employer selects the fund manager, an arrangement that raises the danger that the employer will hire a manager whose affiliate firms provide subsidized loans to the employer at the cost of low performance of the workers' investment portfolio.

The solution to these problems is supervision and regulation of voluntary occupational plans; however, small countries with little specialized human capital may find that performing this function is difficult. Again, one option may be to rely on foreign infrastructure that outlaws voluntary occupational plans that fail to meet internationally recognized actuarial, disclosure, and regulatory standards. Although precedents are scarce, foreign supervisory bodies could be paid to supervise occupational pension plans in small countries. Alternatively, external supervisors could agree with an association of providers of voluntary saving and insurance mechanisms for old age that member firms put a self-regulatory framework in place as in New Zealand or South Africa, where external supervisors examine the safeguards imposed by the association (see Glaessner 1994).

Investment

Two critical areas in small countries are the extent of funding and international portfolio diversification. In each of these areas initial conditions present in a specific country have a significant impact on the optimal design of pension reform.

Funding. Funding refers to the type of backing of pension promises. Two types of backing are (a) apparent or explicit funding, that is, the extent to which pensions are backed by securities covered by the constitutional protection of property rights, as opposed to backing by legislated promises to pay benefits, which usually give rise to pay-as-you-go financing; and (b) ultimate funding, which is the extent to which pension promises are backed by outside physical assets, foreign assets, or both. Ultimate funding excludes government debt, which is backed by future tax collections, and also excludes consumer debt to the extent that it is backed by future earnings. The national saving rate will increase in response to pension reform only if it results in a greater degree of ultimate funding. An increase in explicit funding increases financial depth without an obvious impact on national saving. For example, if a pension system backed by legislated promises with pay-as-you-go financing is replaced by an explicitly funded system where all funds are invested in newly issued government bonds, national saving would not increase.

A pension system in which pension rights are covered by constitutional protection for property rights requires explicit funding. This is because, according to most constitutions, property rights over securities can be established much more finely than property rights over legislated promises to pay benefits in the future. One gain from this reform is that pension promises are made more secure, because their backing obtains constitutional protection for property rights. Another gain is associated with international portfolio diversification.

If the initial condition in the country is no mandatory system for private sector workers and the reform means that mandated contributions will begin to be imposed on them, then adopting both explicit and ultimate funding is advisable. If there is already an explicit funding regime, the recommendation is to maintain it and avoid any move toward pay-as-you-go financing. If the country is in a stage of mature pay-as-you-go financing, then the recommendation is to shift to explicit funding. This entails replacing government promises to back the pension institution's promises to individuals with newly issued government bonds or with shares in state enterprises to be held by the social security institutes. The interest paid by those bonds and equities will provide the social security institutes with the income they need to meet their promises to individuals. Finally, if the country is in a stage of immature pay-as-you-go financing, as most mandatory systems in the developing world are today, the recommendation is to shift immediately to explicit funding (see Valdés-Prieto 1996 for more details).

International Portfolio Diversification. For a small country international portfolio diversification allows both a large increase in expected returns and a large reduction of risk. The higher expected return allows a substantial reduction in the contribution rate required to finance the same benefits, which translates into a substantial gain for workers. As explained earlier, reducing the contribution rate is especially valuable in a small country because of its higher international labor mobility. In a large country where asset markets are sufficiently developed, the gains from international portfolio diversification are smaller because the domestic portfolio is already quite diversified. The prerequisite for international portfolio diversification is explicit funding.

To achieve the gains of international portfolio diversification, the social security institutes must rebalance their portfolios away from government debt and purchase private sector assets instead, mostly foreign assets. A massive unloading of government debt could produce problems in the domestic debt market of a large country; however, the impact would be much smaller in a small country, because foreign investors are available to acquire the government debt without requiring large increases in interest rates. Similarly, the potential balance of payments problems that can arise from a massive purchase of foreign assets by the social security institutes are much less significant in small countries, because foreign portfolio capital will flow in to buy the government bonds, thereby balancing the foreign exchange market.

The foregoing argument is subject to two provisos: (a) that some small countries have adopted policies that interfere with international capital flows, and (b) that the international financial community tends to invest little in small countries about which scant information is available. In such cases a move toward international portfolio diversification could bring about the problems predicted for larger countries. Therefore a precondition for successful pension reform in small countries in these circumstances is for them to abandon interference with international capital flows and to invest in promoting themselves to the international financial community. International organizations can play a valuable role by permitting initial access to international capital markets.

Observers sometimes argue that a reform toward explicit funding is insufficient because it fails to increase national saving rates, and therefore fails to reach a better endogenous growth path based on higher investment and its externalities. Some critics would prefer that a country move toward ultimate funding or backing by outside assets. However, in the case of a small country with an open capital account, the extra growth resulting from the effect of ultimate funding on savings accumulation is relatively less important than international portfolio diversification. This is because growth in a small country is more dependent on openness to international trade in goods, services, and factors of production than on domestic savings accumulation. Even though an increase in ultimate funding increases national savings, it does so at the expense of living generations. If this sacrifice is mandatory, it entails higher tax rates, fewer public goods, or both, which may be relatively harder to bear in small countries, where international factor mobility constrains the level of net tax rates relatively more than in large countries. The conclusion is that in small countries the critical pension reform is toward explicit funding, while the net gains of moving toward ultimate funding are more debatable than in large countries.

A common worry about pension systems is that they are vulnerable to local population risks, such as a drop in the local birth rate or an increase in domestic life expectancy. Explicit funding plus international portfolio diversification greatly reduces these risks in small countries. For example, consider the risk that population growth rate in a small country falls for a decade. If the pension benefits were backed by legislated promises alone (pay-as-you-go), the diversification task would be transferred to the local political system. Even if the political system reacted optimally from the perspective of intergenerational risk sharing, which would mean increasing the level of contributions and reducing benefits as soon as the birth rate begins to fall, each generation would bear substantial population risk. In practice, most political systems do nothing until contribution revenue actually drops, which is too late. By then the risk of a fiscal crisis becomes large, and that risk is worse in a small country, because it has little scope for increasing tax rates in response to high international factor mobility. Contrast this with the outcome when the pension system is explicitly funded and the portfolio is internationally diversified. In this case pension benefits are barely affected because the international capital market easily absorbs the population risks of any one small country, so contribution rates do not have to be altered. In sum, a shift to explicit funding significantly reduces the level of population uncertainty each generation bears.

Concluding Remarks

This chapter has taken a largely microeconomic perspective and has considered only the supply-side aspects of pension reform; thus it does not analyze important issues relating to the fiscal implications of pension reform and to demand issues in detail. Neither does the chapter focus on the many improvements that can be made to pay-as-you-go social security systems (for such improvements see World Bank 1994; Valdés-Prieto 1994). Because of fiscal and political reasons, these improvements in existing pay-as-you-go schemes need to be undertaken simultaneously or prior to pursuing privatization and moving toward funding. Finally, the analysis mentions, but does not focus in detail on, the design and regulation of occupational pension plans, nor on the voluntary, individualized, defined contribution schemes often found in small countries.

Pension reforms are complex to design. Implementation is even more demanding, because it must take into account how reforms will interact with existing pension policies and with related reforms in the areas of health, labor markets, securities and capital markets, privatization of nonfinancial companies, and housing finance. Moreover, these reforms raise issues in such areas as the political economy and the legal and constitutional rights of contributors and existing pensioners. Such issues would need to be carefully examined when implementing any of the recommendations in this chapter.

Some of the issues that deserve further investigation are the design of transitions at the fiscal, microeconomic, and political economy levels. In particular, all transitions in Latin America have resulted in the coexistence of new, privately managed, funded pension systems with the old pay-as-you-go financed and government-managed pension schemes. Countries such as Mexico are beginning to examine options that may not involve the coexistence of the two regimes. This coexistence has not been smooth in several instances; thus the analysis of such types of reforms will be particularly important in the future.

Notes

1. This calculation assumes a flat age-earning profile, 40 years of continuous contributions, and 20 years of retirement.

2. The suggestion that trustees be chosen by impersonal bidding made by Arrau and Bitran (1992) is not practical, because such bidding would be extremely vulnerable to adverse selection. In this context adverse selection means that some people would be disproportionately attracted to offer low bids, such as criminals, people willing to sell their decisions to rich business groups, and political administrators willing to use their power to obtain favors and contributions for their own parties. Although bidding coupled with adequate screening processes for checking trustees' background and qualifications could be employed in theory, trustees have never been chosen by bidding in any country.

3. The so-called master trustee is a vertically integrated pension services company that has a misleading name. It integrates all functions except that of sponsor or trustee, which has the final say about investment strategy and voting in shareholders' meetings. Given a board of trustees, that board can separately subcontract the portfolio managers, a custodian, a collection firm, and an account processing provider.

4. One way to keep these costs in check is to allow the use of the formula developed by the Teachers Insurance and Annuity Association College Retirement Equities Fund for self-insured annuities, whereby pensioners as a whole bear this risk (Greenough 1990).

References

The word *processed* describes informally produced works that may not be commonly available through libraries.

Arrau, P., and E. Bitran. 1992. "Introduccion de un Sistema Previsional de Capitalizacion Individual en Paraguay." Inter-American Development Bank, Washington, D.C. Processed.

Demsetz, H. 1968. "Why Regulate Utilities?" *Journal of Law and Economics* 11(1): 55–65.

Glaessner, T. 1994. "External Regulation Versus Self-Regulation: What Is the Right Mix? The Perspective of the Emerging Securities Markets of Latin America and the Caribbean." World Bank, Washington, D.C. Processed.

Godoy, O., and S. Valdés-Prieto. 1994. "Democracia y Prevision en Chile: Experiencia con Dos Sistemas." *Cuadernos de Economia* 31(93): 135–60.

Greenough, W. 1990. "It's My Retirement Money, Take Good Care of It: The TIAA-CREF Story." Philadelphia: University of Pennsylvania Press.

Holzmann, R. 1994. "Pension Reform Concept for Latvia." University of Saarland, Saarbrücken, Germany. Processed.

Mesa-Lago, Carmelo. 1991. "Portfolio Performance of Selected Social Security Institutes in Latin America." Discussion Paper no. 139. World Bank, Washington, D.C.

Mitchell, O., and P. L. Hsin. 1996. "Public Pension Governance and Performance." In S. Valdés-Prieto, eds., *The Economics of Pensions: Principles, Policies, and International Experience.* Cambridge, U.K.: Cambridge University Press.

Pontusson, J. 1984. *Public Pension Funds and the Politics of Capital Formation in Sweden.* Stockholm: Arbetslivscentrum.

Tiglao, R. 1990. "Pinched Pensions: Government Institutions Called on to Help Philippine Cash Squeeze." *Far Eastern Economic Review,* November 29.

Valdés-Prieto, S. 1994. "Earnings-Related Mandatory Pensions." Policy Research Working Paper no. 1296. World Bank, Washington, D.C.

_____. 1995. "Vendedores de AFP: Producto del Mercado o de Regulaciones Ineficientes?" Working Paper no. 178. Catholic University of Chile, Institute of Economics, Santiago.

_____. 1996. "Financing a Pension Reform towards Private Funded Pensions." In S. Valdés-Prieto, ed., *The Economics of Pensions: Principles, Policies, and International Experience.* Cambridge, U.K.: Cambridge University Press.

Willig, R. 1994. "Public Versus Regulated Private Enterprise." Proceedings of the World Bank's 1993 Annual Conference on Development Economics. *World Bank Economic Review* (suppl.).

World Bank. 1994. *Averting the Old Age Crisis: Policies to Protect the Old and Promote Growth.* New York: Oxford University Press.

9

Promoting Pension Funds

Gregorio Impavido, Alberto R. Musalem, and Dimitri Vittas

Publicly managed pension schemes cover an estimated 800 million people worldwide, or roughly one-third of the world's total labor force. More than 80 percent of these 800 million people are covered by mandatory, publicly managed, defined benefit schemes: nearly 50 percent by pay-as-you-go schemes and more than 30 percent by partially funded schemes. The rest of the workforce is covered by a mix of funded, public and private, defined benefit and defined contribution plans (Palacios and Pallares 2000). In mature countries with flat demographic structures, like Italy, Poland, and Slovenia, where universal coverage is the norm, public pension expenditures can reach 15 percent of gross domestic product (GDP), and the gross implicit pension debt can be as high as 400 percent of GDP, as in Brazil and Macedonia. In other countries population aging will increase pension cost pressures. The alternatives of encouraging massive immigration, delaying the compulsory retirement age, reducing benefits, or increasing contributions to maintain or improve the financial viability of unfunded schemes are politically unfeasible.

The result has been a move to reform pension systems. To date 25 to 30 countries have undertaken systemic pension reforms and many others are in the process of formulating reform proposals. The trends that have emerged from the recent wave of reforms are (a) more funding of current liabilities, (b) more private management of assets, (c) more defined contribution schemes, and (d) more individual responsibility and choice.

Countries of all sizes face financial pressures in their pension systems. Nearly half of all countries that have undertaken systemic reforms in recent years fall into the category of countries with small financial systems that are the object of this book. The question of how best to organize the private management of pension funds is a major policy issue in many such countries, specifically because of the small size of their financial systems.

Small countries cannot fully exploit economies of scale and scope in the provision of financial services. Moreover, their financial systems are often too small to generate much competition. Establishing payment systems and sound regulation and supervision are expensive. As a consequence, small financial markets are generally opaque, incomplete, poorly regulated, illiquid, prone to lack of competition and high concentration in the provision of services, inefficient, and characterized by relatively high transaction costs. Furthermore, because of their openness, small economies are more vulnerable to external shocks and are thus more volatile (see for example, Bossone, Honohan, and Long 2002; Easterly and Kraay 2000).

Despite the risks associated with financial openness, external financial liberalization can compensate for low economies of scale and scope. This implies allowing foreign ownership of intermediaries, participating in regional markets, and creating regional market and regulatory infrastructure. More fundamentally, it also implies sound and credible macroeconomic policies and exchange rate regimes that facilitate international integration. Small financial systems could integrate with larger systems as regions within a country integrate.

This chapter discusses the options available to policymakers for promoting pension funds in countries with small financial systems. It draws on the experience of both small and larger countries alike, and it analyzes the impact of adopting many of these different options on local financial markets. The first section of the chapter discusses the minimum prerequisites for the successful implementation of systemic pension reform. It then reviews the likely benefits of pension fund development in small financial systems for the rest of the financial sector. The third section considers the options available to policymakers in these countries for the institutional and regulatory structure of private pension funds. The final section draws conclusions.

Prerequisites for Pension Reform

If a fully fledged and efficient financial system and institutions were a prerequisite for the successful development of private pension schemes, few countries would be able to undertake systemic pension reform. However, the experience of countries in Eastern Europe and Latin America suggests that the practical prerequisites are far less demanding unless reformers aim to begin with a nearly perfect system with low costs, high returns, and highly diversified risk, an ideal that is both unnecessary and counterproductive. Although a fully fledged financial system with an entire array of efficient institutions and a full range of financial instruments would be desirable, the minimum that is required seems to be (a) a hard core of sound banks and insurance companies; (b) a long-term commitment by the government to pursue financial sector reforms signaled, among other things, by the implementation of sound macroeconomic policies; and (c) a long-term commitment to the creation of a sound regulatory and supervisory framework (Vittas 2000).

Sound Banks and Insurance Companies

Pension reforms are unlikely to succeed in countries in which the dominant banks and insurance companies are state owned, financially insolvent, and operationally inept. Banks need to inspire confidence that they will be able to collect loans, compensate depositors, and transfer funds to their rightful owners. Funded pensions typically hold some bank assets; thus weak banks threaten the security of retirement income (Mitchell 1998). Banks—as providers of services like collateral, clearing, and settlement—are also necessary for securities markets to grow and provide alternative pension fund investments. Insurance companies must also be financially sound and able to offer basic insurance policies. Nevertheless, the role of banks and insurance companies in the early years of pension reform can easily be exaggerated. Collecting contributions, allocating them to the accounts of their rightful owners, and directing accumulated funds to the selected asset management companies are parts of a major logistical exercise that requires considerable preparation and the development of computerized systems, but does not require fully developed, sound banking and insurance sectors.

For example, Chile's new pension system became operational in May 1981, but was not seriously affected by the collapse of the entire banking system in 1982–83. The pension funds placed their assets in government bonds and waited for the restoration of banking soundness before once again investing some of their funds in bank deposits (Vittas and Iglesias 1992). In Argentina and Mexico, the gyrations of their banking systems in the mid-1990s did not have an adverse effect on the fledgling pension funds that were operated, more often than not, by subsidiaries of the same banks that were facing serious financial problems.[1] Banks in Eastern

European countries, such as the Czech Republic and Hungary, have been in weak financial condition, but this has not impeded the implementation of systemic pension reform and the creation of funded pension pillars.

Effective segregation and safe custody of pension fund assets are two crucial aspects of pension funds operation that may explain the insulation of pension funds from the adverse effects of widespread banking crises. If asset segregation is to be ensured for any country, large or small, legislation mandating it is needed, together with a proactively effective supervisory agency to ensure compliance. Safe custody requires an institution with the financial, human, and technical resources to fulfill this function. In the absence of sound and efficient local banks two solutions are available. First, the central bank can perform this demanding function if it has the inclination and resources to do so. In Chile the central bank was the only authorized custodial institution for the pension system for at least its first 10 years (Ariztia 1998; Vittas and Iglesias 1992). Second, the country can take advantage of globalization and use one of the global custodial banks, such as State Street, Northern Trust, Morgan Chase, or Citigroup, to perform this function.[2] The development of central securities depositories and the concomitant dematerialization of marketable securities have made custodial services somewhat easier and more economical to offer, but the issue remains an important one.

Long-Term Government Commitment

Long-term government commitment to broad financial sector reforms is important, because pension reforms should be accompanied by extensive reforms in fiscal and financial policies, as well as in capital and labor markets. The absence of well-developed capital markets is not a major obstacle at the beginning of a pension reform program, because accumulated assets are initially small. However, capital market reforms are required in the long run, as pension fund assets are likely to continue to grow steadily over time. This is one of the main characteristics of long-term contractual savings. Countries have 5 to 10 years to reform their capital markets and expand the range of available financial instruments, but unless they succeed in these reforms, the funded pillar of the pension system will be unable to fulfill its fundamental objective, which is to help provide retiring workers with better and more secure pensions.

Emphasizing the need to develop local capital markets should not be construed as an argument for maintaining a closed capital account and for prohibiting pension funds from investing overseas. Such a policy could result in the mispricing of domestic assets, which would not contribute to the sound development of capital markets. Pension funds in countries with small financial systems, especially those with nondiversified economies, would need to invest in foreign securities to attain a satisfactory level of risk diversification for pensioners. The amount of overseas investment would depend on the extent of international integration (global or regional) of key sectors of the economy, such as banking, insurance, and utilities. However, pension funds would rarely invest all or almost all of their resources in foreign assets. The development of local markets for government bonds, mortgage bonds or mortgage-backed securities, leasing and factoring facilities, and small and medium enterprise and venture capital finance would be important to provide efficient outlets for the resources of pension funds that would be invested locally (as discussed later, this argument is linked to the home bias exhibited in the investment policies of pension funds in most countries). At the same time, the development of fully funded pensions will spur the growth of these markets by generating a demand for long-term assets.

Governments signal their long-term commitment by adopting sound and credible macroeconomic policies. Institutional investors cannot survive in a volatile macroeconomic environment even if indexed instruments are used. Fiscal policies must be prudent. As long as the level of nominal debt is too high, the credibility of the government's anti-inflationary stance would be undermined and long-term maturities would be difficult to attain (Missale and Blanchard 1994). The credibility of macroeconomic policies would also suffer if pension fund reserves and other types of contractual savings were used as captive sources of government funding. Pension funds can have a beneficial impact on government finances and the development of the local financial system by lengthening debt maturities and lowering risk premiums. Realization of these benefits depends, however, on avoiding extensive reliance on pension fund captivity, which in the end will be costly to both contributors and taxpayers.

Finally, the adoption of sound macroeconomic policies and the existence of sound banks and insurance companies would allow small countries to keep their capital accounts open and permit free trade of international financial services. This would allow small countries to overcome many of the obstacles to systemic pension reform that stem from their small size.

Sound Regulation and Supervision

Governments should also be committed to the creation of a sound and robust supervisory and regulatory framework. This does not necessarily mean that the existence of a sophisticated and effective supervisory authority is a necessary prerequisite for the implementation of systemic pension reform. Regulation and supervision involve sunk costs and need developing together with the appropriate institutions. However, a minimum level of regulation and supervision should be in place to ensure that only qualified institutions obtain licenses, that contributions are paid in a timely manner, and that contractual terms are enforced. Over time the supervisory agency could develop all its other functions, including creating a strong capability for undertaking off-site surveillance, conducting on-site inspections, or contracting out these or any other functions.

Benefits for Small Financial Systems

Countries with small financial systems generally display different degrees of integration with the rest of the world and vary in terms of the quality of their macroeconomic policies and banking and insurance sectors. These differences affect their ability to benefit from pension reform. Small financial systems can be grouped into three categories: (a) those that are incomplete, but the segments that operate are sound and are associated with high per capita income, credible macroeconomic policies, and open capital accounts (with close, but not perfect, substitution between domestic and international financial instruments); (b) those that are incomplete, but the segments that operate are predominantly unsound and stagnant and are associated with low per capita income, noncredible macroeconomic policies (caused, for instance, by a long history of macroeconomic imbalances), and closed capital accounts; and (c) those that fall between these two extremes.

The first category, demonstrated, for example, by Cyprus, Iceland, Malta, and Mauritius, offers the best case for successful implementation of systemic pension reform. Several reasons account for this, namely:

• Contractual savings is a luxury financial service that is demanded when a country has high rather than low per capita income. This is because with a high per capita income the time preference or discount rate is lower, thereby increasing the value of purchasing coverage for future contingencies. In addition, in countries where family ties are stronger, self-insurance within the family reduces demand for external insurance.

• Credible macroeconomic policy provides an enabling environment for the development of long-term financial instruments, including contractual savings.

- Sound banks provide a vehicle for channeling long-term savings as long-term loans to borrowers such as the government, enterprises, and individuals, even when financial markets are incomplete.
- Open capital accounts do not force pension funds and other contractual savings institutions to invest solely in the local market.

Systemic pension reform in countries with small and incomplete, but sound, financial systems could result in several benefits, even if only some of their resources were invested locally. First, it could increase the options available to citizens and enterprises for obtaining sound coverage against contingencies (for example, longevity, death, unemployment). Second, it could increase the supply of long-term savings, thereby promoting financial deepening and innovation and improving financial risk management. Third, it could increase the national saving rate. All these changes would foster economic growth and welfare.

The development of pension funds and other contractual savings institutions, supported by adequate regulation, supervision, and tax treatment, could provide incentives for increasing demand for these products beyond what could have been the case through offshore purchases of similar products. The higher demand could trigger the establishment of local companies as well as subsidiaries or branches of foreign providers of such products. The industry's location within the country may create opportunities for investing in the country rather than overseas by increasing investors' knowledge about local markets. In addition, the presence of pension funds and insurance companies may encourage the creation of domestic venture capital funds, which could identify investment opportunities that would otherwise not have been seized. Even where contractual savings institutions are not bound by rigid rules about the allocation of investments, but instead are regulated by what is known as the "prudent expert" rule, their investments will consist of long-term deposits in local and foreign banks; capital market instruments, namely, government and corporate bonds, asset-backed securities, and company shares; and small equity investments in domestic and foreign venture capital funds and in leasing and factoring companies. Investments in company shares would likely be effected and traded abroad, as the local economy would be too small to develop an efficient local stock exchange; nevertheless, the benefits of easier access to equity finance for local companies would still accrue.

Mandatory contributions to pension funds could increase the national saving rate, but only if some members of the population do not have sufficient access to credit (Baillliu and Reisen 2000). (With perfect access to credit they would not need to save more in total, as they could use borrowing to smooth out their consumption over their life cycle, despite having made the mandatory pension contributions.) In addition, the national saving rate would increase if governments did not use these funds as a captive source of finance. The development of pension funds and other contractual savings institutions would foster growth, because they have the potential to increase national saving, and hence investment. In addition, these institutions would require lower liquidity and risk premiums because of their long-term liabilities, thereby reducing the cost of capital, which in turn would increase investment and foster growth. Furthermore, the development of long-term savings would reduce borrowers' refinancing risk while funding contingent liabilities. Also banks would be able to lend long term while reducing their term transformation risks. The improvement in risk management would reduce the country risk premium and interest rates, which will foster investment and growth. Finally, the development of long-term savings will flatten the term structure of interest rates, thereby encouraging entities to undertake investment projects with longer maturities. As such projects have a higher rate of return, they would also foster economic growth.

Furthermore, mandatory funded schemes tend to promote the development of securities markets, especially in countries with closed capital accounts and strong legal frameworks (Impavido, Musalem, and Tressel 2002b).[3] The development of contractual savings in shallow financial markets stimulates stock market development, though there may also be a reverse causality (Catalan, Impavido, and Musalem 2000). It also increases competition in financial markets as evidenced by reduced bank spreads (Impavido, Musalem, and Tressel 2002c). Furthermore, the development of contractual savings helps reduce output volatility, because it increases the resilience of banks and enterprises to interest rates and demand shocks by improving their financial structure. It also reduces refinancing risks by lengthening the maturity of debts and improves resilience to shocks by favoring equity finance relative to debt finance. In bank-based financial systems the development of contractual savings increases firms' debt to equity ratios, but increases the maturity of their debt. By contrast, in market-based financial systems it reduces firms' debt to equity ratios (Impavido, Musalem, and Tressel 2002a). Finally, the development of contractual savings is associated with greater resilience to banking system credit and liquidity risks (Impavido, Musalem, and Tressel 2002c). Developed financial markets, in turn, are crucial for sustainable and high economic growth (Levine 1999; Levine, Loayza, and Beck 2000).

The second group of countries, those with chronic macroeconomic imbalances and other limitations, provide little room for the development of pension funds and other contractual savings institutions. Long-term saving instruments cannot prosper in a macroeconomic environment of high and volatile inflation, while contractual savings are unaffordable when per capita incomes are low. Furthermore, these countries' financial systems are limited to banking institutions, which are usually weak. They also tend to have closed capital accounts, which prevents pension funds from investing abroad. Thus before trying to develop contractual savings institutions, the authorities should focus on establishing a credible long-term macroeconomic framework and strengthening bank prudential regulation and supervision.

As for the intermediary category of small financial systems, the situation varies from country to country. Countries in this group may have a credible macroeconomic policy, a relatively sound banking system, and an open capital account; however, they are likely to have incomplete financial markets (underdeveloped securities and mortgage markets and insurance and pension sectors) and low to medium per capita income. While these countries meet the prerequisites for implementing systemic pension reform, their low to medium per capita income would impede a rapid expansion of contractual savings. Initially, the portfolios of pension funds and other contractual savings institutions are likely to be placed primarily in government bonds and bank certificates of deposit. In addition, they might have small holdings of company shares and foreign securities, and possibly of leasing companies. Gradually, as financial markets develop, investment regulations should allow more diversified portfolios by permitting larger investments in shares, foreign securities, corporate bonds, and asset-backed securities and small shares in venture capital companies.

Figure 9.1 shows changes in the investment allocation of Chilean pension funds' financial assets. In 2001 the pension funds had around 17 percent of their financial assets in cash and long-term deposits, 43 percent in bills and bonds, 10 percent in shares, 13 percent in foreign securities, and 15 percent in other securities (mainly mortgage notes). Once investments in stocks were authorized and investment limits on specific assets were relaxed, the Chilean pension funds, which were established in 1981, gradually reduced their holdings in cash, deposits, and debt and increased the proportion of assets in stocks. At the start of Chilean pension reform investment regulations allowed up to 100 percent in government securities, up to 60 percent in corporate bonds, and up to 70 percent in each of the following categories: mortgage-backed securities, letters of credit, or fixed-term deposits. As the market developed, the government relaxed these regulations to permit investments in company shares (first allowed in pension fund portfolios in 1985), mutual

Figure 9.1 Portfolio Allocation of Chilean Pension Funds, 1981–2001

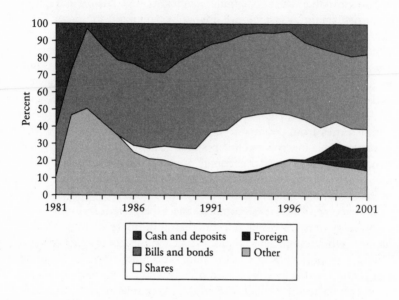

Source: World Bank contractual savings database.

funds, real estate funds, venture capital funds, securitized credit funds, foreign securities, and hedging instruments.

In summary, countries with a minimum core of sound banks and insurance companies and with sound macroeconomic conditions are likely to benefit from the development of pension funds and other contractual savings institutions. Gains from financial sector development will initially be concentrated in development of the government bond market and long-term lending through banks. At the next stage benefits would derive from the development of corporate bond markets and asset-backed securities, but at a later stage the equity market will be complicated by the country's small size.

Options for Pension Fund Development

Countries with small financial systems generally have small capital markets. As Glaessner and Valdés-Prieto (chapter 8 in this volume) note, the small scale of these countries' capital markets means they have few profitable and liquid assets in which funds can be invested. Such countries are characterized by a relative scarcity of human capital that generally leads to poor regulation and supervision. In addition, because of their small populations these countries have a relatively small number of contributors, which reduces the economies of scale in the operation and regulation of pension systems. This section discusses the options available to policymakers who wish to reform pension systems in this type of environment.

Alternative Institutional Arrangements

An important question facing pension reformers concerns the institutional setup of a fully funded pension pillar. Should they authorize only one institution to manage the funds so as to maximize economies of scale and ensure the same net returns for all workers, at least all workers of the same generation or cohort? Or should the centralized funding system offer limited investment options to members and outsource fund management through a bidding process? Or should the reformers authorize several institutions to encourage competition, innovation, and efficiency, but at the risk of duplication of services and the higher costs involved with a smaller scale of operations? In the latter case should they authorize specialized institutions with specialized funds or should they introduce special retirement accounts and allow all financial institutions to offer them?

Many authors have addressed these issues (see Dowers, Fassina, and Pettinato 2001 or Glaessner and Valdés-Prieto in this volume and the references therein), and different countries have experimented with different approaches. The single fund approach exists in many countries in the form of a public fund, either a national provident fund operating a defined contribution plan or a partially funded social security corporation operating a defined benefit plan. Among the former, the Central Provident Fund of Singapore has an excellent operating record, although the investment returns offered to account holders have been low. Workers are allowed to withdraw funds for housing purposes, with the remaining funds being invested by two other government agencies, the Singapore Monetary Authority and the Government of Singapore Investment Corporation. The investment returns of the latter corporation have probably been high given the excellent economic record of Singaporean public corporations; however, this corporation's accounts are not available for public scrutiny, and little is known about its overall performance (Asher 2001; Vittas 1993).

The performance of the national provident funds in India, Malaysia, and Sri Lanka and of the social security organizations in The Gambia and Jordan have been acceptable, combining reasonably low operating costs with positive real investment returns. Yet even if these funds deliver positive real rates of return, these rates almost always fare badly compared with wage growth, and hence can provide only modest income replacement (Iglesias and Palacios 2000, part I). By contrast, the national provident funds of several African countries and the social security organizations of some Latin American countries have suffered from disastrous financial results, obtaining highly negative real returns over long periods.

At the other end of the spectrum is Kotlikoff's (1994) proposal for all countries, especially those with underdeveloped financial systems: hire a multinational financial group to manage the assets of accumulated funds and require it to invest passively in a world index fund. A periodic bidding process would ensure a low asset management fee, while use of the world index would maximize risk diversification and benefit from the high returns obtainable in equity markets.

The Kotlikoff approach allows for age-specific portfolio allocations and has the advantage of avoiding massive marketing costs while offering the same returns, at least to all workers of the same cohort. Yet despite its intellectual appeal, this approach has yet to be adopted by any country, or even by any of the thousands of company pension plans in the United States and other Anglo-American countries. While a growing number of large company pension plans are opting for passive investment strategies, they tend to focus on national markets and have avoided allocating all their funds to a world index fund. This may reflect dissatisfaction with the construction of the world index or the well-known home bias that characterizes the operations of pension funds in most countries (Reisen 1995), but until some of the larger or more advanced countries adopt this solution, smaller countries are unlikely to do so.

The pension plan that comes closest to the Kotlikoff proposal is the U.S. federal Thrift Savings Plan, instituted in the mid-1980s for federal government employees in the United States. This initially mandated the use of three indexed funds (specializing in equities, bonds, and money market instruments), although two more funds (specializing in small caps and international stocks) were added in 2000. The Thrift Savings Plan hires asset managers after an elaborate bidding process that contains extensive safeguards for ensuring an unbiased selection process. The plan's early experience has been encouraging. It has earned market rates of return on highly diversified portfolios, while its gross expense ratio has declined steadily as the fund's assets have grown, from an average of 0.67 percent of funds in 1988 to 0.07 percent in 1999 (Hustead and Hustead 2001).[4] Note, however, that even in this case the plan does not mandate the use of a world index fund, but rather tracks U.S. securities markets.

Some countries do have public pension funds that have moved in the direction of passive investment policies resembling the use of a world index approach, with the most prominent examples being Canada, Ireland, and Norway. In most of these countries, however, public pension funds represent a fraction of accumulated assets. Moreover, the approaches are new, and the extent to which they will be able to meet their objectives and resist political interference in their investment policies remains to be seen.

Most countries that have implemented systemic pension reforms that involve the creation of mandatory or voluntary fully funded pension pillars have followed policies that fall between these extremes. Bolivia, for example, has adopted a system closer to the centralized system of fund management by organizing an international bidding process for the award of a small number of licenses. After a protracted process it has selected two companies led by Spanish banks that satisfied the eligibility criteria (von Gersdorff 1997). The criteria mainly emphasized international expertise in operating pension plans and individual accounts. Note that the two Spanish banks that were awarded the two licenses, Banco Bilbao Vizcaya and Argentaria, later merged, creating a monopoly situation in the Bolivian pension market. The Bolivian authorities resolved this impasse by arranging for the sale of one of the pension funds to Zurich Finance.

The Bolivian case underscores that institutional structures are not immutable, and that if anything, they are in a constant state of flux. In Chile 13 pension fund administration companies, known as *administradoras de fondos de pensiones* (AFPs), were initially authorized when the system started in 1981. Two of these companies merged early on. The 12 companies that existed during the 1980s employed fewer than 3,000 agents and were able to recruit most of the workers who were required to participate in the system.[5] After suffering large losses during the first five years of the new system, AFPs became highly profitable in the late 1980s and attracted considerable new entry. By the early 1990s the number of AFPs had increased to 21, which led to a massive expansion in the number of selling agents from less than 3,000 in the 1980s to more than 15,000 by 1994 (Acuna and Iglesias 2001; Vittas 1995). New companies hired agents in an attempt to lure workers from existing AFPs, while existing companies were forced to fight back by expanding their own sales forces. An undesirable outcome of the growth in the number of companies was a vast increase in marketing costs, which reached two-thirds of total operating costs, and an explosion in account switching. At its peak, the annual volume of account transfers involved one out of every two active accounts.

Few of the new companies were able to reach critical mass. Most eventually withdrew from the market, either by being taken over by other AFPs or by closing down. The liquidation of a small number of companies proceeded smoothly without any financial losses for the workers who had accounts with the liquidated companies. By the end of 2001 only seven AFPs remained. The Herfindahl index of concentration, measured by the size of fund assets, initially fell from 0.217 in 1981 to 0.125 in 1994, but subsequently rose to 0.207 in December 2000 (Acuna and Iglesias 2001).

The size of the national market should be a determinant of the optimal number of independent pension funds in countries that opt for open, nonemployer funds. Thus among reforming countries Colombia, El Salvador, and Peru have authorized a small number of funds (Queisser 1998). Even so, subsequent mergers resulted in increased consolidation, and El Salvador now has three funds and Peru has five. Argentina and Mexico started with a larger number of funds, 25 and 17, respectively, but a wave of mergers has reduced the number of funds in these countries as well. At the latest count Argentina had 13 and Mexico had 11.

In Eastern Europe, Hungary started with 270 active funds in its voluntary system in 1994. Even after consolidation, the voluntary pillar still had 160 funds in 1999 (Rocha and Vittas 2002; Vittas 1996). The Czech Republic initially authorized 44 funds, but the number has since fallen to 20. The Czech Republic is the only country where the liquidation of failed pension funds has resulted in financial losses for workers; however, the impact on workers has been mitigated given that the losses have not exceeded the contributions paid by the government. In the compulsory pillars of Hungary, Kazakhstan, and Poland the number of funds has been much smaller, though at 25, 16, and 19, respectively, it has been higher than the number of surviving funds in Latin American countries. This implies considerable scope for further consolidation in these countries' pension systems.

In contrast to the countries of Eastern Europe and Latin America that have undertaken systemic pension reform in recent years, a plethora of employer-based pension funds characterizes the pension systems of countries of the Organisation for Economic Co-operation and Development with large private pension pillars. The United States has more than 700,000 funds and the United Kingdom has more than 200,000 (Rocha, Gutierrez, and Hinz 2001). Australia reports well over 100,000 funds, although the vast majority of these are so-called "mom and pop" funds that cover owners of small firms and a selected number of employees and are exempt from the regulatory rigors imposed on employer, industry, and open funds. Switzerland has more than 11,000 funds, but of these only about 4,000 have affiliated members and function like traditional funds.[6]

Employer funds incur lower marketing and operating costs than independent funds, because they do not need to engage in expensive advertising and pay high commissions to selling agents, and because their operating system can piggyback onto the preexisting company payroll system. Employer funds, unlike public funds, also tend to have a satisfactory level of investment performance, especially in countries that have not imposed quantitative restrictions but have relied on the so-called prudent expert approach (Davis 1998).

Workers covered by employer funds face different problems than those covered by independent funds. If the fund operates a defined benefit plan, there are restrictions on eligibility, vesting, and portability of pension rights (Vittas and Skully 1991), while the security of promised benefits depends on the continued solvency and integrity of the sponsoring employers (Bodie 1990; Bodie and Merton 1992). Initiatives to tighten the regulations covering these aspects of employer pension funds have resulted in an accelerated conversion of employer funds from defined benefit to defined contribution plans. This trend has been most pronounced in Australia, New Zealand, and South Africa, but is now spreading to other countries with a predominance of defined benefit plans.

In the case of defined contribution plans, large employers tend to operate efficient funds or to negotiate with specialized financial institutions that offer investment and other services on advantageous terms. Small employers, however, tend to sponsor plans that incur high operating costs and/or have low investment returns, either because small employers have weaker negotiating powers or because they are offered advantageous terms on other types of financial services.[7] Thus the record of employer funds is more mixed than may appear at first sight. Unfortunately, the lack of timely, transparent, and comprehensive data has impeded a thorough analysis of this issue even in countries such as Canada, Switzerland, the United Kingdom, and the United States, where employer pension funds have long been a dominant feature of the pension system.

The new Swedish approach involves a central public agency for collecting contributions, maintaining individual account records, and paying benefits with a decentralized asset management system. Workers have the right to direct their funds to several hundred authorized mutual funds (Palmer 2000). The latter receive the total funds allocated to them by workers but do not know the identity of their customers. This system of blind accounts offers few incentives for direct selling, and marketing expenses are limited to the creation of a brand name. Unlike as in Chile, the fee schedule is heavily regulated by the central agency (James, Smalhout, and Vittas 2001; James and others 1999). The system is highly complex and its introduction experienced considerable delay. Its success depends on the presence of a highly efficient central agency and robust and effective regulation and supervision of the participating mutual funds. Nevertheless, it is a promising innovation that moves in the direction of regulated, constrained choice.

This brief overview of different countries' experiences indicates that the institutional structure of the pension system depends on its basic design. Countries that rely on closed, employer-based funds tend to have a much larger number of funds than countries that rely on open, nonemployer funds. Employer funds avoid marketing costs and enjoy some economies of scope (and of scale for large employers), but their performance depends on the solvency and integrity of employers as sponsors of pension plans. The record seems to be positive for large employers' pension funds, but somewhat mixed for the smaller firms' plans.

Countries that rely on open, nonemployer funds tend to experience a consolidation process that results in the survival of only a small number of funds. A consolidated and highly concentrated pension system based on a small number of open funds enjoys economies of scale and may avoid excessive marketing costs, but it poses a serious policy challenge: how to ensure that competitive and efficient services continue to be offered. This problem is exacerbated in small economies, where the small size of the market already inhibits competition. One solution could be to allow employers to opt out of the system by permitting plans sponsored by groups of employers. Another solution would be a centralized fund management scheme that gives members investment options and outsources fund management, for example, the Thrift Savings Plan in the United States and the new Swedish system. However, the issue of how much to invest offshore so as to offer contributors greater possibilities for portfolio diversification remains, particularly for small countries.

Centralized Versus Decentralized Services. Services like the collection of contributions, data processing, maintenance of records and accounts, channeling of funds to asset managers, and payment of benefits are likely to benefit from significant economies of scale (Glaessner and Valdés-Prieto, chapter 8 in this volume; James, Smalhout, and Vittas 2001; James and others 1999). Several countries have tried to lower the operating costs of the funded pension pillar by mandating the use of a central agency. Many commentators have long pointed to the cost benefits of using a centralized agency, citing the excellent operating record of Singapore's Central Provident Fund (Asher 2001; Vittas 1993). Several countries, including Argentina, Costa Rica, Hungary, Kazakhstan, Mexico, Poland, and Uruguay, have tried to avoid Chile's example and have mandated the use of central collection agencies. However, almost all these countries made the serious mistake of assigning this important function to pre-existing public institutions with long records of inefficiency and incompetence. The result, as exemplified by Kazakhstan's and Poland's experiences, has been a long period of lost records, unaccounted-for money, misdirected funds, asset management companies that could not tell their customers where their money had gone, and workers who did not know if their employers had forwarded the contributions withheld from their salaries to the central agency (see Hausner 2002 for the Polish experience).

Mexico seems to be the only reforming country that has assigned this function to a central clearing agency jointly owned by private sector institutions. This agency's record appears to be better than that of the central public agencies of Poland and other countries, but in Mexico the new agency was built on the lessons of the previous, ill-fated program of 1992 (Grandolini and Cerda 1998). No other country seems to have come anywhere near Singapore's excellent operating record.[8]

Glaessner and Valdés-Prieto (chapter 8 in this volume) note that the small size of the market for pension services in small countries limits the interest of foreign direct investors in providing such services locally. The total revenues in terms of commission fees could be much less than US$10 million per year in countries with fewer than 500,000 active contributors and wage rates of less than US$500 per month. In such cases, major foreign companies would have little interest in investing directly in setting up a local branch or agency.

Whenever the small size of a country does not justify the capital costs that characterize some pension services, it might be necessary to allow foreign firms to centralize these services in a foreign location, where production costs could be lower and provided that communication services are efficient and data privacy can be ensured. Several large financial groups already use shared local services in their operations in different countries. For instance, the pension fund operated in the Czech Republic by the Internationale Nederlanden Group (ING) shares many services with the local subsidiary of Nationale Nederlanden, the insurance arm of ING, while the investment of funds is subcontracted to the local ING asset management company. Using centralized services in another country would reduce operating costs further, both because of greater economies of scale and because of the location of such centralized services in countries with lower labor costs.

Allowing the subcontracting of services in the open market and the use of cross-border providers would permit a more efficient unbundling of services and the emergence of greater competition in specific services, such as asset management, where economies of scale may be less dominant. In this way, the markets for the provision of pension services would become more contestable and would limit the potential adverse effects of the growing concentration of these markets (Dowers, Fassina, and Pettinato [2001] also advocate this approach).

Financial Expertise. The main rationale for subcontracting is that countries with small financial systems have small populations, and hence are likely to have a small pool of human capital with the required expertise to operate pension funds efficiently. When Chile initiated its new system no foreign companies were involved. As the rules did not allow participation by banks, several of the early AFPs were set up by trade unions (despite the government's opposition) and trade associations (the association of construction companies established Habitat, one of the most successful AFPs). Foreign companies entered the system in the early 1980s, probably in response to the problems the new pension system had experienced early on.[9] Bankers Trust acquired a controlling stake in Provida, the largest company in the system; Aetna Insurance acquired a controlling stake in Santa Maria; and in a joint venture with the Bank of Boston, which is now part of Fleet Boston, American International Group acquired a controlling stake in Union. Bankers Trust sold its stake in Provida at a big profit in the early 1990s, benefiting from its success, while American International Group and Fleet Boston withdrew from the market after failing to gain a significant market share.[10] Today the AFP system is dominated by two Spanish banks (Banco Bilbao Viscaya Argentaria, which has bought a controlling stake in Provida in recent years, and Banco Santander Central Hispano in Summa Santander), an American bank (Citibank in Habitat), a Canadian insurance company (Sun Life in Cuprum) and an American insurance company (Aetna in Santa Maria).

Other Latin American countries that reformed their pension systems more than 10 years later have allowed, even encouraged, foreign participation in their private pension pillar. In some cases Chilean pension funds played a prominent role, for example, in El Salvador and Peru. In other cases foreign banks and insurance companies submitted applications in joint ventures with large local institutions. In Argentina, when the system was set up in 1994 the four or five largest *administradoras de fondos de jubilaciones y pensiones* were joint ventures by foreign and local institutions (Vittas 1997).

In the Czech Republic and Hungary, the foreign presence was not very large at the launch of the voluntary pillars in 1994, but the presence of foreign institutions grew over time. Foreign institutions now control more than 85 percent of the assets of pension funds in both countries. The growing foreign presence was linked to the consolidation of the banking and insurance sectors and the privatization of large local institutions by selling them to foreign strategic investors (Rocha and Vittas 2002).

When Hungary introduced its mandatory pillar in 1998, foreign banks and insurance companies held a dominant stake in the small number of mandatory funds that were authorized. Foreign institutions were also present at the establishment of Poland's mandatory pillar. In Argentina, and more recently in Mexico, the sale of large private banks and insurance companies to foreign strategic investors has resulted in a consolidation and expansion of the already significant presence of foreign banks and insurance companies in the pension system.

Reputable foreign institutions benefit from a number of operational advantages. They know how to operate systems with a large number of individual accounts efficiently, they have experience in cross-selling and in exploiting economies of scale and scope, they have well-established expertise in asset management, and they are in a better position to resist government pressure and political interference in their day-to-day operations. They are also better able to integrate their local operations with their global activities and, by implication, with global markets. Finally, during the course of their activity foreign institutions train local staff and help improve skills.

However, as Bossone, Honohan, and Long (2002, p. 113) put it, "the easy equation 'foreign equals good'" is not always valid. The authors make this comment in relation to foreign banks' strategic investments in Hungary, where not all the purchasers were prime institutions and where some were suspected of money laundering. However, even in the absence of criminal activities, the record of foreign institutions is far from stellar. For instance, the performance of pension funds owned by foreign institutions has been erratic, especially in Eastern Europe. Investment returns and operating fees have been unremarkable, the quality of service has left much to be desired, and the expected contribution toward creating a competitive and efficient system has been less than expected. Nevertheless, as in the case of banking and insurance, foreign pension funds have been able to operate with fewer problems, have not engaged in fraudulent or imprudent activities, and have taken steps to enhance their operating and investment efficiency. Those institutions that have used significant management resources and have placed local nationals in key management positions have performed better than those that have adopted a passive approach and have relied on expatriate management.

Countries with small and underdeveloped financial systems that engage in pension reform need to invite reputable foreign banks, insurance companies, and asset managers to play an active and central part in establishing the new private pillars. Ideally, foreign institutions should be encouraged to join forces with local groups that know the local markets and can help them overcome any public opposition to the reform program. However, when procuring financial expertise from abroad, small countries need to be particularly careful in allowing only highly reputable institutions to service their market. Highly reputable companies also have the incentive to perform up to expectations, as their reputation costs are high.

Moreover, by attracting reputable foreign companies reforming countries would reduce the costs of supervision, which may take time to develop to meet adequate standards. Reforming countries usually also need to enhance their prudential supervision, competition regulation, and market conduct regulation as they reform their pension systems. Reputable foreign companies are usually based in industrial market economies with strong home country regulation. Such a company could provide the host country with a transition period during which it updates its regulatory and supervisory systems while the company's home country carries out effective regulation and supervision. International regulators are increasingly sharing information about questionable international companies. Given such a framework, the host country needs to develop strong links with the home country's supervisory authority and sign a memorandum of understanding in relation to the exchange of such information.

Fiduciary Responsibility of Pension Fund Managers

Governments in developing countries often see pension funds and contractual savings as a captive source of finance for fiscal deficits or targeted industries. If not a direct alternative to debt monetization, they often see pension funds and contractual savings as a pool of funds for "developing" the economy. This forced development often means direct government control of asset management and direct investment in target industries, housing, and failing banks. Another tool widely used to achieve this forced development is to prohibit foreign investments by pension funds and insurance companies.

Trustee Services. Unfortunately, in the developing world state intervention in the allocation of pension funds is the norm rather than the exception. Many countries regularly treat public pension funds as captive sources of funds, a feature that has seriously undermined the provision of old-age pensions. Iglesias and Palacios (2000) survey the management of public pension reserves. They find that "public pension funds are usually subject to a series of restrictions and mandates that produce poor returns" (p. 35). Governments' nonpension objectives often lead to socially and economically targeted investments and forced loans to the government to finance its deficits. These investments yield returns that are often below bank deposit rates and almost always below the rate of income growth. This contrasts with returns to privately managed pension funds, which generally exceed income growth. For instance, Iglesias and Palacios (2000, p. 35) observe: "The worst returns are produced by publicly managed pension funds in countries with poor governance records."

Figure 9.2 summarizes the foregoing statement by plotting the average real return on public pension assets for 20 developing and industrial countries against a governance index. The relationship is highly nonlinear with rapidly diminishing marginal utility of governance. Note, however, that this relationship does not imply causality, but merely a correlation. The correlation coefficient between the annual real rate of return and the governance index is 0.49 and significantly different from zero with a p-value of 2.7 percent.

Iglesias and Palacios (2000) use these data to compare the returns of private pension funds with those of public pension funds. They find that public funds have been mismanaged in many countries and that private pensions are one way to introduce discipline in asset management. Government interference can be detrimental when investment policies are guided by objectives unrelated to the maximization of returns on pension assets.

Figure 9.2 Public Pension Assets: Annual Real Returns and Governance, Selected Countries, Various Time Periods

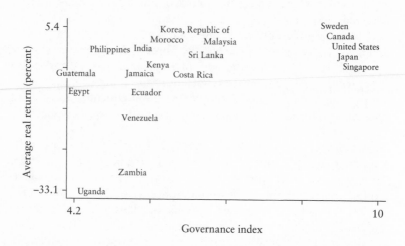

Note: The governance index is the one used in Mauro (1995) for all countries except Costa Rica, Guatemala, Uganda, and Zambia, for which the Transparency International corruption index was used. Higher levels of the index indicate better governance.
Source: Iglesias and Palacios (2000).

　　Analysis of the relationship between trustee services (and governance more generally) and fund performance is also available for more developed countries. Mitchell and Hsin (1997), Useem and Hess (2001), and Useem and Mitchell (2000) use different surveys of U.S. state and local pension systems to show that the governance of public pensions affects investment strategies, and therefore overall investment returns. In general, these authors find strong links between governance and information disclosure variables, funding levels, and practices and performance.

　　The significant impact of governance on public pension performance appears to explain why public pension funds in both industrial and developing countries perform worse than private pension funds. The literature cited finds that inconsistent performance is associated with indicators of poor governance; however, a direct link between governance and investment performance cannot be established with U.S. data. A few results are contradictory, such as the impact of the size and composition of the board of trustees.

Other results are more clear-cut, for instance, independent performance evaluation is associated with better investment policies and frequent performance evaluation is not significantly associated with performance. Evidence for developing countries—some empirical, most factual—clearly indicates that poor governance, that is, the inability to isolate fund management from political risk, is an important determinant of poor performance (Impavido 2002).

Low rates of return on pension contributions induce distortions in the labor market as workers increasingly perceive contributions as income tax. In addition, low rates of return imply that savings are not allocated to the most efficient uses. Clearly governments want to overcome a situation of economic impasse by targeting key industries; however, the recourse to coercive regulation and captive sources of funds is a short-term solution to a credibility problem on the part of the government that prompts investors to impose high risk premiums on future nominal interest rates.[11] What is not realized, or is probably underestimated, is that the use of captive sources of funds only reinforces investors' expectations and seriously undermines the development of financial markets. When financial markets are not developed, financial innovation is hampered and the cost of capital remains high. Hence, efficient mobilization of savings and allocation of resources are impeded. Furthermore, when these captive sources of funds involve social security schemes, this undermines the provision of adequate pension benefits and inflates the government's implicit debt.

These considerations are valid even in the context of countries with extremely small financial systems because, as already noted, it is unlikely that all or nearly all available funds will be invested overseas. Thus the need to develop efficient national markets for government bonds, housing finance, and venture capital would remain. In recent years several high-income countries, including Belgium, Canada, France, Ireland, New Zealand, Norway, Sweden, and the United States, have created public pension funds with better incentives to attain higher investment returns and to implement strong safeguards to insulate the funds from political interference. In all cases the public pension funds represent a fraction of total pension fund assets under management, which makes isolating them from political interference easier and avoids the distorting effects of public sector dominance of financial innovation and efficiency. However, the new investment rules for such public funds have yet to pass a test of political interference.

The necessary prerequisites for successful implementation of well-insulated public pension funds do not seem to exist in most developing countries. In small developing countries the reduced dimension of institutional relationships, the relative scarcity of human capital, the greater concentration of wealth, and a relatively less independent civil service facilitate the concentration of functions, interference by third parties, and weak governance more generally. Glaessner and Valdés-Prieto (chapter 8 in this volume) argue that the supply of trustee services and governance must be maximized in the provision of pension services in small countries. Not only is it important to procure services from highly reputable companies, maybe foreign companies as previously mentioned, but supplying highly independent trustee services is equally important. These greatly influence the performance of pension funds by hiring and selecting asset managers, determining investment policies, and selecting auditors and asset custodians. The number of trustees per pension fund should be high enough not to expose them to undue interference. The number of trustees should be higher the larger the share of the portfolio invested locally.

International Investments. Policymakers in small developing countries often look with suspicion at the option of liberalizing foreign investment by pension funds and insurance companies. The economic literature looks at capital controls from the point of view that free intertemporal trade enhances welfare.[12] Hence controls reduce social welfare, but could be considered if their introduction were to mitigate the effects of some other market failure. Exchange controls are generally used in developing countries to protect the tax base and prevent capital flight. Capital inflows are controlled to reduce moral hazard when the state maintains explicit or implicit guarantees for bank liabilities. Other market failures relate to sticky prices in product and labor markets, anticipated trade reforms, and short-term private speculation ("hot money"). Small open economies are particularly exposed to the consequences deriving from capital mobility. Countries with weak financial systems also control capital flows to reduce the possibility of financial crises. For instance, net capital inflows in the Asian crisis–affected countries went from 6.3 percent of GDP in 1995 and 5.8 percent in 1996 to –2 percent in 1997 and 5.2 percent in 1998 (Takaoshi and Kreuger 2001). Such large swings can induce volatility of the real exchange rate. If the authorities are interested in avoiding real exchange rate volatility, which is considered detrimental to export-led growth, they will try to discourage these flows through taxes and controls. In extreme cases only exchange rate controls can prevent the exhaustion of foreign reserves.

In his survey Dooley (1996) finds evidence that capital controls have succeeded in maintaining interest differentials in both industrial and developing countries. These controls, together with other forms of financial repression, have been used to increase net fiscal revenues (Aizenman and Guidotti 1994). However, the data do not support the idea that capital controls have succeeded in affecting the volume and composition of private capital flows, the level of international reserves, or the level of the exchange rate, or even in fending off speculative attacks in countries with inconsistent macroeconomic policy regimes or stances.

Whatever the rationale for exchange controls, should they be applied to contractual savings? Fontaine (1997) surveys Chile's experience in allowing foreign investment by pension funds. Pension funds have only been allowed to invest abroad since March 1990, almost 10 years after the implementation of pension reform. At that time the authorities permitted pension funds to invest up to 3 percent of their total assets in fixed income securities issued by low-risk countries and banks. In 1995 the authorities also allowed investment in foreign shares with a limit of 12 percent of the total portfolio. Fontaine (1997) concludes that there are no good macroeconomic reasons for treating international investment by pension funds differently from local investment. In other words, foreign investment by pension funds should be subject to the same rules of diversification applied to domestic investments. However, Fontaine (1997, pp. 269–70) does argue that "imposing restrictions on foreign investment by pension funds is desirable during the transition phase of a pension reform." This would serve the dual purpose of developing the domestic capital market and helping the public sector ease the fiscal cost of transition from a pay-as-you-go scheme to a fully funded scheme. The authorities should also impose restrictions on flows only during balance of payment crises and if asset stocks are large relative to international reserves. This would limit the volatility of capital flows and its impact on the real exchange rate (Davis 1999; Fontaine 1997).

Restrictive rules on foreign investments by pension funds and other contractual savings institutions need to be assessed in the context of the extent of international economic integration in particular countries. In countries where foreign entities hold strategic ownership positions in large utilities, industrial firms, and financial institutions, a blanket prohibition on foreign investments would force pension funds to invest in large local companies that are unattractive to foreign strategic owners or in companies that are too small to elicit any foreign interest. This argument is particularly important for those Eastern European countries seeking European Union membership, but may also be relevant for countries in other regions. Its validity is reinforced by recent developments in international capital markets. First-class firms in countries with less developed securities markets list their shares in well-established and more efficient and liquid international financial centers. If pension funds were prohibited from investing overseas, they would be taking excessive risks by investing in second-class firms listed on domestic stock markets. This policy would lead to an underpricing of domestic risks and would discourage other investors from investing in domestic stock markets.

When restrictions are imposed for balance of payment reasons or to prevent institutionalized capital flight, consideration should be given to the use of international asset swaps with pension funds based in other countries (Bodie and Merton 2002). In this way the international diversification of pension fund assets would not involve a large outflow of capital: the only movement of capital across the exchanges would be to cover the net gains or losses incurred by national pension funds as a result of these asset swaps. The use of international asset swaps and other derivative products could be authorized on an individual basis to pension funds that demonstrated the use of effective systems of asset management and internal control.[13]

Even in the absence of any investment restrictions on foreign assets, pension funds are likely to invest a substantial part of their assets in domestic assets. The share of domestic assets would be smaller in the case of small, nondiversified economies, especially those dominated by a small number of firms, and in the case of countries that were already highly integrated, regionally or internationally. However, asset allocations would be far removed from the weights implicit in a world index fund, even one that was properly constructed and was based on all assets, not just corporate equities, and took account of market liquidity and not just market capitalization.

The main reason behind this home bias (Reisen 1995) relates to the existence of foreign currency risk and the lack of long-term hedging facilities. Countries that required their pension funds to follow the prudent expert rule and to implement modern asset and liability management systems would not be exposed to institutional capital flight and would be protected from unduly volatile capital flows. Thus all countries, but especially those with small financial systems, should refrain from imposing unduly restrictive rules on foreign investments. They should instead focus on establishing and maintaining macroeconomic stability, without which neither pension funds nor any other form of contractual savings institutions would be able to prosper.

Conclusions

Countries with small and incomplete financial systems are generally small, open economies with a relatively low supply of financial sector expertise. Countries with a minimum core of sound banks and insurance companies, with sound macroeconomic conditions, and with medium to high per capita income are highly likely to benefit from the development of pension funds and other contractual savings institutions. As their capital markets are likely to be too small, gains from financial sector development will initially be concentrated in the development of the government bond market and long-term lending through banks. At the next stage benefits would come from the development of the corporate bond markets and asset-backed securities, and at a later stage the equity market though these will be complicated by the country's small size. This could increase the options for obtaining sound coverage against future contingencies, increase the supply of long-term savings, promote financial deepening, complete the development of financial markets, and improve financial risk management. It might also increase the national saving rate and foster economic growth.

In developing private pension funds, the options available to policymakers are similar to those available to countries with larger financial markets. Countries that rely on closed, employer-based funds tend to have a much larger number of funds than countries that rely on open, nonemployer funds. The latter tend to experience a consolidation process that results in the survival of a small number of funds, but such a system poses a serious policy challenge: how to ensure the continuance of competitive and efficient services. This problem is exacerbated in small economies where the small size of the market already inhibits competition. One solution could be to provide employers with the opportunity to opt out of the open system by allowing multi-employer-sponsored plans as well. Another solution could be to adopt a centralized fund management scheme that provides members with investment options and to outsource fund management, for example, the Thrift Savings Plan in the United States and the new Swedish scheme.

Whenever the small size of a country does not justify the capital costs that characterize some pension services, it might need to allow foreign firms to centralize these services in a foreign location where production costs could be lower, and provided that communication services are efficient and data privacy can be ensured. Allowing the subcontracting of services in the open market and the use of cross-border providers would permit a more efficient unbundling of services and the emergence of greater competition in specific services, such as asset management, where economies of scale may be less dominant. In the process of subcontracting and the use of cross border services, local governments must attract highly reputable international firms that would ideally join forces with local groups. By attracting reputable foreign companies reforming countries would reduce the costs of supervision, which may take time to develop to meet adequate standards.

Finally, the authorities should emphasize the quality of services provided by local pension funds trustees. This is especially relevant in countries with small financial sectors, where the limited pool of qualified human capital reduces the likelihood that governing bodies are independent from political power. The surveyed literature underlines how good governance is a key determinant of fund performance. The development of a sound investment policy is an important fiduciary responsibility of pension trustees. This needs to be supported by adequate regulation to allow investment abroad.

Notes

1. Private pensions funds have continued to operate during Argentina's current major economic and financial crisis, despite the serious problems facing the country's banking system. The most serious adverse impacts are a result of the asymmetric "pesification" program, the ill-advised changes in regulations, and the default of dollar- and peso-denominated government bonds.

2. Despite the importance of asset segregation and safe custody, note that few, if any, countries of the Organisation for Economic Co-operation and Development impose sufficiently robust requirements in this regard. In the United Kingdom the infamous case of Robert Maxwell, who, it was found after his death in 1991, had stolen from the pension funds of companies that he controlled, resulted in some tightening of custodial rules, but neither the United Kingdom nor any other leading country has requirements for strict segregation of assets and safe custody by a totally independent custodian. In this respect Chile is still a leader among countries with funded pension pillars.

3. Note that this does not imply support of the idea that countries should keep their capital accounts closed to maximize the impact of private pension development on securities markets. Indeed, closed capital accounts have strong negative consequences in terms of overall economic development.

4. These expenses include the investment management cost of funds but do not include the administrative costs of the employing agencies.

5. Participation is compulsory for workers employed by others. Self-employed workers can participate on a voluntary basis, and about 10 percent of self-employed workers are affiliated with the AFP system.

6. The remainder are funds without members, set as financing vehicles, often for "top hat" benefits, or they are funds in the process of closing down (Queisser and Vittas 2000).

7. A study commissioned by the Pension and Welfare Benefit Administration of the U.S. Department of Labor on the fees and expenses of 401(k) plans reports that the total fees, including asset management fees, incurred by small plans ranged from 0.57 to 2.14 percent of assets, with a mean of 1.32 percent. The study did not elaborate on the reasons explaining this wide variation (Economic Systems, Inc. 1998).

8. Yet, as noted earlier, the poor performance of Singapore's Central Provident Fund in relation to the investment returns offered to account holders has marred its record. On a net investment return basis, which is what ultimately counts for individual workers, the record of the Central Provident Fund is far from enviable (Valdés-Prieto 1998).

9. These included the adverse effects of the 1982–83 banking crisis, but especially local operators' inability to maintain the high level of capital reserves that the regulatory framework initially required (Ariztia 1998).

10. American International Group also withdrew from Argentina and Mexico after a similar failure to build a critical market share.

11. The U.S. Social Security trust fund can only be invested in nontradable government securities; however, the credibility of the U.S. government's macroeconomic policy is not at stake.

12. The literature on multiple equilibriums argues that capital controls are a first-best temporary solution that enables governments to increase their reputations and improve fundamentals so that self-fulfilling speculative attacks are less likely. Markets may see the removal of controls as a further commitment on the part of governments toward establishing even better reputations (see, for example, Bartolini and Drazen 1997; Laban and Larrain 1997; Obstfeld 1986a,b, 1995, 1996).

13. This approach was formally introduced in Switzerland in 2000, although it had been practiced informally for some time.

References

The word *processed* describes informally produced works that may not be commonly available through libraries.

Acuna, R., and A. Iglesias. 2001. "Chile's Pension Reform after 20 Years."
Social Protection Discussion Paper no. 0129. World Bank, Washington, D.C.

Aizenman, J., and P. E. Guidotti. 1994. "Capital Controls, Collection Costs, and Domestic Public Debt." *Journal of International Money and Finance* 13(1): 41–54.

Ariztia, J. 1998. *AFP: A Three-Letter Revolution.* Santiago, Chile: Corporación de Investigación, Estudio y Desarrollo de la Seguridad Social.

Asher, M. 2001. "Managing National Provident Funds in Malaysia and Singapore." Paper presented at the World Bank conference on Public Pension Fund Management, September 24–26, Washington, D.C. Available on: www.worldbank.org/finance/.

Bailliu, J., and H. Reisen. 2000. "Do Funded Pensions Contribute to Higher Aggregate Savings? A Cross-Country Analysis." In H. Reisen, ed., *Pensions, Savings, and Capital Flows: From Aging to Emerging Markets.* Paris: Organisation for Economic Co-operation and Development.

Bartolini, L., and A. Drazen. 1997. "Capital-Account Liberalization as a Signal." *American Economic Review* 87(1): 138–54.

Bodie, Z. 1990. "Pensions as Retirement Income Insurance." *Journal of Economic Literature* 38(1): 28–49.

Bodie, Z., and R. C. Merton. 1992. "Pension Benefit Guarantees in the United States: A Functional Analysis." In R. Schmitt, ed., *The Future of Pensions in the United States.* Philadelphia: University of Pennsylvania Press.

_____. 2002. "International Pension Swaps." *Journal of Pension Economics and Finance* 1(1): 77–83.

Bossone, B., P. Honohan, and M. Long. 2002. "Policy for Small Financial Systems." In G. Caprio, P. Honohan, and D. Vittas, eds., *Financial Sector Policy for Developing Countries.* New York: Oxford University Press.

Catalan, M., G. Impavido, and A. R. Musalem. 2000. "Contractual Savings or Stock Market Development: Which Leads?" *Journal of Applied Social Science Studies* 120(3): 445–87.

Davis, P. E. 1998. "Regulation of Pension Fund Assets." In H. J. Blommenstein and N. Funke, eds., *Institutional Investors in the New Financial Landscape.* Paris: Organisation for Economic Co-operation and Development.

_____. 1999. *Investment of Mandatory Funded Pension Schemes.* London: Birkbeck College, The Pension Institute.

Dooley, M. P. 1996. "A Survey of Academic Literature on Controls over International Capital Transactions." *IMF Staff Papers* 43(4): 639–87.

Dowers, K., S. Fassina, and S. Pettinato. 2001. *Pension Reform in Small Emerging Economies: Issues and Challenges.* Sustainable Development Department Technical Papers Series no. IFM-130. Washington, D.C.: Inter-American Development Bank.

Easterly, W., and A. Kraay. 2000. "Small States, Small Problems? Income, Growth, and Volatility in Small States." *World Development* 28(11): 2013–27.

Economic Systems, Inc. 1998. "Study of 401(k) Plan Fees and Expenses." U.S. Department of Labor, Pension and Welfare Benefit Administration, Washington, D.C.

Fontaine, J. A. 1997. "Are There (Good) Macroeconomic Reasons for Limiting External Investments by Pension Funds? The Chilean Case." In Salvador Valdés-Prieto, ed., *The Economics of Pensions: Principles, Policies, and International Experience.* Cambridge, U.K.: Cambridge University Press.

Grandolini, G., and L. Cerda. 1998. "The 1997 Pension Reform in Mexico." Policy Research Working Paper no. 1933. World Bank, Washington, D.C.

Hausner, J. 2002. "Poland: Security through Diversity." In Martin Feldstein and Horst Siebert, eds., *Social Security Pension Reform in Europe.* Chicago: University of Chicago Press.

Hustead, E. C., and T. Hustead. 2001. "Federal Civilian and Military Retirement Systems." In O. S. Mitchell and E. C. Hustead, eds., *Pensions in the Public Sector.* Philadelphia: University of Pennsylvania Press.

Iglesias, A., and R. J. Palacios. 2000. "Managing Public Pension Reserves." In R. Holzmann and J. Stiglitz, eds., *New Ideas about Old-Age Security.* Washington, D.C.: World Bank.

Impavido, G. 2002. "Governance Issues in Public Pension Fund Management: Preliminary Considerations." In R. Litan, M. Pomerleano, and V. Sundarajan, eds., *Financial Sector Governance: The Role of Public and Private Sectors.* Washington, D.C.: The Brookings Institution Press.

Impavido, G., A. R. Musalem, and T. Tressel. 2002a. "Contractual Savings and Firms' Financing Choices." In S. Devarajan and F. H. Rogers, eds., *World Bank Economists' Forum,* vol. 2. Washington, D.C.: World Bank.

_____. 2002b. "Contractual Savings and Impact on Securities Markets." World Bank, Washington, D.C. Processed.

_____. 2002c. *Contractual Savings Institutions and Banks' Stability and Efficiency.* Policy Research Working Paper no. 2752. Washington, D.C.: World Bank.

James, E., J. Smalhout, and D. Vittas. 2001. "Administrative Costs and the Organization of Individual Account Systems: A Comparative Perspective." In R. Holzmann and J. E. Stiglitz, eds., *New Ideas about Old Age Security: Toward Sustainable Pension Systems in the 21st Century.* Washington, D.C.: World Bank.

James, E., G. Ferrier, J. Smalhout, and D. Vittas. 1999. "Mutual Funds and Institutional Investments: What Is the Most Efficient Way to Set Up Individual Accounts in a Social Security System?" Policy Research Working Paper no. 2099. World Bank, Washington, D.C.

Kotlikoff, L. J. 1994. "A Critical Review of the World Bank's Social Insurance Analysis." World Bank, Educational and Social Policy Department, Washington, D.C.

Laban, R. M., and F. B. Larrain. 1997. "Can a Liberalization of Capital Outflows Increase Net Inflows?" *Journal of International Money and Finance* 16(3): 415–31.

Levine, R. 1999. "Law, Finance, and Economic Growth." *Journal of Financial Intermediation* 8(1/2): 8–35.

Levine, R., N. Loayza, and T. Beck. 2000. "Financial Intermediation and Growth: Causality and Causes." *Journal of Monetary Economics* 46(1): 31–77.

Mauro, P. 1995. "Corruption and Growth." *Quarterly Journal of Economics* 110(3): 681–712.

Missale, A., and O. J. Blanchard. 1994. "The Debt Burden and Debt Maturity." *American Economic Review* 84(1): 309–19.

Mitchell, O. S. 1998. "Building an Environment for Pension Reform in Developing Countries." Social Protection Discussion Paper no. 9803. World Bank, Washington, D.C.

Mitchell, O. S., and P. L. Hsin. 1997. "Public Pension Governance and Performance." In S. Valdés-Prieto, ed., *The Economics of Pensions: Principles, Policies, and International Experience.* New York: Cambridge University Press.

Obstfeld, M. 1986a. "Capital Controls, the Dual Exchange Rate, and Devaluation." *Journal of International Economics* 20(1): 1–20.

_____. 1986b. "Rational and Self-Fulfilling Balance of Payments Crises." *American Economic Review* 76(1): 72–81.

_____. 1995. "The Logic of Currency Crises." In B. Eichengreen, J. Frieden, and J. von Hagen, eds., *Monetary and Fiscal Policy in an Integrated Europe.* Heidelberg, New York, London: Springer.

_____. 1996. "Models of Currency Crises with Self-Fulfilling Features." *European Economic Review* 40(3-5): 1037–47.

Palacios, R. J., and M. Pallares. 2000. "International Patterns of Pension Provision." Social Protection Discussion Paper no. 9. World Bank, Washington, D.C.

Palmer, E. 2000. "The Swedish Pension Reform Model: Framework and Issues." Social Protection Discussion Paper no. 0012. World Bank, Washington, D.C.

Queisser, M. 1998. "The Second Generation of Pension Reforms in Latin America." Aging Working Paper no. 54. Organisation for Economic Co-operation and Development, Paris.

Queisser, M., and D. Vittas. 2000. "The Swiss Multi-Pillar Pension System: Triumph of Common Sense?" Policy Research Working Paper no. 2416. World Bank, Washington, D.C.

Reisen, H. 1995. "Liberalizing Foreign Investments by Pension Funds: Positive and Normative Aspects." Aging Working Paper no. 5.3. Organisation for Economic Co-operation and Development, Paris.

Rocha, R., and D. Vittas. 2002. "The Hungarian Pension Reform: A Preliminary Assessment of the First Years of Implementation." In M. Feldstein and H. Siebert, eds., *Social Security Pension Reform in Europe*. Chicago: University of Chicago Press.

Rocha, R., J. Gutierrez, and R. Hinz. 2001. "Improving the Regulation and Supervision of Pension Funds: Are There Lessons from the Banking Sector?" In R. Holzmann and J. E. Stiglitz, eds., *New Ideas about Old Age Security: Toward Sustainable Pension Systems in the 21ˢᵗ Century*. Washington, D.C.: World Bank.

Takaoshi, I., and A. O. Krueger, eds. 2001. "Regional and Global Capital Flows: Macroeconomic Causes and Consequences." In *East Asia Seminar on Economics*, vol. 10. Chicago: University of Chicago Press.

Useem, M, and D. Hess. 2001. "Governance and Investment of Public Pensions." In O. S. Mitchell and E. C. Hustead, eds., *Pensions in the Public Sector*. Philadelphia: University of Pennsylvania Press.

Useem, M., and O. S. Mitchell. 2000. "Holders of the Purse Strings: Governance and Performance of Public Retirement Systems." *Social Science Quarterly* 81(2): 489–506.

Valdés-Prieto, S. 1998. "The Private Sector in Social Security: Latin American Lessons for APEC." In Asian Development Bank, ed., *Promoting Pension Reform: A Critical Assessment of the Policy Agenda*. Manila: Asian Development Bank

Vittas, D. 1993. "Swiss Chilanpore: The Way Forward for Pension Reform?" Policy Research Working Paper no. 1093. World Bank, Washington, D.C.

_____. 1995. "Strengths and Weaknesses of the Chilean Pension Reform." World Bank, Washington, D.C. Processed.

_____. 1996. "Private Pension Funds in Hungary: Early Performance and Regulatory Issues." Policy Research Working Paper no. 1638. World Bank, Washington, D.C.

_____. 1997. "Private Pension Funds in Argentina's New Integrated Pension System." Policy Research Working Paper Series no. 1820. World Bank, Washington, D.C.

_____. 2000. "Pension Reform and Capital Market Development 'Feasibility' and 'Impact' Preconditions." Policy Research Working Paper Series no. 2414. World Bank, Washington, D.C.

Vittas, D., and A. Iglesias. 1992. "The Rationale and Performance of Personal Pension Plans in Chile." Policy Research Working Paper no. 867. World Bank, Washington D.C.

Vittas, D., and M. Skully. 1991. "Overview of Contractual Savings Institutions." Policy Research Working Paper Series no. 605. World Bank, Washington, D.C.

Von Gersdorff, H. 1997. "Pension Reform in Bolivia." Policy Research Working Paper no. 1832. World Bank, Washington, D.C.

Part V

Regulation

10

Regulatory Harmonization and the Globalization of Finance

Cally Jordan and Giovanni Majnoni

Scholars have considered the convergence of financial regulation across jurisdictions to be at times a precondition of market integration, at times a consequence, but always a key feature of financial integration.[1] In recent decades the relationship between financial integration and regulatory harmonization has changed because of the accelerating pace of financial globalization. Not only have capital flows increased enormously, but the provision of financial services across different jurisdictions has also grown. This growth is a result of the expansion of financial intermediaries internationally and of the direct supply of financial services to foreign entities, as in the case of foreign listings. Some observers argue that the increased provision of financial services and products across national boundaries has already exercised a disciplining effect through stiffer competition; however, the integration of financial products and services and of financial regulatory frameworks represents two different aspects of the same process, namely, the globalization of finance, that move together, but often at different speeds.

Even though market forces can promote regulatory harmonization, regulatory developments should not be left to market forces

We are grateful to Paola Bongini, Jim Hanson, Patrick Honohan, and Larry Promisel for helpful comments on earlier drafts of this chapter.

alone. Market forces and self-regulating institutions share well-known problems. Coordination failures associated with market-led initiatives can generate negative systemic externalities, attracting capital toward less regulated systems and institutions or generating forms of competition that may undermine financial stability. In addition, the costs of financial regulation and supervision may be too high for small countries, a potentially critical issue in the development of sound standards in a world where the number of independent jurisdictions has almost trebled since World War II. Overall, welfare considerations related to the presence of systemic externalities and to the high cost of public goods suggest that regulatory harmonization should not be left to market forces alone.

From the perspectives of national policymakers and analysts of international financial relations the relevant question then becomes how countries should pursue financial regulatory harmonization. How should a specific country overcome the tension between its own national policy and its global economic interests?

This chapter will explore the regulatory dynamic that has emerged as a result of a period of unprecedented internal and external financial liberalization and banking and financial crises around the world. It argues that the globalization of finance has altered the relationship between trade and financial integration and that this has affected the methods and procedures of integration, charting new paths of regulatory harmonization and convergence.

This chapter compares the ongoing dynamic of financial integration with the situation after World War II to assess whether we are moving on familiar ground or into uncharted territory and whether reviewing experience will prove useful. It then explores the role of government-led and market-led initiatives in the transition from segmented to integrated capital markets. Finally, using a deliberately stylized characterization of the ongoing process of regulatory harmonization, it focuses on the main strengths and weaknesses of the emerging international trend in the globalization of finance represented by the worldwide dissemination of codes and standards of best practice.

The How and When of Financial Integration

Countries facing the many policy questions raised by the integration of financial markets are likely to look to experience for guidance. Thus a logical first step is to characterize the current process in terms of its similarities to or differences from past instances of financial integration and regulatory harmonization.

For this purpose we shall consider three aspects of the regulatory process over the last 50 years: the interaction between the financial regulatory process and other components of the overall legal and regulatory framework, the nature of the rule-setting institution, and the level of cogency of the rules. Looking at the dynamic of the regulatory process we shall consider what sequence of regulatory events (trade versus financial integration), of the rule-setting institutions (political versus technical authorities), and of rules (binding versus indicative) has best characterized the evolution of financial regulation in the past and now.

While the sequence trade → finance may have characterized past episodes of economic integration, it is losing relevance today. In the 1960s and 1970s economic integration between countries followed a relatively standard pattern, with trade liberalization coming first as a necessary precondition for the prospective integration of productive sectors.[2] Financial integration was the outcome of increased provision of foreign financial services associated with the trade of goods rather than as an independent phenomenon (Aliber 1984).[3] The provision of financial services across jurisdictions has traditionally been viewed as performing an ancillary function, reflecting the general perception that successful commercial integration was the first and most relevant policy objective, while financial integration played at best a supporting role.[4] The European integration process followed this pattern, moving from a restricted number of goods markets (steel and coal) to the entirety of goods and then of financial markets. However, the current globalization of international finance markets is depriving the trade → finance sequence of its relevance. Financial integration takes place independently from the level of economic integration and, even though evidence still supports the notion that trade liberalization is "essential to reap the full benefits of capital account liberalization" (IMF 2002, p. 131), the traditional trade → finance sequence appears to have been increasingly substituted for in practice by a new finance → trade sequence.

One effect of this new course of events is the observed diffusion and adoption of financial codes and standards of good practice across economies at different levels of development and of openness. This is a process that considers finance as instrumental to the process of economic integration instead of residual, and that therefore tries to anticipate the timing of desirable regulatory harmonization to limit the destabilizing effects of international capital movements.[5]

A second feature of interest concerns the difference in the involvement of rule-setting governmental and nongovernmental institutions, where the notion of nongovernmental institutions is extended to include technical bodies such as supervisory authorities. Traditionally governments have set the rules for more intense economic cooperation among countries, both at a bilateral and at a multilateral level, through treaties, memorandums of understanding, or other official agreements. In the past official agreements usually paved the road for closer interactions between private sector actors and institutions, but since the 1970s initiatives by the nongovernmental sector have often taken the lead in setting the pace of, and even forcing, government interventions in the financial area. Thus with increasing frequency initiatives stemming from the private sector and technical and professional bodies have tilled the ground to be sown by political authorities. The best known and one of the first of these nongovernmental technical institutions is the Basel Committee of Banking Supervision, created after the failure of the Herstatt bank in 1975 (an event that affected correspondent banks operating in several different jurisdictions) to coordinate and strengthen the supervision of internationally active banks.

A third feature of economic integration relates to the regulatory tools used to promote integration. In the past government involvement was primarily limited to bilateral or multilateral treaties. The time needed to negotiate and approve international treaties compared with the speed of financial innovations in the marketplace has made these traditional tools of international diplomacy ineffective in the financial domain. Now nongovernmental bodies stemming from both the private and official sectors have taken the lead in defining new rules of behavior. Sometimes these new rules take the form of codes of conduct or of benchmarks against which to compare and assess individual behavior. Governments have also used this approach, for example, compiling lists of noncompliant tax havens or offshore financial centers. These rules are quite different from traditional treaties in that they are intended to shape common behaviors without necessarily affecting the legal framework.[6] The sequence of integration rules has changed from the traditional sequence treaties → codes of conduct to codes of conduct → treaties.

The dynamics of global financial integration and the related process of regulatory harmonization have taken a considerably different form than in the not so distant past. The tremendous growth of capital movements related to technological developments and to current and capital account liberalization has made the when of financial integration less dependent on other aspects of economic integration than in the past. In turn, the change in the when has inevitably affected the how, making replicas of past solutions of limited use and requiring a new pragmatic approach to regulatory harmonization that is based on a process of trial and error, and in which the received wisdom is constantly tested against the new emerging reality. Few features of past approaches to regulatory integration have survived this reality check. The next two sections single out such features from past episodes of government- and market-induced regulatory harmonization as a step toward characterizing the emerging approach to regulatory harmonization, namely, the standards and codes approach.

Government-Induced Regulatory Convergence

Between World War I and the early 1980s capital controls largely insulated national economies, reflecting the lack of interest in financial integration and the ease with which capital flows could be controlled compared with today. In the few cases where governments actively pursued integration among different financial systems, this was largely the result of political decisions. Recent experience has shown that government-induced integration has been significant under three clearly defined sets of circumstances.

Probably the most economically important set of the three is the trade-induced case. This refers to those countries where a tight network of trade relationships has induced governments to promote a stronger form of integration by partly waiving their national sovereignty in deference to a supranational regional authority. The typical example is those Western European countries that, building on strong commercial ties, have successfully moved toward an economic and a monetary union. Similar objectives and ambitions have been pursued by governments elsewhere less successfully, for example, the Latin American countries of the Andean Pact and the Southern Cone Common Market.

The second set of circumstances can be labeled as the dominant neighbor case, where a country's economy is significantly affected by the proximity of a large neighbor that dominates the region in economic terms. In this situation national governments are induced to harmonize their financial laws and regulations with those of their large neighbor to improve domestic firms' and financial intermediaries' access to larger and more liquid foreign financial markets. Such a pattern characterizes the relationship between Western Hemisphere countries and the United States and between Eastern European and North African countries and the European Union (EU).

The third set of circumstances, more nuanced but still relevant, is represented by the common colonial heritage case. The colonial heritage generally persists in the legal and regulatory frameworks of former colonies, but in some cases it also extends to the selection of monetary arrangements similar to those that prevailed during the colonial period. This is the case of the West African Monetary Union and of the Central African Monetary Union among former French colonies and of the Eastern Caribbean Currency Union among former United Kingdom colonies. A significant feature of these monetary unions is that, contrary to the European Monetary Union, they have not always been preceded by full trade liberalization. Tariffs may still apply to trading between countries that share the same currency and monetary authority, which is an example of the inversion of the traditional sequencing.

While government-induced integration has presented specific challenges in each of these three cases, the European experience is probably more instructive given its complexity, the number and size of participating countries, and the extent of financial integration. It is also a context in which the criteria for government-induced regulatory harmonization across countries have been spelt out more clearly than anywhere else.

The current convergence of macroeconomic and financial conditions throughout Europe should not obscure the strong initial differences, both structural and economic, that prevailed among the 12 EU countries. Different regulatory frameworks, degrees of capital market openness, roles of commercial banks (universal versus specialized), and corporate governance arrangements (bank-based versus market-based control) were the norm among Western European countries until the 1980s, and to some extent still are. To fully appreciate the extent of regulatory harmonization note that all four legal families made popular by the current debate on the interaction between law and financial systems (La Porta and others 1998) were and still are represented among the EU member countries.

These deeply rooted structural differences showed no sign of diminishing between the 1950s and the 1970s, when the EU pursued an objective of full harmonization. Starting in the mid-1970s EU members embarked on a new strategy based on the principles of subsidiarity and minimum harmonization. The subsidiarity principle implies that supranational authorities should limit their rule-making activity only to those areas that national jurisdictions cannot cover. The minimum harmonization principle requires that two ancillary principles be in effect: the mutual recognition of foreign regulatory systems (a recognition of the validity of foreign regulation) and the principle of home country control (a recognition of the validity of foreign supervisory authorities).

The strategy's longevity from a regulatory point of view is indicative of its effectiveness, even if the integration of financial markets may not have followed suit. The key feature of this new approach has been the substitution of the traditional top-down process—based on compulsory compliance with a detailed list of centrally issued regulations—with a new process whereby only a minimum number of common rules had to be defined while further harmonization was left to market forces. Competition among regulations and regulatory systems was allowed to operate while the minimum set of rules prevented a "competition in laxity." Note that minimum harmonization has been successful where it has been inclusive, that is, all the participants in the harmonization process have participated in defining the minimum standards. Harmonization of regulatory systems is not an easy process at the best of times, and often proves illusory where distorted by asymmetries in size and influence (Greene, Braverman, and Sperber 1995; Scott 2000).

Finally, a new set of issues has recently entered the European debate on regulatory harmonization that concerns the need for different standards for wholesale and retail markets. The EU has determined that an approach focused uniquely on defining minimum regulatory standards for the three main actors in the marketplace—banks, insurance companies, and securities intermediaries—is inadequate unless it is tailored to the size of the transactions and of the intermediaries involved (European Commission 1998). With the inception of the euro and the progressive despecialization of financial intermediation, distinguishing between the requirements applicable to large players—be they corporations, asset management companies, or payment systems—or to retail investors in the furtherance of consumer protection has become increasingly important.

Thus to summarize, two main lessons from the European experience may be applicable to financial integration more broadly. First, the principle of minimum harmonization, together with mutual recognition principles, underlines the potential for leaving integration to market forces once national legal and regulatory frameworks share common minimum standards. Second, in a financially integrated world size matters both for regulated entities and for regulators, and the same set of rules may not be efficient and equitable for both large and small players.

Market-Induced Regulatory Convergence

All regulatory convergence must start with markets, but markets themselves are institutions that represent a shared set of rules whose existence rests on some initial agreement or shared regulatory principles. This implies the existence of a more intimate relationship between private forces and the rule-making process than is frequently perceived. Private contracts have almost invariably shaped the initial development of most financial institutions up to the point where the emergence of externalities of some sort has required intervention by the public regulator. Notwithstanding the emphasis that the analysis of regulatory convergence in financial markets, and in particular capital markets, has put on formal regulation, the role of private legal rules as a factor in regulatory convergence remains relevant.

The relationship between private contracts and formal regulation should not be viewed as static, but as a dynamic continuum (Jordan and Lubrano 2002). The same rule can take multiple forms and over time swing between the two extremes of private legal rules based on a contract or convention and formal legislation. For example, fairly standardized private legal solutions found in shareholder agreements or private company bylaws have taken the form of regulatory requirements embedded in commercial codes or securities regulation. Several contractual governance mechanisms developed in the context of private companies, such as tagalong rights for minority shareholders in the event of a change of control, were adapted and crossed over to the realm of public corporations. Their outlines can be seen, for example, in the 1964 Williams Act in the United States, the source of U.S. tender offer rules. In turn, legal restrictions have determined the appearance of new variants of the original contracts.

Overall, market-induced regulatory harmonization has operated in two ways: first, through the dissemination of best practices by opening markets to new players and new products consistent with these practices and, second, through the creation of new contractual standards. Some have argued that opening domestic markets to qualified foreign institutions has favored the interaction of supervisory agencies in disseminating good-quality supervisory regulation and practices (Levine 1996). Analogously, the attractiveness of listing on foreign stock markets has resulted in good quality accounting standards being disseminated across different jurisdictions without the imposition of formal regulatory requirements.

Moreover, market-led initiatives can help define new contractual standards. New contractual arrangements motivated by regulatory arbitrage have not always survived the removal of the arbitrage opportunity, but in a few cases new market standards have brilliantly outlived their originating cause, as in the case of the standardized practices underpinning the development in the 1960s and 1970s of the so-called Euromarket (a banking and securities market mainly centered in London for business denominated mainly in U.S. dollars) and of the placement standards for American depository receipts (ADRs).

The Euromarket has sometimes been erroneously characterized as an unregulated market. In reality it is a highly specialized wholesale market, originally tailored to U.S. issuers raising debt financing from European investors, that over time has attracted issuers of other nationalities and has diversified into different instruments, such as derivatives and equities. Taking advantage of the difference in the fiscal and legal characterization of the transactions between the United States and Europe, market practitioners have skillfully flown below the radar screen of formal national regulation. U.S. regulators looked at the nature of the transaction, and if it was centered in Europe they let it go. European regulators looked at the nationality of the issuer, and non-European issuers did not trigger a regulatory response. The Euromarket flourished in the interstices.

The Euromarket, like the derivatives markets it fostered, has operated for decades on the basis of standard contractual forms and industry association rules and practices without indications of egregious market abuses. When the threat of formal regulatory intervention loomed in the early 1990s in the form of the European Commission's Investment Services Directive, industry associations and practitioners quickly closed ranks, beefed up their rule book, and bolstered their industry oversight.[7] The Euromarket has demonstrated all the usual virtues of private legal rules—responsiveness to market conditions and participants, flexibility, and consensualism—virtues of contract that make private legal rules especially suited to regional or supranational specialized markets. Of course, this approach is not suitable for every market or for every aspect of a market but is highly effective given the right conditions.

ADRs represent another interesting example of standardized practices that have led to the creation of a cross-border market. ADRs have provided a means for U.S. investors to diversify internationally from the comfort of home while providing some U.S. banks with a tidy fortune in fees for their services as intermediaries and custodians. The popularity of ADRs soared during the 1990s. During 1990–99 the number of ADR programs grew from 352 to 1,800 and the number of countries involved from 24 to 78 (Claessens, Djankov, and Klingebiel 2000). The ADR market, like the Euromarket, began as a private market based on regulatory arbitrage. The receipts, carefully named to avoid characterization as a security, were issued in the United States by a number of U.S. banks, backed by the deposit of non-U.S. issuer securities. As a result of negotiations between the industry and the Securities and Exchange Commission, ADRs were a compromise solution in terms of regulation and disclosure requirements, which exceptionally avoided U.S. bank liabilities under U.S. securities law.[8]

The critical lesson of the previous examples is that markets have the capacity not only to spread existing standards across jurisdictions, but also, and more important, to develop contractual and regulatory standards through arbitrage and competition. Financial innovations, frequently devised to circumvent regulatory inconveniences such as prospectuses or taxation as in the case of euroloans and ADRs, often address more general financial needs and achieve significant and stable development. Market-induced regulatory convergence can therefore be characterized as a process that operates through competitive selection and refinement of contractual standards.

Market forces alone are not always able to successfully enforce the standards that they have helped to set, however. Market discipline is exerted through the pricing mechanism and is as good as the quality of the available information or of the incentives to price risk properly. Where these conditions are not attained, the traditional mechanisms of public censure and reputation costs—the traditional forms of sanctions levied in cases of market abuses—may lose their effectiveness. Nevertheless, for markets characterized by a limited number of large players, reputational costs have provided a relatively effective disciplining instrument as confirmed by the lack of episodes of market abuse over extended periods of time.

The New Consensus on Minimum Standards and Codes

As noted earlier, government-induced regulatory convergence has led to different forms and models of regulatory harmonization. In a few but significant areas of the world it has allowed the establishment of monetary unions, as in the case of Western European, Eastern Caribbean, and African franc zone countries. In other regions the gravitational pull of one or more large and successful countries has acted as a catalyst, prompting a process of regulatory alignment. Experiences in these regions have shown that the difficulties of top-down harmonization, whereby a political authority imposes common rules across jurisdictions, can be reduced by invoking the principles of minimum harmonization. It is difficult to overestimate the importance of the minimum harmonization principle for the process of global financial integration.

Market mechanisms have also had some success in developing and enforcing financial standards through reputational discipline.

Reputational discipline has been important where market-determined standards prevail and where a limited number of large institutions dominates the marketplace. In these cases standardized market practices have proved to be effective for extended stretches of time, even in the absence of public administrative or penal sanctions.

These principles—minimum harmonization and mutual recognition on the one side and reputationally induced discipline on the other—represent probably the most effective lessons that past episodes of financial integration carry over to a world of integrated capital markets. Both play a major role in the regulatory response to the globalization of capital that is currently represented by the standards and codes approach. This approach has taken the form of a minimum set of rules embedded in codes of best practice voluntarily adopted by national policymakers to improve the strength and reputation of their financial systems in the international marketplace. Reputationally induced discipline has been strengthened by such "official" incentives as the "name and shame" practice associated with the Financial Action Task Force's lists of noncooperating jurisdictions or with the Organisation for Economic Cooperation and Development list of offshore financial centers responsible for harmful tax competition.[9]

The combination of these two components has favored the unquestionable popularity of the approach for at least three reasons. First, its hybrid nature, which combines elements of both market and regulatory discipline, appeals to a potentially large constituency within each national financial system, including market regulators and market practitioners. Second, its generality has favored receptiveness on the part of countries with different histories, levels of development, and geographical locations. This has proved to be tremendously important during a period characterized by the largest process of regulatory and legal reforms in history, both in terms of the number of countries involved and of the extension and pervasiveness of the reforms. Finally, the relative conceptual simplicity of minimum harmonization approaches may have conveyed the fallacious impression that the standards and codes approach could represent an easy solution to complex issues posed by financial regulatory reforms and that compliance with standards and codes could act as a means of signaling good conduct.

The popularity of an approach whereby countries have pursued national adherence to a set of international standards and codes on a voluntary basis raises several questions. Are we observing a wholly new pattern? How effective is this regulatory approach? What are the approach's potential shortcomings?

The process is by no means a new one. The presence of norms of behavior that fall short of having the binding force of legislation has been commonly observed at a national level, especially in Commonwealth countries.[10] Such conventions or standards have generally been referred to as soft law because of the lack of a codified procedure for their definition and lack of means of legal enforcement (Giovanoli 2001). The ongoing process of disseminating international standards and codes represents an adoption of the notion of soft law at the international level. As in the case of national soft law, the adoption of codes of best practices is purely voluntary and is the expression of a social consensus that, at the international level, has taken the form of nontreaty international pronouncements such as "codes of conduct, guidelines, recommendations, declarations, and resolutions of international organizations" (Kim 2001, p. 3). Even though soft law shares common advantages over formal law both at the domestic and at the international level, such as greater flexibility and timeliness, a few important differences persist between their national and international versions.

The first difference between the role of soft law in the international and national financial context is that international soft law represents a substitute for and not a complement to hard law provisions, given the substantial absence of international hard law (Giovanoli 2001). As a consequence, international soft law is deprived of the opportunity, available for national soft law provisions, to find formal expression in national hard law and regulations over time. Instead, soft law provisions pertaining to finance tend to percolate down from the international to the national level, often transforming themselves into national hard law and formal regulations rather than international treaties. This differs from practices in the international trade domain, where the traditional hard law strategy is still followed, for example, the World Trade Organization. We shall refer to the interaction between international soft law and domestic hard law as the complementarity issue.

A second difference is represented by the proliferation of international standards and codes. One possible explanation for this is that standards and codes are a substitute for legal provisions at the international level, that is, they fill the void left by the absence of international laws. As a result, the system of international codes and standards has reached a complexity that is a source of concern. An effort to coordinate the different codes is required to avoid potential inconsistencies or simply different scopes of coverage across standards. Lack of coordination is one of the main shortcomings of market-led development, and if not adequately dealt with may ultimately reduce the effectiveness of a soft law approach. We shall refer to this problem as the coordination issue.

A third difference that is common to soft law provisions both at the national and at the international level is related to the inclusiveness of the process. Nongovernmental bodies are ill suited to address and regulate the consequences of their own actions when they fall outside their constituency. Soft laws are similar to club arrangements and are therefore not well suited for effectively addressing the impact of club members' actions on external constituencies (externalities). The question then becomes what weight should be given to nonclub members in the decisionmaking process? Or alternatively, how can the soft law approach become a more inclusive process? The issue is one of legitimacy (Giovanoli 2001), and we shall refer to it as the fair representation issue.

The following subsections provide a more in-depth discussion of these three issues to focus on the challenges the standards and codes approach currently faces and on some gray areas where further research is needed to refine the current course of action.

The Complementarity Issue

The process of transforming consensus views into national laws— the complementarity between soft and hard law—is particularly complex at the international level. Consistent interpretation of standards and codes across jurisdictions with different cultural and legal backgrounds cannot be taken for granted, and this has been the main difficulty with the application of the subsidiarity principle in the EU. In addition, compliance with different standards and codes is purely voluntary. These factors have led to institutions that represent a large number of national jurisdictions and are mandated to promote conditions for economic stability and development internationally, such as the International Monetary Fund (IMF), the World Bank, and the regional development banks (the international financial institutions or IFIs), taking on the responsibility for disseminating and monitoring codes and standards (see IMF and World Bank 2002).

Observers claim that the dissemination activity performed largely, although not exclusively, by the IFIs has triggered substantial national legislative and regulatory activity (Kim 2001). The case of the Republic of Korea provides an example of the complementarity of international soft law and national hard law, as well as of some of its disadvantages. Following the 1997 Asian financial crisis, the Korean government revised its financial sector legislation to

give legal force to several international best practices. The Basel
capital requirements for commercial banks were adopted by law
and regulation; mutual funds, previously not present in the Korean
market, were introduced; and corporate governance criteria were
revised and regulated by law. The laws that were revised included
the Korean Banking Act; the Law on Merchant Banking
Companies, amended to adapt it to the Basel capital requirements;
the Korean Stock Exchange Act, revised to ensure compliance with
sound asset management procedures and to protect small shareholders; and the Securities Investment Company Acts, which led to
the introduction of mutual funds (Kim 2001).

Critics of the process in Korea have questioned the timing and
sequencing of the reforms more than the relevance of the process
itself. Park (2001, p. 2) summarized the concerns as the dilemma of
"restructuring out or growing out," suggesting that if countries cannot pursue recovery and reform simultaneously, they must decide
whether to intensify structural reform efforts at the risk of interfer-
ing with the ongoing recovery or to give priority to the fragile
recovery, even if doing so means derailing the reform process.
According to this view, "Due to the speed of recovery it is now not
so easy to argue that the legal changes and institutional reforms
have significantly contributed to the rebound of the Korean economy" (Kim 2001, p. 16).

Criticism has not prevented the dissemination of international
standards and their incorporation into national law. The phenomenon has become widespread and has not been limited to crisis countries, where IFI conditionality may have played a significant role.
Assessments of compliance with the major codes and standards performed by the IMF and the World Bank as part of the Financial
Sector Assessment Program (FSAP) and for the Reports on
Observance of Standards and Codes indicate a truly worldwide
interest in aligning national legal and regulatory frameworks with
international best practices.[11]

The number of countries that have voluntarily participated in the
FSAP also confirms the attractiveness of the soft law approach. As
of December 2002, three-and-a-half years after the launch of the
program, more than 60 countries had already participated in the
program, equally split into one group of high- and upper-middle-
income countries and a second of low- and lower-middle-income
countries. The initiative's popularity is even more remarkable given
that (a) reforms of legal and regulatory systems have traditionally
been an exclusively national domain,[12] and (b) most international
standards have been drafted in the past five years and represent

first-generation efforts that have yet to undergo revisions and refinements as experience with their application accumulates.

Whether the popularity of the approach hides some weaknesses remains to be verified. The question of implementation is, of course, important given the differences in countries' cultures and legal backgrounds. In addition, some national governments might even perceive compliance with international codes as a signaling reputational device, and this may actually mitigate pressures to fully enforce changes to law on the books. Poor enforcement and its potential causes could well be among the central issues to be addressed by the next generation of standards and codes. In this context two elements may prove to be particularly relevant: (a) the degree of effectiveness of legal transplants in countries with different legal infrastructures and different levels of development, and (b) the role that the size of the financial sector plays in the design of an effective regulatory infrastructure.

The popularity of various international standards and codes has resulted in the proliferation of transplanted legal concepts into national legal systems, which has attracted the attention of legal commentators (see, for example, Berkowitz, Pistor, and Richard 2000; Jordan and Lubrano 2002). The debate on the effectiveness of legal transplants suggests that insofar as they represent transformations of national practices, institutions, and legal concepts prevailing in industrial countries, international standards may not travel well to emerging or transition economies (Pistor 2000). Some of these transplants thrive; some are patently ineffective. They may be incompatible with the underlying domestic legal system (for example, common law fiduciary duties in Roman law legal systems), be introduced by "special" legislation that is inconsistent with and superseded by civil or commercial codes, or be implemented in a form that the particular domestic legal system does not recognize.[13]

The most common difficulty in the area of financial regulation is the absence of a broad concept of fiduciary duty under Roman law legal systems. Fiduciary duty is indigenous to the Anglo-American legal system and supports a wide range of institutions and regulatory structures. It is the "hidden assumption" upon which much of capital markets regulation and corporate governance rests in the common law world. As a legal concept, fiduciary duty is difficult to replicate under Roman law systems for a variety of reasons; however, Roman law legal systems are the most prevalent in the world, found across Europe; North, West, and South Africa; Latin America; and many parts of Asia. Thus the adoption of the institutions and regulatory structures proposed by international standards rooted in the Anglo-American legal tradition, without a compensatory mechanism to mimic fiduciary duties, may be creating a widespread regulatory hazard. The widespread looting of newly privatized entities in Central and Eastern Europe, and the subsequent collapse of capital markets in small countries like Slovakia, were partly attributable to this phenomenon. A more recent example would be the difficulties Korea encountered with investment trust company structures.

Whether standards developed in and designed for large, industrial economies fit small, emerging countries—which account for the majority of jurisdictions around the world—equally well is also questionable. Even aside from the level of development, the size of an economy is by itself an important determinant of the desirable structure and size of its financial and regulatory system. The fixed costs in setting up a regulatory structure, a market, and a banking system are such that few countries can be expected to have all the required financial intermediation services and regulatory structures the standards and codes currently in circulation call for.

In many countries the classical division into banking, insurance, and securities markets may not be conducive to a proper assessment of financial systems' strengths and weaknesses, and such a distinction is too elaborate for small economies and too blunt for larger ones. Drawing again from the EU's experience, where the European Commission (1998) presented a financial services action plan that focused on the distinction between wholesale and retail markets, alternative schemes may pay more attention to the role that size plays in the production of financial and supervisory services. For example, for countries with small, illiquid stock markets,[14] assessing the conditions for establishing regional markets or for firms to access liquid foreign markets may be more useful than assessing national compliance with International Organization of Securities Commissions standards, which reflect regulators' experience with markets of average size and liquidity. One of the weaknesses of the standards and codes approach and of its operational legs (the FSAP and the Reports on Observance of Standards and Codes programs) is to consider small, emerging economies as Lilliputian replicas of large, industrial ones.

The Coordination Issue

As noted earlier, the proliferation of international standards and codes may exemplify the lack of coordination that often precludes "first-best" approaches to market regulation. The establishment of the Financial Stability Forum (FSF) was specifically directed toward preventing such an outcome. The FSF was established to assess the vulnerabilities of the international financial system and to enhance coordination among the many different authorities responsible for financial stability (banks, insurance companies, securities markets).

One of the FSF's first initiatives was to evaluate and rank the different best practice codes proposed by various industry and regulatory bodies. As of February 2000 the FSF had identified 43 different codes and was considering 23 more for inclusion. Of this list the FSF defined 12 codes as being of high priority, of which 5 (the Basel Core Principles on Banking Supervision, the International Organization of Securities Commissions principles, the International Association of Insurance Supervisors principles, the Committee on Payment and Settlement Systems principles, and the IMF Code of Transparency in Monetary and Financial Policies) are typically assessed by the IMF and the World Bank as part of the FSAP.

A serious difficulty that dogs efforts to coordinate standards and codes is the relative absence of empirical evidence demonstrating a relationship between compliance with standards and financial stability. The initial evidence that linked indicators of legal and regulatory structures to the stability of banking and financial systems is based on extremely aggregate indicators of structure (Demirgüç-Kunt and Detragiache 1998; Rossi 1999). Only recently has new empirical work started to test the nature of the relationship between specific and more detailed specifications of regulatory structures and financial development and stability (Barth, Caprio, and Levine 2002). Generally, however, the empirical evidence that links indicators of efficiency and stability to legal and regulatory frameworks (see Schleifer and Wolfenzon 2000 for the effects on the cost of capital) has been based on indicators that have only an indirect relationship with the degree of compliance with international standards and codes.

The only available empirical evidence of the effectiveness of international codes refers to the Basel Core Principles and shows the existence of a weak and indirect link between the degree of compliance with the Basel Core Principles and financial instability (Sundarajan, Marston, and Basu 2001).[15] The compliance of bank supervision with the Basel Core Principles may therefore be read as an indicator of a system's degree of resilience to financial crises rather than of its vulnerability to financial crises (Chen and Majnoni forthcoming). Thus the dissemination of international standards and codes may represent a strategy directed at promoting the overall efficiency of financial services by means of an improved quality of supervisory infrastructures rather than a specific crisis prevention tool.

A second coordination issue concerns the resolution of divergences that are holding back international consensus on such relevant issues as international best practices in relation to accounting procedures, an area where the lack of agreement among large industrial countries—exemplified by the different positions of the International Accounting Standards Board and the United States Financial Accounting Standards Board—has impeded the definition of an international consensus view. In general, the reconciliation of different views at the international level has proven to be harder for those standards and codes more heavily conditioned by the prevailing legal framework, such as those related to corporate governance, accounting rules, and securities markets.

Clearer empirical evidence of the impact of best practices on economic stability would strengthen the credibility of the approach. In addition, there are certain controversial aspects on which consensus has not yet been reached. Progress on these two fronts should help address a list of unanswered questions. Are, for instance, all five standards typically assessed by the FSAP equally relevant from the perspective of economic growth or stability? Do they always represent a priority with respect to accounting or corporate governance standards? Should a standard be defined for the role of competition authorities in promoting access to financial services for different economic sectors (retail, small and medium enterprises, corporate)? These are questions that the next generation of codes and standards should answer, not only to improve the approach's internal consistency, but also, and more important, to avoid arbitrariness in the selection of key standards, which may weaken consensus in relation to the approach itself.

The Fair Representation Issue

The fair representation issue is a general feature of soft law, but it may have particular characteristics at the international level. Soft laws, as an expression of conventions, not of laws, often materialize in the form of understandings or guidelines. Soft law represents consensus within a particular social or professional group of individuals, and therefore cannot be expected to fully address the issues and problems that fall outside the group's scope. As an expression of the views and opinions of specific constituencies, they do not regulate potential externalities.

The fair representation issue has two aspects. The first is best described by Giovanoli (2001, p. 30):

> Fair representation of all parties is crucial for the acceptance
> of standards with no legally binding character. On the other
> hand, it must be recognized that rules are much easier to draft

in relatively small and manageable groups, as broad groups, especially if they are not homogeneous, move slowly and may fail to achieve the necessary degree of consensus. Reconciling at the international level the conflicting requirements of legitimacy and effectiveness is akin to squaring the circle.

A second fair representation issue is not related to the country composition of major international groups, but rather is inherent to the composition of groups of standards setters. Standards setters may pay insufficient attention to the impact of their decisions outside the areas of concern facing their profession. A typical example is the frequently raised concern that bank regulators represented in the Basel Committee devote too little attention to the procyclical effects of new banks' capital discipline (Borio 2002). While the Basel Committee has renewed its attention to the problem, modifying some of the most procyclical features of the new capital discipline, the different emphasis placed on stability and liquidity issues by different constituencies (namely, financial supervisors and economic policymakers) remains a generally pertinent policy issue.

Full integration of the work on standards and codes with systemic considerations requires a macro-prudential approach to financial regulation (IMF 2001). However, the debate on the systemic implications of the dissemination of codes and standards has focused more on financial systems' ability to withstand macroeconomic shocks (IMF and World Bank 2002) than on the macroeconomic effects of new regulatory standards. For example, while considerable attention has rightfully been devoted to evaluating financial intermediaries' capital adequacy by means of appropriate stress testing exercises, to date only a modest effort has focused on assessing the effects of new solvency ratios on the allocation of credit.

Another example of issues likely to fall outside the domain and interests of professional standards setters is the definition of standards for financial crisis management and resolution (Giannini 2001). Responding to the lack of guidelines in this area the World Bank, together with the IMF and other interested parties, has recently begun to formulate principles for dealing with bank and corporate insolvency at both the individual and systemic levels.

Conclusions

The formulation of a new discipline for an international financial system has proven to be harder than in the past. The process of financial globalization has shifted the balance of power from governments to markets and has made the traditional solution, resorting to international treaties, less viable. Historic references are often lacking, and new institutional solutions are being tested through a process of trial and error. The dissemination of international codes and standards supported by IFIs represents an innovative and constructive effort to coordinate national regulatory dynamics. It combines some of the key features of the most successful instances of regulatory harmonization—minimum harmonization and reputationally induced discipline—and, despite its limitations, represents a structured approach to the problems raised by the globalization of capital markets.

The ongoing adaptation of financial regulation in transition economies and the reforms of financial systems in crisis countries and in countries exposed to different degrees of financial contagion have generated a worldwide wave of financial reforms, which probably has no historical antecedent in terms of geographical coverage and extension within each financial system. In this unprecedented environment the standards and codes approach has come to play an important role in promoting regulatory harmonization and reducing the risk of instability related to weak regulations and regulatory arbitrage.

The standards and codes approach aims to offer regulatory benchmarks for individual countries embarking on the process of reforming their financial systems, and for this reason faces the difficult tradeoff of pursuing a general objective without disregarding the needs of countries of different sizes, legal traditions, and levels of financial development. The simple transposition of rules across different institutional frameworks may lead to unintended consequences, as demonstrated by the implementation of privatization schemes in transition economies during the last decade. The standards and codes approach has faced only an initial set of tests, and the process of revision based on initial experience has just begun.

A refinement of standards and codes appears to be warranted— and is under way in some cases—to accommodate different legal traditions and to deal with the specific needs of financial systems of different sizes and complexities. For small developing countries, which represent the majority of independent jurisdictions, the costs of financial regulation may require different regulatory structures than those prevailing in larger economies. A clearer definition of the role different standards play in promoting economic growth and financial stability would also help set priorities among different regulatory reforms and would improve the overall effectiveness of the standards and codes approach. Finally, the application of international standards and codes may benefit from further development of the macro-prudential approach, which considers not only the effects of systemic shocks on financial stability but also the effects of different regulatory strategies on macroeconomic stability.

The approach's success will ultimately depend on its capacity to add operational content to its basic underlying principles of minimum harmonization and reputational discipline, and to address not only conditions for access to international capital markets but also conditions for access to finance, whether provided locally or internationally.

Notes

1. Regulatory harmonization has been pursued as a preliminary step to the single market for financial services in the European Union. Financial reforms have, instead, accompanied or followed the liberalization of financial services in most Latin American countries.

2. Rousseau and Sylla (2001) find that trade integration in the postwar period was not affected by financial integration.

3. Countries that deliberately liberalized capital movements more than or before trade are concentrated in Latin America. An International Monetary Fund report (IMF 2002) finds that the region has the highest concentration of countries that are closed to trade but are financially open and the largest vulnerability to episodes of financial instability.

4. More generally, financial integration was a concern given the additional constraints imposed by greater capital mobility on the pursuit of objectives of monetary policy different from those of balance of payments objectives (Eichengreen 1998).

5. The inversion of the sequence trade → finance has not been limited to financial regulation. Coffee (2001) reports the case of new Israeli firms, which after accessing U.S. markets for funding purposes eventually decided to move their entire productive activity to the United States. In this specific case production has followed finance.

6. Note that a parallel shift from multilateral (formal) to noninstitutional (informal) forums, such as the Group of Seven, the Group of 10, and the Group of 20, has characterized international economic cooperation since the mid-1980s (Padoa-Schioppa and Saccomanni 1999).

7. A second threat has loomed with the proposed European Prospectus Directive. In July 2001 the U.K. Law Society warned that the proposed directive risked killing the only truly pan-European securities market, and accommodations were subsequently made to the proposals.

8. Three tiers of ADR programs are recognized, with graduated disclosure requirements ranging from an exemption from formal Securities and Exchange Commission filings to full U.S. prospectus registration (see SEC 1991).

9. Additional "official" incentives also play a role in the standards and codes approach and are related to the surveillance activity performed by the

international financial institutions. They do not, however, appear to be as central to the characterization of the approach as the reputation factor.

10. "English common law system demonstrates a surprising aversion to law as legislation, to *ex-ante* public legal rules. Large and complex swathes of English law are found in no written legislated form. Trust law, from which is derived the concept of fiduciary duties is a prime example; its fundamental principles remain judge-made, their source being *ex-post* public legal rules. England is a country with no written constitution for example" (Jordan and Lubrano 2002, pp. 27–28).

11. The Reports on Observance of Standards and Codes can be found for a growing number of countries at http://www.worldbank.org/ifa/rosc.html.

12. The confidentiality of the assessment of compliance conducted during FSAP reviews has favored full cooperation between national governments and the IFIs, giving the assessments the nature of an external audit for use by national authorities to determine institutional weaknesses and define policy priorities. However, the IMF and World Bank encourage national governments to make the main findings of the FSAP public.

13. The reliance of Commonwealth countries on judge-made (ex post) legal rules, which differs from the reliance of the non-Commonwealth world on written (ex ante) laws, has often facilitated the implementation of voluntary codes of conduct in the first group of countries while creating problems of legal compatibility of voluntary standards in the second group (Jordan and Lubrano 2002).

14. Only 16 of the more than 150 stock exchanges worldwide (Coffee 2001) have an annual equity trading volume that exceeds 75 percent of the equity market capitalization, as reported by Shah and Thomas (chapter 6 in this volume).

15. The prevailing uncertainty about the effects of international standards and codes is best expressed in a recent empirical paper on the effectiveness of bank regulation, according to which "there is no evidence that best practices currently being advocated by international agencies are the best ones for promoting well-functioning banks. There also is no evidence that successful practices in the United States, for example, will succeed in countries with different institutional and political environments" (Barth, Caprio, and Levine 2002, p. 1).

References

The word *processed* describes informally produced works that may not be commonly available through libraries.

Aliber, Robert. 1984. "International Banking: A Survey." *Journal of Money, Credit, and Banking* 16(November): 661–95.

Barth, James, Gerard Caprio, and Ross Levine. 2002. "Bank Regulation and Supervision: What Works Best?" World Bank, Washington, D.C. Processed.

Berkowitz, Daniel, Katarina Pistor, and Jean Francois Richard. 2000. "Economic Development, Legality, and the Transplant Effect." Working Paper no. 410. The William Davidson Institute, Ann Arbor, Mich.

Borio, Claudio. 2002. "Towards a Macro-Prudential Framework for Financial Supervision and Regulation." Bank for International Settlements, Basel. Processed.

Chen, Xin, and Giovanni Majnoni. Forthcoming. "What Are Basel Core Principles Meant to Signal: An Empirical Analysis." World Bank, Washington, D.C. Processed.

Claessens, Stjin, Simeon Djankov, and Daniela Klingebiel. 2000. "Stock Market in Transition Economies." Financial Sector Discussion Paper no. 5. World Bank, Washington, D.C.

Coffee, John, Jr. 2001. "The Coming Competition among Securities Markets: What Strategies Will Dominate?" Columbia Law School, New York. Processed.

Demirgüç-Kunt, Ası, and Enrica Detragiache. 1998. "The Determinants of Banking Crises in Developing and Developed Countries." *International Monetary Fund Staff Papers* 45(1): 81–109.

Eichengreen, Barry. 1998. *Globalizing Capital: A History of the International Monetary System.* Princeton, N.J.: Princeton University Press.

European Commission. 1998. "Financial Services: Building a Framework for Action." Document number COM (1998) 625.28.10.98. Brussels.

Giannini, Curzio. 2001. "Broad in Scope, Soft in Method. International Cooperation and the Quest for Financial Stability in Emerging Markets." Bank of Italy, Rome. Processed.

Giovanoli, Mario. 2001. "A New Architecture for the Global Financial Market: Legal Aspects of International Financial Standard Setting." In M. Giovanoli, ed., *International Monetary Law: Issues for the New Millennium.* Oxford, U.K.: Oxford University Press, Oxford.

Greene, Edward F., Daniel A. Braverman, and Sebastian R. Sperber. 1995. "Hegemony or Deference: U.S. Disclosure Requirements in the International Capital Markets." *Business Lawyer* 50(2): 413–45.

IMF (International Monetary Fund). 2001. "Macroprudential Analysis: Selected Aspects." Washington, D.C. Processed.

_____. 2002. *World Economic Outlook: Trade and Finance.* Washington, D.C.

IMF (International Monetary Fund) and World Bank. 2002. "Assessing the Implementation of Standards: A Review of Experience and Next Steps." Washington, D.C. Processed.

Jordan, Cally, and Mike Lubrano. 2002. "How Effective Are Capital Markets in Exerting Governance on Corporations?" In *Financial Sector Governance: The Roles of the Public and Private Sectors.* Washington, D.C.: The Brookings Institution.

Kim, Hwa-Jin. 2001. "Taking International Soft Law Seriously: Its Implications for Global Convergence in Corporate Governance." *Journal of Korean Law* 1(March): 1–50.

La Porta, Rafael, Florencio Lopez-de-Silanes, Andrej Schleifer, and Robert Vishny. 1998. "Law and Finance." *Journal of Political Economy* 106: 1113–55.

Levine, Ross. 1996. "Foreign Banks, Financial Development, and Economic Growth." In Claude Barfield, ed., *International Financial Markets*. Washington, D.C.: American Enterprises Institute.

Padoa-Schioppa, Tommaso, and Fabrizio Saccomanni. 1999. "Managing a Market-Led Global Financial System." In P. B. Kenen, ed., *Managing the World Economy Fifty Years after Bretton Woods*. Washington, D.C.: Institute for International Economics.

Park, Jung Chul. 2001. *The East Asian Dilemma: Restructuring Out or Growing Out*. Essays in International Economics no. 223. Princeton, N.J.: Princeton University.

Pistor, Katharina. 2000. "Patterns of Legal Change: Shareholder and Creditor Rights in Transition Economies." *European Business Organization Law Review* 1(1): 59–108.

Rossi, Marco. 1999. "Financial Fragility and Economic Performance in Developing Economies: Do Capital Controls, Prudential Regulation, and Supervision Matter?" Working Paper no. 66. International Monetary Fund, Washington, D.C.

Rousseau, Peter, and Richard Sylla. 2001. "Financial Systems, Economic Growth, and Globalization." Working Paper no. 8323. National Bureau of Economic Research, Cambridge, Mass.

Schleifer, Andrei, and Daniele Wolfenzon. 2000. "Investor Protection and Equity Markets." Working Paper no. 7941. National Bureau of Economic Research, Cambridge, Mass.

Scott, Hal. S. 2000. "Internationalization of Primary Public Securities Markets." *Law and Contemporary Problems* 63(3): 71–104.

SEC (Securities and Exchange Commission). 1991. Release no. 33-6894. Washington, D.C., May 23.

Sundarajan, V., David Marston, and Ritu Basu. 2001. "Financial System Standards and Financial Stability: The Case of the Basel Core Principles." Working Papers no. 62. International Monetary Fund, Washington, D.C.